Anonymous

Intermediate education in Ireland

Anonymous

Intermediate education in Ireland

ISBN/EAN: 9783337215118

Printed in Europe, USA, Canada, Australia, Japan

Cover: Foto ©Paul-Georg Meister /pixelio.de

More available books at **www.hansebooks.com**

INTERMEDIATE
EDUCATION IN IRELAND.

BY

A COMMITTEE OF IRISH CATHOLICS.

DUBLIN:
M. H. GILL & SON, 50, UPPER SACKVILLE-STREET,
1877.

PRINTED BY M. H. GILL AND SON, 50, UPPER SACKVILLE-STREET, DUBLIN

CONTENTS.

	Page
Preface,	v
Introduction,	1
Chapter I. Historical Survey of the Educational Institutions of the last Three Centuries,	23
Chapter II. The Diocesan Free Schools of Queen Elizabeth,	36
Chapter III. The Diocesan Free Schools of Queen Elizabeth (continued),	52
Chapter IV. Royal Free Schools of James the First—The Plantation of Ulster,	65
Chapter V. Schools of the Irish Society of the new Plantation,	81
Chapter VI. Schools and other Foundations of the Governors of Erasmus Smith,	95
Chapter VII. Various other endowed Grammar Schools,	115
Chapter VIII. The Charter Schools and the Incorporated Society,	112
Chapter IX. Model Schools.—I. History,	166
Chapter X. Model Schools.—II. Organization,	18J
Chapter XI. Constitution of Irish Educational Boards and Commissions,	207
Chapter XII. The Educational Penal Code, Past and Present,	224
Chapter XIII. Catholic Intermediate Education,	256
Chapter XIV. Summary.	270

PREFACE.

A few years ago a leading newspaper of this city, *The Freeman's Journal*, published a series of articles on Intermediate Education in Ireland, which at the time attracted considerable attention. These articles were collected into a small volume and published in that form at the end of the year 1871. The Chief Secretary for Ireland having declared, in the House of Commons, on the 14th of this month, that Her Majesty's Government has before it a scheme for the settlement of the important question of Intermediate Education, the circumstances of the present time seem to call for a republication of this most valuable and trustworthy work.

The writers—a Committee of Irish Catholics—explain how they and their brother Catholics find themselves practically excluded from participation in the advantages of a great system, which is spread like a net-work all over the land, at an annual charge to the country, either by way of endowment or of direct parliamentary vote, of over £50,000. All ranks of the Protestant population are permeated by its influence, and in turn sustain it by the kindred sympathy of self-interest. The laws and all the civil institutions of the country recognise it, are in harmony with it, and foster it to their utmost ability. To render it complete, and, if possible, unassailable, it has been permitted to cement by a double University development its monopoly of educational privilege.

In the face of this legal proscription, the Catholics have established for themselves, and support out of their poverty, schools and colleges, which educate three times the number of youths to be found in the richly-endowed nurseries enjoying the exclusive favour of the State. Moreover, by their exclusion from the educational system which identifies, for their mutual advantage, the Protestant and Mixed Schools and the Universities, the Catholic Colleges are deprived of the benefit of those University influences which are of vital importance for the education of a country. Thus we have at this day a triple disability imposed upon Irish Catholics in this single matter of Intermediate Education. They are excluded from all participation in the public endowments and parliamentary votes; they are deprived of the advantages of University influences; they are compelled to defray all charges for this object out of their own overtaxed resources.

The heads of both the great English political parties have more than once admitted that Irish Catholics have some cause of complaint in the matter of University education. But no recognition has as yet been made of this heavy grievance—not sentimental, but social and pecuniary—that Irish Protestants have over £50,000 annually provided for their intermediate education out of the national wealth, and are furnished with two amply endowed Universities for their own benefit, while Irish Catholics have to provide their education altogether for themselves, and have no University assistance in the matter.

The Education Question has now reached such a critical point, and public attention has become so thoroughly awakened to its importance and urgency, that we believe many will be desirous to see, placed within easy reach of the public, the facts which the Committee collected with so much industry respecting the Intermediate Schools of Ireland. Let us hope that in the decision at which Her Majesty's advisers may arrive on this important question, they will give due weight to the statements put forward in the following pages, based as they are on incontrovertible public documents.

DUBLIN, *February 22nd,* 1877.

INTERMEDIATE AND UNIVERSITY EDUCATION IN IRELAND.

INTRODUCTION.

Mr. Gladstone's promise to deal with the Education Question; the fulfilment of this promise cannot be longer postponed. Conditions which a measure for dealing with this question should fulfil; public opinion requires to be enlightened; the task of doing so as regards Intermediate and Higher Education undertaken by a Committee of Catholics. The Education Question now ripe for settlement.

Education one of the first thoughts of Catholics after the Emancipation Act of 1829: Mr. Wyse's Memorial to Earl Grey; his Select Committee; his scheme of Collegiate and University Education; his Memorial to Parliament; this memorial, the basis of the system of National Education. Occupation of Parliament unfavourable to Educational Legislation for some years after Report of Mr. Wyse's Committee. Agitation for Provincial Colleges in the south of Ireland; Queen's Colleges Bill of Sir R. Peel; previous to passing of the Bill, Catholics had discussed only the need of Intermediate and University Education, and not the principles upon which it should be founded; causes of this; the Queen's Colleges Bill evaded the true end of legislation on the subject; English Statesmen never realize the fact that the people of Ireland are not the people of England. Character of Sir T. Wyse's scheme. Government avoided direct legislation on the Intermediate branch of the question, and attempted to indirectly graft a scheme on the National System. Sir R. Peel's Colleges made more unsatisfactory by the manner in which they were organized. Effect of the Famine on the Irish policy of the government.

The opinion of the country clearly in favour of Catholic education. Synodical Address of the National Council of Thurles. Episcopal Resolutions of 1869. Establishment of Catholic University; amount of money contributed for the purpose; circumstances under which it was subscribed; it showed the agreement of bishops and laity. Sir R. Peel's movement for the establishment of scholarships in the Queen's Colleges was a test of Catholic opinion : Committee appointed for the purpose ; extraordinary address issued by it ; analysis of subscriptions made by Catholics to the fund ; protest of the Catholic laity ; foundation of scholarships in the Catholic University. Deputation of Corporate Bodies to Lord Palmerston ; his reception of the deputation and its political effect.

Facts which show that Catholics are as interested as ever in the Education Question : Election addresses ; Declaration of Catholic Laymen ; Declaration of Parliamentary Electors. Conclusion—that there is a thorough agreement in principle between bishops and laity, and that it would be a mistake for a statesman to calculate on a disagreement: Mr. Leslie Foster's recommendation in 1811 is equally applicable now.

In the debate in the House of Commons on the 1st of April, 1870, on Mr. Fawcett's motion respecting Trinity College, Dublin, Mr. Gladstone said—" The Government has taken office for a variety of purposes connected with the profession of what is called the Liberal creed in politics, but the first and the greatest of those purposes was to find a solution for the Irish Church, the Irish Land, and the Irish Education questions—the latter including especially the subject of higher education in that country. These questions were pointed out for solution by previous decisions of the house, and in acceding to office on the understanding that they were to be settled, if possible, the government acted strictly in accordance with the spirit of the constitution". Again, " With respect to the future, I have not the smallest scruple in saying, that if the time of parliament admits of our dealing with the question of higher education in Ireland, we shall deal with it in the same spirit in which we have endeavoured to deal with the question of the Church and the land in that country". This pledge is about to be fulfilled in the ensuing session of parliament, if we may trust public reports. Indeed, the state of intermediate and university education is so anomalous, and the position of Catholics with respect to both so intolerable, that the redress of this, perhaps the greatest of the three great grievances which Mr. Gladstone's government undertook to remove, cannot be postponed any longer.

The general principles upon which a measure should be based in order to effect this object in a way that will satisfy Catholics are simple enough. There are, however, so many different institutions to be dealt with, most of them branches of that gigantic trunk of injustice and oppression which was cut down in the year 1869, and so many opposing interests to be reconciled, that the details must necessarily be complicated and troublesome. It therefore becomes the duty of Irish Catholics to show the character of their educational disabilities, the way they are affected by them, and the nature of the remedies that would satisfy them; with a view to aid the government in devising such a measure as would, on the one hand, be in harmony with the religious principles and fulfil the reasonable wishes of Catholics, and, on the other, satisfy the legitimate requirements of the advocates of secular education.

As to the first of these conditions, or the purely religious element of the education question, the views of Irish Catholics are definite and unchangeable, and though well known to all who really understand our people, it may be useful to reassert them at the present time, in order that those who shall have to legislate on the subject may not be unmindful of the firm determination of Irish Catholics to secure a thoroughly Catholic education for their children.

The second condition which the forthcoming measure should fulfil is, the full realization of educational equality. To ensure this, public opinion requires to be enlightened regarding the different institutions which must be abolished or reformed.

The third, or purely educational condition, though of primary importance to the future welfare of the country, is one which, it is to be presumed, all have alike at heart, and therefore need not be specially discussed in relation to Catholic claims.

The duty which we have said above devolves upon Irish Catholics in view of the approaching legislation on the education question, we will endeavour to perform as far as in us lies. We will confine ourselves to intermediate and university education, because we believe that this portion of the subject can be best studied apart. The Royal Commission which lately sat, having, in their report on primary schools, gone a good way to support Catholic claims, the discussion of the question of primary education is less urgent at the present moment than it might otherwise have been. This course will not, however, preclude us from incidentally referring to the question of primary schools whenever our special subject may require it. We naturally begin by showing that, like the questions of the Church and of the land, that of higher education has been sufficiently long under public discussion to be ripe enough for settlement; that, just as happened with those questions, an unsuccessful attempt was made to evade the necessity of legislating on the subject upon the only basis which could satisfy Irish Catholics; and, lastly, that the latter have shown in practice and expressed in words, that this basis must be the recognition of their right to have a system of intermediate and higher education provided for them, not only free from danger to their faith, but one under which the mind of Irish Catholic youth may be able to freely develope itself after its own intellectual type.

One of the first thoughts of the Irish Catholics after the passing of the Emancipation Act of 1829 was the state of education. Mr., afterwards Sir Thomas, Wyse, who had been returned for the city of Waterford at the general election of 1830, presented at the end of that year a memorial, on the organization of education in Ireland, to Earl Grey, the premier of the first really Liberal administration which held office since the death of the Marquis of Rockingham in 1782. This memorial, which referred to primary, intermediate, and university education, had a large share in determining the basis of the system of National Education introduced the following year by Mr. Stanley. The question of intermediate and higher education was much more intricate, and involved many interests at that time still very powerful, and nothing was therefore done to complete the educational edifice. Mr. Wyse was not, however, discouraged. In 1832 he moved for a select committee to inquire into the diocesan schools of Ireland, with a view of opening up these little known institutions and clearing the ground for legislation. Owing to the fierce contests about the Reform Bill, and other parliamentary obstacles, this Committee was not appointed until 1835. It sat in 1835, 1836, and 1838, when it finally reported. The report recommended that the diocesan and Royal schools should be thoroughly reformed and re-organized, and that county schools or academies and provincial colleges should be established. Mr. Wyse also laid a memorial before parliament, in which he pointed out the necessity of connecting the proposed colleges with a university. He proposed three alternative schemes as to the university; 1st, to take the University of Dublin as it stands, with its one college, removing all restrictions as to religion, adding other colleges, some of which might be theological; 2nd, if the first plan should be found impracticable, to found and endow a Catholic university equivalent to the University of Dublin and its single college, Trinity College; and 3rd, "if the merits of this plan shall not be conceded", to found in each province, several provincial colleges, which should form together a university:—that is, in fact, four universities.

No action followed this report. The time of parliament being occupied in 1833 with many important judicial reforms, and in 1834 and 1835 with, among other matters, the Irish Church Reform and the Tithes, there was little chance for an Irish education question receiving attention; while in Ireland itself the tithe agitation absorbed the whole attention of the people. During 1836, 1837, and 1838, Canadian affairs, English Poor Law Reform, and the Irish Municipal Reform, left no opening for legislation on education. In Ireland itself the matter was, however, seriously taken up, especially in Munster, and a great meeting was held in Cork in November, 1838. This agitation produced no immediate result; for the Irish Municipal Reform Act—passed in 1839—the settlement of Canada, the great Free Trade debates on sugar and corn within parliament, and the Corn Law and Chartist agitations outside, completely silenced the voice of Ireland. Perhaps the circumstance that Mr. Wyse, who had made the question of intermediate and higher education his own, held office from 1839 to 1841, may have had some share also in the lull in the agitation of the subject which took place in Ireland during those years, as well as for its resumption in 1842. Although every other question was thrown into the shade by the great question of the repeal of the legislative union, the subject of higher education made considerable progress during the repeal agitation, mainly through the support which it received from the national party. Another meeting was held in Cork in November, 1844, and the subject was at length mentioned in the Queen's speech in 1845, and the bill establishing the three Queen's Colleges, introduced by Sir Robert Peel, became law.

The question of intermediate and higher education had now entered on a new phase. Up to this the conduct of the movement was left, as is the usage in such cases, in the hands of the man who had first taken it up. Hitherto the speeches, pamphlets, letters, and newspaper articles on the subject, were almost exclusively devoted to pointing out the want of high schools and colleges in the country, and the many benefits their establishment would confer, and had barely begun to touch upon the principles upon which the constitution of the schools and colleges should be based. The truth is, the majority of the people knew too little about the office and work of colleges and universities, though instinctively feeling the want of them. to rightly understand, or even to perceive at first, the importance of the question of principle. There were a few Catholics whose education, no doubt, qualified them for thinking more seriously on abstract principles than is the usual habit of Irish politicians. But at that time Irish Catholics of education and position were subject to influences which rendered it very difficult for them to form a sound judgment on such a question. In the first place, the influence of the philosophy of the eighteenth century still operated on those who had received their education abroad, or from teachers who had been so educated. Many had been educated in the Protestant University of Dublin, and were necessarily to a great extent Protestantized. The principles of the *doctrinaire* school, then dominant in the liberal party, also largely affected Irish Catholic thought. And, lastly, the effects of the intellectual, moral, and political slavery of centuries still weighed upon the people. Even the majority of the clergy, especially those whose education and habits would naturally incline them to take a special interest in the abstract question of education, did not yet fully realize the altered position of Ireland. They had been so accustomed to obtain justice by small and halting instalments, that, though holding in the abstract the same views as to the principles upon which the education of the country of all degrees should be based as the majority of Irish Catholics do now, they instinctively dreaded those who declined to be satisfied with justice by such instalments, and who demanded their rights in full. Like men who have just escaped from a prison house, they were always timidly looking behind them, fearing that a conscious display of liberty on their part might provoke their ancient enemies to re-impose their chains. It would, however, be unreasonable to expect that men who had grown up in political slavery should be able in a few years to acquire the self-consciousness which can only belong to those who have not been slaves. It would be still more unreasonable to hold that the views of such men should bind irrevocably men of another generation, living under different social and political circumstances.

There is yet another and very important reason why, previous to 1845, Irish Catholics did not give more prominence to their views respecting the principles upon which the higher education they asked for should be based. It is this. They believed that the question was practically a Catholic one. The agitation begun in the south of Ireland was mainly confined to that province, and found no favour among the Protestants of Ulster. Liberal Protestants, it is true, took an active part in the movement; but as Protestants were already richly provided with all the means of higher education, their coöperation was deemed sympathy with the cause of justice, as in the case of Emancipation. Hence Catholics believed that the proposed schools and colleges would be practically left to themselves, and consequently that it would be unnecessary to demand guarantees for faith and morals, the guardianship of which would be in their own hands.

In 1844 the Government seem to have been inclined to complete Sir Thomas Wyse's original scheme of education; but the measure actually laid before parliament in 1845 not only fell far short of what had been expected, but directly evaded the chief end of legislation on the subject—the satisfaction of the just claims of Catholics. English statesmen never seem to realise the fact that the people of Ireland are not the people of England; that we have had a different history, political and religious, and have different idiosyncracies. They forget, too, in the case of Ireland, that legislation, to be acceptable and successful, should express the real wants, and be in harmony with the intellectual, moral, and political instincts of the people. Not so, however, when England is concerned. The members of the Anti-Corn Law League, while pressing their demand for a "cheap loaf" for the British workman on the acceptance of a reluctant parliament and an unwilling ministry, with a persistency which would not brook disappointment, were not solicitous about the principles on which the commercial policy of England was to be reformed. It became the duty of Sir Robert Peel and his President of the Board of Trade, Mr. Gladstone, to discover those principles, and develope out of them the *via media* which should reconcile a revolution in the commercial system with the doctrines of political and economic science. Had those statesmen shown equal intelligence in understanding the demands of Irish Catholics for educational reform, equal willingness in hearkening to them, and ingenuity in devising ways for satisfying them, we should not in 1871 find ourselves face to face with the self same educational difficulty which twenty-six years ago they evaded in 1845.

Although, in some points, we differ considerably from Sir Thomas Wyse's views on education, we freely admit that his proposed scheme was distinguished by largeness of conception and unity of purpose. It was a part of his scheme to found an academy or high school in every county, to serve as a seminary for the middle classes and a feeder of the university colleges. Had the plan submitted to parliament by Sir Robert Peel in 1845 embraced this portion of the scheme, and had it in its original form been as much at variance with the true wants and wishes of our people as the Bill which actually passed the House of Commons, there can be no doubt, the Irish Catholic middle class would have better seen than they did the dangerous character of the measure. Instead, therefore, of legislating for intermediate as well as for collegiate education, it was determined to attain the same end indirectly by grafting a scheme of intermediate schools on the National System. It was hoped that under the protection of the then popular system those schools would escape observation until they should have become firmly rooted in the country. The Commissioners of National Education, who for nine years had forgotten that, from the first, Model Schools formed an essential element of the National System, suddenly advert, in their Report for the year 1844, published in April, 1845, "to a communication which they had already made to [his] Excellency, as to the necessity of having model schools established under [their] own immediate direction in [their] several school districts". In order to acquire sites for these schools by direct conveyance to themselves, they asked to be incorporated—a request which was granted a few months afterwards. How this cunningly-planned system of intermediate schools, so different from the model schools originally contemplated, grew up, and how, when their true character was discovered, they decayed, will be discussed hereafter.

Unsatisfactory as was the Colleges Bill of Sir Robert Peel, the scheme as it was ultimately carried out was still more so. Even the promise of Lord Clarendon, the Lord Lieutenant of Ireland, into whose hands had passed the carrying out of the Act, that "*in the council, professorships, and other posts of each college, the Catholic religion will be fully and appropriately represented*", was obliterated from the memory of the Irish government by the famine, which the English press fondly hoped had for ever crushed Irishmen, and especially Irish Catholics.

Even during those fearful times the real opinion of the country began to find voice according as the true character of the Queen's Colleges and the certain results of their action became more and more apparent. That that opinion is unquestionably for a thoroughly Catholic system of education, no one will deny who impartially considers the attitude of the Irish people during the last quarter of a century. The opinions of the Catholic bishops on the Queen's Colleges have been over and over again expressed in unmistakeable terms. We shall confine ourselves to the earliest and latest unanimous declarations of their views to Irish Catholics. The former was the synodical address of the fathers of the National Council of Thurles, issued in 1850; the latter the resolutions of the Catholic archbishops and bishops of Ireland, passed at their meeting in Maynooth on the 18th of August, 1869. The following passage from the synodical address shows their opinion of the Queen's Colleges in their infancy:

"It is by the sternest sense of duty—by a painful, but irresistible feeling of necessity that we are compelled, dearly beloved, to announce to you, that a system of education, fraught with grievous and intrinsic dangers, has, within the last twelve months, been brought to your own doors. It is presented to you, we deplore to say, in those collegiate institutions which have been established in this country, and associated with the name of our august, most gracious, and beloved sovereign. Far be it from us to impugn for a moment the motives of its originators. The system may have been devised in a spirit of generous and impartial policy; but the statesmen who framed it were not acquainted with the inflexible nature of our doctrines, and with the jealousy with which we are obliged to avoid everything opposed to the purity and integrity of our faith. Hence, those institutions, which would have called for our profound and lasting gratitude, had they been formed in accordance with our religious tenets and principles, must now be considered as an evil of a formidable kind, against which it is our imperative duty to warn you with all the energy of our zeal and all the weight of our authority".

The following, being the first of the episcopal resolutions of 1869, shows the opinions of the bishops, after twenty years' experience of the system:

"They reiterate their condemnation of the mixed system of

education, whether primary, intermediate, or university, as grievously and intrinsically dangerous to the faith and morals of Catholic youth; and they declare that to Catholics only, and under the supreme control of the Church in all things appertaining to faith and morals, can the teaching of Catholics be safely entrusted. Fully relying on the love which the Catholics of Ireland have ever cherished for their ancient faith, and on the filial obedience they have uniformly manifested towards their pastors, the bishops call upon the clergy and the laity of their respective flocks to oppose, by every constitutional means, the extension or perpetuation of the mixed system, whether by the creation of new institutions, by the maintenance of old ones, or by changing Trinity College, Dublin, into a mixed College".

In their memorial to the Lord Lieutenant in 1859,* and in their official letters to the Right Hon. E. Cardwell, when Chief Secretary for Ireland,† and the Right Hon. Sir George Grey, Secretary of State for the Home Department,‡ they have been equally explicit in their condemnation of the mixed system, and in stating the principle upon which the government should legislate for the education of Irish Catholics.

At the Synod of Thurles the bishops resolved to found a Catholic University, which should serve as a support of Catholicity and as an intellectual centre for the Catholics of the Irish race. The satisfaction with which the announcement of the project was received, and the readiness with which the funds for its maintenance have been supplied, are sufficient proofs, if none other were forthcoming, of the views of the Irish Catholic laity on the kind of education they want.

* Memorial to the Earl of Carlisle, etc., 28th November, 1859; Parl. Paper, No. 26 (1860).
† Letter to Mr. Cardwell, March, 1860; Parl. Paper, No. 206 (1860).
‡ Letter to Sir Geo. Grey, 14th January, 1866; Parl. Paper, No. 84 (1866).

More than £150,000 has been already contributed for this purpose, the greater part by Catholics at home, but many thousands by Irishmen in America and Australia also. The latter fact has scarcely attracted the notice of statesmen or of the English public, and yet it affords strong evidence of the real opinions of Irishmen on the education question. These men, besides sharing in the support of the civic institutions of their adopted countries, have had to build and maintain missionary churches, convents, charitable institutions, colleges, and schools—for the Irish are the apostles of the voluntary system,—and yet, though living amidst republican societies, away from the influences of their early home associations, they freely contribute to support the Catholic University, because they see in it the embodiment of the views and wishes of their brethren at home.

The actual amount of money contributed to establish and maintain the Catholic University, considerable as is the sum, is not the only element we have to take into account. We should remember that the country, only just recovering from one of the most frightful disasters on record, was politically prostrate when the University was set up; and also that within the period of its existence, vast sums have been expended on the foundation and maintenance of churches, convents, charitable institutions of all kinds, colleges, diocesan and other schools—all the colleges and schools being based on the denominational principle. We purpose in another chapter to show, as evidence of Irish opinion, what Irish Catholics have done within a century in founding and maintaining colleges and schools.

We have now brought down the history of the education movement to the foundation of the Catholic

University. This was the practical expression of the views of the bishops on higher education put forward in the synodical address from Thurles. The money subscribed to support the University was, on the other hand, evidence that the laity agreed with the bishops as to the principle of that education.

But, besides the general evidence which the pecuniary support of the Catholic University affords of the opinion of the laity on the question of intermediate and higher education, several opportunities have occurred within the last ten years of directly testing their views on the subject. Who does not remember the attempt of Sir Robert Peel, when Chief Secretary, to enlarge the resources of the Queen's Colleges by raising a subscription to found additional scholarships in connection with those institutions? He was led to believe that not only would a considerable sum of money be collected, but that his appeal would produce such an expression of opinion from Catholics in favour of the system of education represented by the Colleges, as would silence all further opposition to them on the part of the Catholic clergy.

We have no doubt that Sir Robert Peel sincerely believed that, in establishing the Queen's Colleges, his father showed himself a true benefactor of this country, and that the colleges themselves were really doing well the work that many intended they should do. That work was two-fold. First, the teaching of physical science, and of ancient and modern literature, chiefly from the artistic and philological point of view—this side of literature being thought more suitable to the imaginative turn of the Celtic mind, than the historical, which is reserved for the more robust Teutonic intellects of our neighbours. Secondly, the slow disintegration of the Catholics, as a religious party, by producing a number of one-sided and imperfectly trained young men, more or less weaned from Catholic habits of thought, who, being necessarily spread through middle class society, would, it was hoped, leaven it with ideas at once antagonistic to Catholicity and incompatible with Irish national traditions. Like other English statesmen who came to Ireland to make their apprenticeship, Sir Robert Peel mistook the interested opinion of placemen, the intolerant exaggerations of a few members of the coming Scientific Church, and the nauseous untruth of shallow and ignorant candidates for the honours in the gift of the Irish government, for the healthy opinion of the country.

But even this does not help us to understand how he selected the following committee, of which he himself was chairman, and Mr. George Johnstone Stoney, secretary of the Queen's University, honorary secretary— the Duke of Leinster, Right Hon. Abraham Brewster, Sir James Emerson Tennent, James W. Napier, Esq., Alexander Thom, Esq., Benjamin Lee Guinness, Esq., and William Malcolmson, Esq. Are we to conclude that he could not find, even among government officials, one Catholic willing to connect his name with the project? This exclusively Protestant committee— some of whom belonged to the party which, in the name of liberty, deprived Catholics of every constitutional right, and in the name of knowledge condemned them to ignorance—had the hardihood to publish an address, in which the following paragraphs occur:

"Founded by Parliament from a foresight of the great good they [the Queen's Colleges] are destined to confer, they have won their way into popular esteem: their prestige is established, and the Irish people have recognised the claim of this university to take rank among the national institutions of the country. It is essential, however, to limit, as much as possible, the weight of governmental influence in the administration of such educational establishments by restricting their burden on the public purse.

"We believe, therefore, that by appealing to the public spirit of the country, we appeal to motives as commendable and powerful as any which prompted the liberality of our forefathers.

"They fought the battle of that freedom which we enjoy: on us devolves the duty of shrinking from no sacrifice to strengthen and confirm it; and as it is to the influence of our example is entrusted the development of those moral and material resources which tend to elevate the character of our country, so we are persuaded that in no way can that development be more effectually promoted than by enlarging the resources of this great national edifice of education, which, free from all denominational bias, is so successfully cultivating friendly feelings and mutual forbearance between the members of different creeds".

The response which Sir Robert Peel received to this extraordinary document was certainly not what he was led to expect, but such as any one knowing anything of this country might have anticipated. The munificent sum of £382 5s., and £15 a-year during the life of the donor—the contributions of forty-two persons—represented the amount subscribed to found the Peel Scholarships by the Catholics of Ireland! Of this sum £145 was subscribed by six professors and officers of the Queen's Colleges; while the liberal sum of £25 5s. formed the united contribution of all other Catholic officials—judges, commissioners, inspectors of all grades, etc. If we deduct these two sums from the total Catholic subscriptions, there remains £212, and £15 a-year as the contribution of Irish Catholics unconnected directly with the State. But even part of this sum was subscribed anonymously, and may have been an official subscription. Far more important as a test of public opinion were the letters, in which more than two hundred Catholic peers, members of parliament, magistrates, and other gentlemen repudiated in indignant terms the attempt of the Chief Secretary to obtain their support for the system of education in the Queen's Colleges. This was, beyond question, one of the most important declarations of opinion which, up to that period, had emanated from the higher classes of the Catholic laity.

The protest against the Peel Scholarship appeal was not confined to words, but in some cases took the form of acts. The laity of the county and city of Limerick, for instance, founded scholarships in the Catholic University for a period of ten years, of the annual value of £200; the late John Conolly founded scholarships for the same period of the annual value of £100, and the bishop and clergy of Cloyne, scholarships also for ten years of the annual value of £120; besides £8,677 subscribed in the same year, by the country at large, for the support of that institution.

The following summer witnessed a more formal declaration of the sentiments of the Catholic middle classes. The corporations and town commissioners of a large number of the cities and towns sent a joint deputation to the late Lord Palmerston, the premier, in order to lay before the responsible ministers of the crown the claims of Irish Catholics respecting the higher education of their children. The disdain with which the prime minister received the delegates of the elected representatives of our civic population, the best exponents of the feelings and convictions of our people, is still fresh in the memory not only of the gentlemen who formed the deputation, but in that of their constituents, and of the whole nation. Lord Palmerston assigned no reason for refusing to listen to the claims put forward by the deputation, though obliged to admit their justice. The discourtesy of that reception, and the injustice of the rejection of claims, which he was obliged to admit were well founded, went far towards filling to the brim the cup of Lord Palmerston's transgressions towards Ireland, and producing that unprecedented alienation of Irish Catholics from the Liberal party which marked the last years of his administration.

During the last two or three years the questions of the Church and the land, which had precedence of that of education, naturally absorbed the attention of the people. Nevertheless, we can refer to three facts which clearly show that Irish Catholics have lost none of the interest they had hitherto taken in this momentous question.

We do not believe that even one of the candidates, who at the last general election sought to represent popular constituencies in Ireland, ventured to ask their suffrages without having first expressly declared his intention to advocate the claim of Catholics to have a system of Catholic education.

In the spring of 1870 there was printed, by order of the House of Commons, on the motion of The O'Conor Don, M.P., a declaration of Catholic laymen respecting university education in Ireland. To this exclusively *lay* document there are appended the names of 960 gentlemen of the first position among Catholics, including noblemen, members of parliament, deputy lieutenants, and a large number of magistrates and professional men. These gentlemen demand such a change in the existing unfair arrangements for higher education in Ireland as will satisfy the just claims of Catholics.

And, lastly, during the last few months, the following declaration has received the signatures of many thousands of Parliamentary electors, and still continues to receive them:

"We, the undersigned Irish Roman Catholics, clergymen and laymen, being registered Parliamentary electors, deem it our duty to declare, as follows, our conscientious convictions respecting the momentous question of education in Ireland:—

"1. That education, to be fruitful of good, must be founded on religion; and that non-religious education tends to subvert religion and morality in Catholic youth. Our practical conviction of the truth of these principles is evinced by our maintaining over 6,000 boys and youths in Catholic schools and colleges, at an annual cost to ourselves of about a quarter of a million sterling.

"2. That, while unwilling to interfere with the rights of our Protestant fellow-countrymen, we claim for ourselves, as Christian guardians and parents, representing four and a-half millions of Irish Catholics, the right—with which we will admit no interference—to give to our children an education based upon and interwoven with the religion which we believe to be true, and conformable to the teachings of the Church of which we are members.

"3. That our fathers, having transmitted unsullied to us our religion, we are determined so to hand it down to those who will come after us; and as, for this purpose, Catholic education is necessary, we are determined to use all constitutional means in resisting, as an encroachment upon our civil and religious liberties, every attempt to force upon us any system of education, university, intermediate, or primary, which is not based upon the Catholic religion.

"4. That we protest against the assertion, that

the just claims of Catholics can be met by the extension or perpetuation of the mixed system, whether by the erection of new institutions, by the maintenance of the Queen's Colleges and model schools, or by changing Trinity College, Dublin, into a mixed college.

"5. That, inasmuch as we, Catholics, who entertain these conscientious opinions, contribute equally with our fellow-subjects to the public taxes, it is but just that endowments and all other advantages afforded by the state to educational institutions, based upon Protestant or upon non-religious principles, should, in the fullest sense of equality, be shared with Catholic institutions, which alone are in accordance with the religious opinions of the great mass of the people of Ireland.

"6. We therefore, demand such a change in the system of public education—primary, intermediate, and university in Ireland—as will place us on a footing of perfect equality with our fellow subjects who entertain no conscientious objections to existing systems, and remove the civil disabilities which are at present inflicted upon us for our religious opinions in this matter of education".

In conclusion, we repeat that there is no one acquainted with Ireland, who looks back over the events of the last twenty-five years, but must admit, as regards the fundamental principles of intermediate and higher education, that the Catholics of Ireland, with some few exceptions—so few that they need not be taken into account—thoroughly agree with their bishops. There is, as there must necessarily be regarding a question of so much importance, and involving so many details, much difference of opinion as to the best way of practically carrying out these principles. But there never has been, and so long as Ireland continues to be

Catholic, never will there be, any fundamental difference between the views, sentiments, or wishes of the clergy and laity of this country. We say with confidence, that the statesman who would calculate upon such a difference in order to evade settling the education question upon the only basis which will ever satisfy Irish Catholics, will be disappointed. Sixty years ago Mr. Leslie Foster, a member of the then Education Board under the administration of Mr. Spencer Perceval, perhaps the most anti-Popery government that ever ruled England, said:—

"Whatever plan may appear to this board most eligible, it should be laid before the heads of the Roman Catholic clergy previous to our report. No person acquainted with the discipline of the Roman Catholic Church in Ireland can doubt that on the sentiments of the bishops will depend the degree of resistance or coöperation which any plan would receive from the subordinates of their religion".

We commend these words to the careful consideration of the statesmen of to-day, who will find that time has not diminished either their wisdom or their truth.

CHAPTER I.

HISTORICAL SURVEY OF THE EDUCATIONAL INSTITUTIONS OF THE LAST THREE CENTURIES.

Existence in Ireland of an Education Question from the Norman Invasion to the present time; this interval divided into two periods; during the first, from 1169 to 1537, education was *political* and *English*, as opposed to *native;* since 1537, when Protestantism was introduced, it has been *politico-religious;* existing educational institutions created during the second period; these institutions can only be rightly understood when viewed from a historical standpoint.

Primary, Intermediate, and University Education so dovetailed into each other, that, in their general aspects, they must be studied as a whole. Chronological table of Irish educational foundations; those founded between 1537 and 1793 were intended to subvert the faith and nationality of the country: failure of both objects. The Parish School Act of Henry the Eighth designed as much for political and social propagandism as for education; failure of those schools; similar politico-religious objects more evident in subsequent foundations,—*e.g.*, the Charter Schools; society for those schools still existing as the "Incorporated Society"; operations of the Society; reasons why this scheme is specially mentioned. Other primary schools of public foundation in operation during the Charter School period; withdrawal of State-grants from all such institutions after 1829, and the establishment of the system usually known as National, mark a new era. Archbishop Whately's hope regarding the system, that it would "gradually undermine the vast fabric of Popery", not realized, owing to the system having gradually drifted into a denominational one. Final result of all educational schemes—the rejection by the country of "secular" or "united" education.

For seven hundred years, there has been an education question, with adverse sides to it, in Ireland. An event of profound importance divides, nearly equally, this long period, and gives a new complexion to the controversy. From the Anglo-Norman invasion, 1169, to 1537, when Protestantism was first introduced, the education question in this country was purely political, involving a conflict of manners, customs, laws, language, traditions, and race, between the natives and the Anglo-Norman settlers of the Pale, who at the latter date only partially occupied four or five counties of Leinster. This period of 368 years saw enacted (1367) the Statute of Kilkenny, abolishing the Brehon laws and forbidding every usage and habit that distinguished the " Irish enemy" —which, from 1169 to 1612, was the legal and technical description of the people of this country. This statute of 1367, the "Head" Act, passed at Trim (5 Ed. IV., c. 2), 1465, and, in fact, the whole legislation of the period, was a declaration, not alone of war, but of extirpation, against the entire native population. With the exception of five regal families—*de quinque sanguinibus*—all " mere Irish " were forbidden, under penalty of death, to obey the Brehon law, or to adhere to native habits, while, on the other hand, they were excluded from the benefits of the political system of the invaders. Their own language, literature, and civilization were proscribed, and none other provided for them. Wherever the Palesman had power, the chief ecclesiastical positions, the direction of most of the abbeys and monasteries, and the charge of the great schools, were a monopoly in Anglo-Norman hands. Unity of faith was inadequate to soften the deep hostility of races. The struggle of nationalities and the ever-recurring reprisals continued between the aliens and the natives, from the landing of the Anglo-Norman to the time of Henry the Eighth. The education of the first period was, therefore, exclusively *political* and *English*, as opposed to *Native*. The introduction of Protestantism in 1537 brought a new and more bitter element of discord. The intense attachment of the Irish to the ancient faith, the attempt to force upon them, by penal statutes, the royal creed, and the alienation, for this purpose, of the church property of the kingdom, superadded to the passions fomented since the invasion, roused a spirit of national resistance that has not since wholly subsided. The education question of this latter period is, therefore, politico-religious—native faith and nationality against an alien established Church and an anti-Irish scheme of education. It is remarkable that the two periods are of much the same extent, the former 366, the latter 336 years.

The existing educational institutions in this country, from the parish school to the university, date from the sixteenth century, and are the slow aggregation of successive foundations, with varying phases of liberality and different sources of endowment. No one of these schemes can be thoroughly realised unless in association with the kindred institutions of the time, and in relation to the frequent changes in the spirit of legislation as regards this country, and it is only in this way that the present phase of the education question can be thoroughly apprehended. Viewing the subject of education in its three divisions—primary, intermediate, and university—it is evident that while the meaning of these names is sufficiently clear, the divisions themselves overlap each other. This is the case in every country, but the intermixture is most marked in Ireland. The higher classes in model schools and in some other primary schools are occupied with subjects of study not inferior to those of undergraduates in the Queen's University, or of freshmen in Trinity College. The same may be said with regard to institutions for intermediate education. The several branches of the educational system in Ireland are, therefore, so related that, to be understood, they must be considered, not only individually, but as a whole, in their bearings on each other. That the entire field may be seen, we give the following chronological table of the introduction into Ireland of the several schemes of schools, colleges, and universities:—

1537.—Act of Supremacy (28 Henry VIII., c. 5) passed, declaring the king to be head of the Church; another act (28 Henry VIII., c. 16) in the same year, vested in the crown the lands of certain great abbeys and religious houses, many of which were educational establishments.

1537.—An "Acte for the English order, habite, and language" (28 Henry VIII., c. 15), out of which grew the existing system of Protestant parochial schools.

1570.—Diocesan free schools (Latin), previously established, placed on a permanent basis by statute, 12 of Elizabeth, c. 1.

1591.—Trinity College and the University of Dublin chartered by Elizabeth, and endowment provided.

1608.—Royal free schools—Order in council, made by James I., for their foundation and endowment out of the confiscated estates in Ulster.

1613.—Irish Society (London Companies of Undertakers) obtain charter of incorporation and grants of the whole city and county of Derry for, among other trusts, the purpose of education.

1657.—Erasmus Smith, one of the Cromwellian settlers, endows schools with large estates, which he obtained under the Plantation of Ireland.

1672.—Blue Coat Hospital (Dublin) Free Schools, founded by Charles II.

1700.—Endowed grammar schools. From the opening to the close of the seventeenth century, more than ten of these schools were founded and in part locally endowed. A few others were established in the early part of the eighteenth century.

1704.—Foundling Hospitals.

1731.—Royal Dublin Society founded; chartered in 1750, for the promotion of Husbandry and the useful Arts, and endowed with parliamentary grants up to the present time.

1733.—Charter schools incorporated. They obtained parliamentary grants up to 1833, and still exist under a modified scheme, known as the Incorporated Society's schools.

1769.—Hibernian Military School. Still enjoys parliamentary grants.

1775.—Hibernian Marine School—obtained parliamentary grants.

1795.—Royal College of Maynooth; parliamentary grants or endowment to 1870.

1800.—Association for discountenancing Vice, schools founded in 1752, and obtained parliamentary grants from 1800 to 1827.

1808.—Belfast Royal Academical Institution enjoyed parliamentary grants up to 1849, when the Queen's College, Belfast, was opened.

1814.—Kildare Place Society's schools, founded in 1811, obtained parliamentary grants from 1814 to 1832.

1819.—Lord-Lieutenant's fund annually granted by parliament up to 1838, for the erection of schools.

1831.—National System of Education for the Poor of Ireland introduced, and still supported by large parliamentary grants.

1832.—Presbyterian Theological College, Belfast, enjoyed parliamentary grants up to 1870.
1838.—Poor Law Act passed, and workhouses opened; workhouse schools supported by rates, but for the last few years aided by grants from parliament.
1845.—Queen's Colleges Act passed, and those Colleges opened in 1849, supported by parliamentary grants.
1849.—National Model Schools opened and extended throughout Ireland. In the case of boys' schools they may, as we shall see later, be looked upon as in a great measure schools for intermediate education.
1851.—Queen's University chartered and supported by the state.
1854.—Convict Prisons Act passed, and their schools, supported by the state, opened.
1858.—Reformatories Act passed, and their schools, aided by the state, opened.
1866.—Royal College of Science, Dublin, developed out of the Museum of Irish Industry, supported by the state.
1869.—Industrial Schools Act passed, which secures state contribution towards the support of those schools.

The above list gives a sufficiently clear idea of the various classes of educational institutions. The institutions founded from 1537 to 1793, to the establishment of which millions of the public taxes and thousands of acres of the confiscated lands had been devoted, were set up for two avowed objects—to subvert the faith, and subjugate the nationality of the Irish people. The wars, rebellions, confiscations, plantations and transplantations, the Penal Laws, and their slow repeal, are a sufficient answer to those—if there be any such—who would still indulge the hope that Irish nationality can be stamped out by state schools and state education. The Protestant incumbent was, from 1537, obliged by oath, on pain of forfeiture of his benefice,

"To endevour himself to learne, instruct, and teach the English tongue to all and everie being under his rule, cure, order, or governance . . . . and for his own part [to] use and exercise the English order and habite, and also provoke as many as he may to the same . . . . . and also [to] keep or cause to be kept within the place, territorie, or paroch where he shall have preeminence, rule, benefice, or promotion, a schole for to learne English . . . . . taking for the keeping of the same schole such convenient stipend or salarie as in the said land is accustomably used to be taken" (28 Hen. VIII., c. 15, § 9).

Thus the intruded clergy were constituted religious, literary, and political schoolmasters, charged "to provoke" all within their cure "to use and exercise" the English "order, habite, and language";—the abolition of the native "manners and the native apparel", including the "coulin", the "glib", and the "crombeal", or the form of wearing their hair and beard, ranking with the extirpation of Popery as objects of the alien ministers' solicitude. Bard, minstrelsy, and beard were alike proscribed, which but increased the attachment to national usages, as the Irish maiden so passionately sets forth in her touching appeal to her lover:

> And I 'll gaze on thy gold hair, as graceful it wreathes,
> And hang o'er thy soft harp, as wildly it breathes;
> Nor dread that the cold-hearted Saxon will tear
> One cord from that harp, or one lock from that hair.

The Act of Henry the Eighth just referred to, for promoting "the English order, habite, and language", clearly indicates that the educational system, even in the parish primary schools, was not confined to literary, moral, and religious instruction, but was also designed as a powerful agency of social and political propagandism. How imperfectly they fulfilled this object may be understood from the fact that in 1825, after the act had been 288 years in operation, a Royal Commission reports that out of the 1,242 benefices of the Established Church, only 782 had parish schools in operation. As there are in Ireland 2,425 civil parishes, we see at once that more than two out of every three civil parishes had no school within the meaning of the act. Nearly all those schools received aid from the Kildare Place Society, some from the Society for Discountenancing Vice, and many from the "Lord Lieutenant's Fund". A considerable number have been closed since 1824. A majority of those which still exist are connected with the Church Education Society, and some receive aid from the National Board. The religious census returns of 1834 and 1861, and the Act of 1869 disestablishing and disendowing the Irish Church, are the verdicts of the total failure of the English parish schools and all subsequent schemes of primary education designed to subvert the faith of the Irish people.

The terms of incorporation of some of the later foundations for (in whole or in part) primary education, are much more explicit, as to their missionary and anti-Catholic, or rather anti-Popery, character, than those of the Parish School Act of Henry the Eighth. Passing over the charter, in 1613, of the Irish Society, and the indenture, dated 1657, of Erasmus Smith, the royal charter of George the Second, dated 24th October, 1733, "for erecting English Protestant schools in the Kingdom of Ireland", rehearses and approves the declaration made in the petition presented to his Majesty by Primate Boulter on behalf of the "Lord Primate, Lord Chancellor, archbishops, noblemen, bishops, judges, gentry, and clergy of our kingdom of Ireland", and says:—

"That in many parts of our said kingdom there are great tracts of mountainy and coarse land, of ten, twenty, and thirty miles in length, and of considerable breadth, almost entirely inhabited by Papists; and that in most parts of the same, and more especially in the provinces of Leinster, Munster, and Connaught, the Papists far exceed the Protestants of all denominations in number. That the generality of the Popish natives appear to have very little sense or knowledge of religion but what they implicitly take from their clergy, to whose guidance in such matters they seem wholly to give themselves up, and thereby are kept not only in gross ignorance, but also in great disaffection to our person and government, scarce any of them appearing to have been willing to abjure the Pretender to our throne. So that if some effectual method be not made use of to instruct these great numbers of people in the principles of true religion and loyalty, there is little prospect but that superstition and idolatry, and disaffection to us and our royal posterity, will, from generation to generation, be propagated amongst them. That amongst the ways proper to be taken for converting and civilizing of the said deluded persons, and bringing them (through the blessing of God) in time to be good Christians and faithful subjects, one of the most necessary, and without which all others are likely to prove ineffectual, has always been thought to be the erecting and establishing of a sufficient number of English Protestant schools, wherein the children of the Irish natives may be instructed in the English tongue and the fundamental principles of true religion".

After one hundred years' trial, state support was withdrawn from the Charter Schools in the year 1832, on the recommendation of the Royal Commission of 1824-26; but the corporation still subsists, under the name of the "*Incorporated Society*", the unpopular and odious designation "*Charter*", having been withdrawn from their schools, of which they have still twenty-one, eight of them boarding institutions. From the donations and bequests received under royal favour and high ecclesiastical and other influence, and the residue of the property remaining after the withdrawal of the parliamentary grant in 1832, the "Incorporated Society" still retains landed estates of 17,240 acres in fifteen counties, besides about £100,000 stock, with an income of £8,000 a-year.—(*Report Comm. Prim. Ed., Ireland*, 1870, vol. 1, page 492).

These few facts are cited as the clearest and most faithful exposition of the spirit of the times, with respect to education. They indicate a continuity of object from the Act of 1537, establishing English Parish Schools, to 1833, or a period of three centuries. The conversion from Popery to Protestantism of the natives, and their civilization through the inculcation of loyalty and of "The English order and habite"—were the avowed motives of the framers and supporters of all those schemes. The king, through the lord lieutenant, gave the charter schools a prominent place in his address from the throne at the opening of almost every session of parliament, and, for many years, subscribed £1,000 annually to the funds. The Irish parliament, besides large annual grants, gave the schools the produce of a tax upon peddlers and hawkers. The Imperial parliament supported them. The whole of the episcopal and clerical influence of the Established Church, the peerage, the judicial bench, and the landed gentry, actively sustained them. The children were boarded and clothed and put out to trades; the girls got marriage portions, if they married Protestants, and the boys were started in life. All these advantages were tendered to the poorest people in Europe, the Catholics of Ireland. Without entering into details of the profligacy which resulted from these institutions—the financial results of the scheme for the first ninety years, 1734 to 1823, may be cited from the first report of the Royal Commission on Irish Education (page 30), dated 30th May, 1825:

"The expenditure of the society during the ninety years it has been in operation, has been no less than £1,612,138, of which the sum of £1,027,715 was derived from parliamentary grants.

"We have in vain endeavoured to obtain any account of the total number of children admitted during the same period. We find, however, that from May, 1821, to January, 1825, 1,012 children were admitted, being on an average 200 yearly. We find also that the total number apprenticed from the beginning has been 12,745, and of whom not more than 1,155 have received the marriage portions of £5 given to all apprentices duly serving their time, *and marrying Protestants*".

"*From these statements it results that 7,905 children apprenticed cost just a million sterling*".

We have referred to this scheme of the Charter Schools because, extending over so long a period, and reaching down even *to the present generation*, it is a standing proof of the cruelty, the wickedness, the infatuation, and the persistency with which it was sought to force Protestant systems of education on the Irish people.

Side by side with the Charter Schools, during the whole period of their existence, were the following *primary* schools of public foundation—the English *parish* schools, those endowed by the Irish Society, chiefly in Londonderry, most of those of Erasmus Smith, the Blue Coat Hospital, and other similar institutions. During the latter portion of the Charter School period there were also in operation, and supported by parliamentary grants, the schools of the Association for Discountenancing Vice and Promoting a Knowledge of the Christian Religion (1780-1827), and those of the Kildare Place Society (1814-1832); several foundling hospitals and orphanages, the Hibernian Military and Marine Schools, while the Lord Lieutenant's Fund (1819-1830) was, with trifling exceptions, devoted to the erection of Protestant schools. All these were openly Protestant (modified somewhat in the case of the Kildare Place Society), as may be understood from the fact that the parliamentary grants were successively withdrawn from every one of them, save the Hibernian Military School in the Phœnix Park, an institution still Protestant in direction, spirit, and operation, although 141 of the 410 boys found there by the Royal Commissioners, 26th February, 1869, were Catholics. The relaxation of the Penal Laws against Catholic Education commenced in 1781, and went forward up to 1793. Such, however, was the perverse spirit of the policy of the time, that between those dates and 1829, many of the anti-Catholic institutions just enumerated were founded, and, along with older kindred foundations were supported by Parliamentary grants. But with the passing of the Emancipation Act in 1829, the civil status of Catholics assumed a new phase, and schemes for the perversion of their faith could no longer be openly undertaken by the Government, or supported by the Legislature. All the grants to these institutions may be said to have been withdrawn immediately after emancipation, when the establishment, at the close of 1831, by Earl Grey's government, of the system of education (usually known as " National") for the poor of Ireland marks the new era of civil and religious liberty.

Despite the hope indulged by Archbishop Whately,

one of the chief promoters of the National System, that it would "gradually undermine the vast fabric of Popery in Ireland", that system has drifted into a denominational one. This fact, previously well known to all, is declared in the Report of the recent Royal Commission on Primary Education, to which we refer our readers, since it is beside our present purpose to enter into that question.

It appears, therefore, that after the many millions spent on primary instruction for 335 years, we stand face to face with those striking results:—secular education, in the modern sense, implying the ignoring of all religious instruction, may be said to be unknown in Ireland; united education, as in the national schools, with a "common Christianity", has proved a total failure; all Ireland, every creed and sect, has settled down into denominationalism, pure and simple—each great religious body having its own schools, under its own management, clerical or lay, with its own religious economy.

It is clear that the discussion of the question of Intermediate and Higher Education could not be understood or appreciated unless preceded by this brief historical review of education in Ireland.

CHAPTER II.

THE DIOCESAN FREE SCHOOLS OF QUEEN ELIZABETH.

English Parish School Act the only constructive educational legislation of Henry the Eighth; his destructive statutes more important. Irish Parliament a mere shadow. Act of 1557 declaring that the Irish Parliament could only pass or reject a Bill, but not frame or alter one; this degrading statute continued in force until 1782; all penal laws passed and anti-Catholic and anti-national institutions founded during this period. Educational measures of Elizabeth.

Act of 1570 for the erection of Diocesan Free Schools; failure of these schools, admitted in several Acts of Parliament. These schools the subject of inquiry by Parliament and Commissions. Report of Commissioners of 1788-91; of Commissioners of 1809; appointment of permanent Commission for Endowed Schools; Report of Commissioners of Education Inquiry of 1826; Parliamentary Inquiry of 1835; Report of Endowed Schools Commissioners of 1858. Tabular view of existing schools, value of premises, income and attendance; analysis of table; summary of statements of Commissions and Committees of Inquiry on Diocesan Schools; number of Catholic scholars and teachers in those schools; value of preceding details.

Diocesan Schools created as a substitute for confiscated Catholic educational foundations; the tax on Protestant clergy for the support of these schools a charge on their income for the benefit of the inhabitants generally; evasion by the clergy of the terms by which they held the property; this opinion justified by evidence of Dr. Kyle. Subsisting incomes of Protestant clergy not relieved from this charge by Act of 1869. Surplus funds of Disestablished Church must bear the charge as a first incumbrance; and also a capital sum as compensation for arrears. The Diocesan Free Schools must occupy a prominent position in connection with the "Equities" of the Education Question.

The Act of 1537, ordering the establishment of an English School in every parish in Ireland, appears to have been the only constructive legislation of Henry the Eighth towards the education of the Irish people. His destructive statutes were, however, even from an educational point of view, more important: the seizing of the great abbeys and monastic foundations, the alienation of the Church lands and of all the other ecclesiastical property of the kingdom, being a general disendowment of Catholic educational institutions. On his death, in 1547, the religious changes began to assume a more decided character, and persecution in support of them was actively employed during the short reign of Edward the Sixth. The brief period of Mary's rule led to no educational legislation; but Elizabeth, who came to the throne in 1558, soon set about founding institutions to propagate the new state creed, and punish all who refused conformity. The great civil wars in Ulster and Munster afforded a pretext for using education to arrest or eradicate the universal hostility to English rule and English religious ideas that pervaded the country. The Anglo-Irish Parliament, never more than a shadow, and never pretending to represent the Irish people, had now been shorn of even the semblance of legislative functions. Poyning's Act of 1495 (10 Henr. 7, c. 4), explained by one passed in 1557, just before the accession of Elizabeth, declared that no bill, nor even the heads of a bill, should be framed by the lords and commons of Ireland, but only by the viceroy and his council, and that the bill thus framed was to be passed into law by the Irish parliament, or rejected, without alteration or debate. This utter degradation of the kingdom continued until 1782—nearly three centuries—within which period all the penal laws were enacted, and all the anti-Catholic and anti-national educational institutions under consideration were founded. The establishment, in 1563, of the Thirty-nine Articles in their present form, gave the finishing touch to the new Reformation in England. The head of the last Earl of Desmond, impaled on London Bridge in 1567, symbolised the defeat of the Irish. Three years after that event Elizabeth commenced her educational foundations in

Ireland by the act of 1570, for the establishment of Free Grammar, or, as they were called, Diocesan Schools. This was followed in 1591 by the foundation of Trinity College and the University of Dublin. These two great measures for superior instruction are the chief features in Elizabeth's reign in connection with public education in this country.

As we have proposed to ourselves to treat, in the first place, of the institutions connected with Intermediate Education, we will now proceed to consider the Diocesan Schools, reserving the consideration of Trinity College and the University of Dublin for a future part of this work.

The Act (12th Elizabeth, c. 1) passed in 1570, placed the Diocesan Free Schools, some of which had been previously in operation, on a permanent footing. The two objects, political and religious, of the educational foundations of the period are explicitly set forth in the preamble of the statute, entitled, " An Act for the erection of Free Schools":—

"Forasmuch as the greatest number of the people of this your Majesties realm hath of long time lived in rude and barbarous states, not understanding that Almighty God hath, by his divine laws, forbidden the manifold and haynous offences, which they spare not daily and hourely to commit and perpetrate, nor that hee hath by his holy Scriptures commanded a due and humble obedience from the people to their princes and rulers; whose ignorance in these so high pointes touching their damnation, proceedeth only of lack of good bringing up of the youth of this realm, either in publique or private schooles, where through good discipline they might be taught to avoid these lothsome and horrible errours; it may, therefore, please your most excellent Majestie that it be enacted, and bee it enacted by your Highnesse, with the assent of the Lords spirituall and temporall, and the Commons in this present Parliament assembled, and by the authority of the same, *That there shall be from henceforth a free* schoole within every diocese of this realm of Ireland, *and that the schoolemaster shall be an Englishman or of the English birth of this realm, and, etc".*

The determined resistance of the Irish people to Protestantism rendered the Diocesan School Act almost a dead letter. Various statutes were passed admitting those schools to be failures, and devising new provisions for giving them efficiency. The act of 1694—7 Will. III., c. 4—the famous statute declaring all Catholic education at home and abroad penal, which will be noticed hereafter—deserves special mention, because it calls them Public Latin Free Schools, and contains provisions for enforcing the Act of Elizabeth. The Act was followed by the 8 George I., c. 9, 1725; 29 George the Second, c. 7, 1755; 21 and 22 George the Third, c. 28, 1781; 53 George the Third, c. 107, 1813; 3 George the Fourth, c. 79, 1822; and 1 William the Fourth, c. 56, 1830.

Besides this copious legislation, the Diocesan Free Schools were also the subject of numerous inquiries by Royal Commissions and by parliament. The reports of these Commissions and parliamentary Committees afford ample proof of the laxity with which the provisions of these statutes were carried out, and of the extent and character of the failure of the diocesan school system. We will now briefly recapitulate their principal statements, beginning with those of the Royal Commissions.

The Commission (1789-91) reported that in the thirty-four dioceses they found only twenty diocesan schoolmasters. In many dioceses there were no schoolhouses, while in others they were in a ruinous state; many of the masterships were mere sinecures. The sums payable by the clergy for the support of the schools in twenty dioceses amounted to only £616 5s. 7d., or an average of £30 16s. 3d. from each, while fourteen of the dioceses contributed nothing. By the Act of 1755 the repairing and rebuilding of the school-houses might be levied off the county in which the school was situated; but the Commission finding this inoperative, recommended that besides the whole expense of building and repairs, half the expense of the schoolmasters should also be borne by county presentment. It was further suggested by this Commission, that these schools might be rendered more useful by having a second master for instructing in mathematical learning; also that, besides an annual clerical contribution of £50 from each of the thirty-four dioceses, parliament should grant £1,924 out of the annual vote to charter schools, with the view of rendering the diocesan schools efficient, and of securing the admission of 20 gratuitous scholars into each, and the foundation of 396 exhibitions, at £9 per annum each, the holders to be elected by the (Protestant) bishops and clergy.

A subsequent Commission in 1809 reported to the Lord Lieutenant that out of 34 dioceses, only 10 were provided with schoolhouses in tolerable repair; that in three others the houses were out of repair, or otherwise insufficient; and that the remainder were wholly unprovided. The whole number of effective schools was only 13; and of scholars only 380. Various recommendations were made, amongst others, that as Diocesan Schools have been found impossible, district schools formed, by a union of dioceses, should be adopted.

With a view to carrying out some of the recommendations of the commission of 1809, the act of 1813 (53 Geo. III., c. 107) provides for the appointment of a Commission to have permanent charge of endowed schools. This act is still in force, and the commissioners appointed under it are known as " The Commissioners of Education for the Regulation of certain of the Endowed Schools in Ireland". Various powers were conferred by this act, amongst others, one enabling grand juries to present the sums requisite for the building and repairs of diocesan and district schools, and also for the purchase of sites. This Commission proposed, in 1823, that 5 of the 34 dioceses should remain separate, and that the other 29 should be united into 13 districts for school purposes.

The Commissioners of Education Inquiry of 1824 were specially directed to report on the Diocesan Schools, which they did in May, 1827, stating that of the eighteen schools, the endowments of which had been fixed in 1824, by the Lord Lieutenant and Council, six were then vacant, the Lord Lieutenant not having exercised his power of appointing masters. Two of the others had no scholars, while in four there were less than eleven boys; so that in only six of the eighteen schools was the attendance of scholars in a satisfactory condition. They further add: " We consider it extremely doubtful whether any attempt to establish permanent schoolhouses appropriated for the diocesan schools will be found ultimately successful. It has been seen that every endeavour hitherto made for that purpose, from the reign of Elizabeth, has failed, and that, in fact, there never were so few, either of schools or scholars, as at the present moment". They condemned the amalgamation of the thirty-four dioceses into eighteen districts; recommended that twenty-seven schools should be established (retaining seven of the unions), viz. three schools in the county of Cork, two each in Down and Galway, and one in each of twenty other counties. No Diocesan Schools were to be established in nine counties—viz., Dublin, Kilkenny, King's County, Louth, and Westmeath, in Leinster; Cavan, Fermanagh, and Tyrone, in Ulster; and Leitrim, in Connaught.

The next Commission which inquired into those schools was that of 1855–58. But before we pass to the consideration of its proceedings it will be well to cast a glance at the results of Parliamentary inquiries. For the sake of brevity we will confine ourselves to the most important—viz., that of 1835, when a select Committee of the House of Commons inquired into and reported on schools of public foundation in Ireland. It appears that there were then in operation but twelve of the eighteen Diocesan Schools, only six of which had more than twenty-five scholars, at an average, for the preceding five years; and six other schools were vacant. The report of the Committee, made in 1838, points out fully and clearly the causes of the failure of these schools, the chief of which are— (1) differences of opinion as to their object, the rights of the public, and the obligations of the contributors, the masters and the Commissioners of Education, appointed under the act of the year 1813, which led to collision of the parties, and neutralised attempts at improvement; (2) objectionable mode of collecting contributions from the clergy; (3) want of security for a good class of buildings; (4) unlimited authority of the masters; and (5) insufficient number of Diocesan Schools for the wants of the country. The Committee states that the Diocesan Schools seem "to have almost exclusively confined themselves to preparation for the learned professions. The commercial classes have found scanty means for the supply of their peculiar intellectual necessities. . . . . The actual course reduces itself to Greek,

Latin, and a small proportion of abstract sciences, with a little geography, history, etc".—(Rep. p. 58).

We may now proceed to consider the state of the Diocesan Free Schools, when, for the last time, they were examined and reported on by the Endowed Schools' Commission in 1858, twenty years after the parliamentary inquiry just referred to. By the statute of 1570, *each* of the thirty-four dioceses should have a free school, whereas, in 1858, only sixteen Diocesan or District Schools were said to be in existence, and four others were only imaginary institutions. The union of the Ballina with the Tuam school in 1857, reduced the number of existing schools to fifteen, of which Wicklow (opened in 1825 and closed in 1834), had not been in operation for many years. The mastership of Mallow was vacant from 1850 to 1857, and the mastership of Tuam was vacant at the time of inspection by the Endowed Schools' Commission, thus reducing the schools found in operation to twelve. Only eight had houses suitable for the purposes of the schools, and satisfactory reports as to the state of instruction could be made with regard to six only. Public complaints were made to the Endowed Schools Commission as to the management of four schools, and three others are in fact described *as private schools for the benefit of the masters.* The majority of the masters examined before the Commission denied the existence of the right of any scholars to free education, although such right had been stated and explained by a circular from the Commissioners of Education in their annual report for 1831, laid before Parliament.

The grand juries objected upon various grounds—some well founded, and others merely technical—to make presentments for the erection and repairs of the diocesan schools. Amongst the former was the objection to the Protestant and supposed exclusive character of the staff, of the instruction, and of the scholars; and, also, the denial, by the masters, of the right of any scholars to free admission. In five counties, however—Antrim, Londonderry, Down, Limerick, and Kildare—liberal sums were voted for the erection of school-houses, and in two others, presentments were made for repairs.

The Endowed Schools' Commission further states that, in 1858, there were no sites for Diocesan Schools in sixteen out of the thirty-two counties of Ireland.

The following table, extracted from the Report of this Commission (p. 44, 45), shows the main facts connected with the Diocesan Schools in 1858:—

Locality of School.	No. of Dioceses in School District	Annual Value of School Premises	Net annual income from tax on clergy.	Master's salary.	No. and Religious Denomination of Scholars on Rolls in 1857.			
					Established Church.	Catholics.	Presbyterians.	Totals.
		£ s. D.	£ s. D.	£ s. D				
Carlow	2	30 0 0	110 15 5	110 0 0	8	—	—	8
Naas	1	32 12 0	64 12 4	60 0 0	13	—	—	13
Mullingar	2	—	120 0 0	132 9 5	2	1	—	3
Wexford	1	44 18 7	64 12 3	64 12 3	43	6	—	49
Wicklow	2	—	92 6 0	92 6 2	—	—	—	—
Cork	1	—	73 16 11	73 16 11	39	1	3	53*
Mallow	1	1 0 0	92 6 2	92 6 2	—	—	—	—
Ross Carbery	1	—	27 13 10	30 0 0	18	9	—	27
Limerick	3	62 3 8	138 9 2	138 9 2	5	—	—	5
Ballymena	2	23 13 10	110 15 5	120 0 0	21	—	4	25
Downpatrick	2	28 10 0	83 1 6	100 8 11	8	3	10†	23‡
Londonderry	1	377 3 10	92 6 2	330 0 0	46	—	5	51
Monaghan	3	48 4 9	120 0 0	120 0 0	12	5	—	17
Tuam	3	—	120 0 0	136 15 4	—	—	—	—
Elphin	1	—	73 16 11	73 16 11	17	13	—	30
Totals	26	653 6 8	1384 12 3	1674 1 3	232	38	22	304

* There were also in Cork five " Friends" and five Wesleyan Methodists.
† Including "Non-subscribing" Presbyterians.
‡ Including two Methodists.

It will be seen that the preceding table refers to only twenty-six out of the thirty-four dioceses. It was intended that the remaining eight dioceses, which are without diocesan schools, should be formed into four district unions of two dioceses each; the localities for such projected schools being Tralee, Thurles, Dungannon, and Loughrea, the aggregate diocesan contributions, fixed by warrant of the Lord Lieutenant and Privy Council for the masters' salaries being £286 3s. The whole annual tax levied under the act upon bishops and clergy—or rather supposed to be levied—was £1,672 15s. The sites of eight of the schools included thirteen acres; the aggregate annual value of the premises of nine schools is £653; two schools, Mullingar and Tuam, have annual endowments from trust funds amounting to £29, while the school at Londonderry has an endowment from the Irish Society of £280 towards the salary of the master, and £150 for exhibitions.

This school at Londonderry was established under a special act of parliament (49 George III. c. 59) passed in 1809, and had in 1857 fifty-one scholars, the largest attendance in any of the Diocesan Schools. It was erected in 1814 at a cost of £13,000, by subscriptions from the Irish Society and the bishop, and by county presentment. It had an annual endowment from the corporation, and also from the London Companies, both now withdrawn, with the exception of £50 from the " Mercers' "; it has £90 from the bishop and clergy, and £430 from the Irish Society. It is the only one of the Diocesan Schools to which exhibitions are attached; and from the peculiar position and endowments of the school, it must be regarded as a special foundation, in which the Diocesan School is merged. Yet, with a tax for its erection, levied off all the occupiers of land in the county, and the large contribution from the Irish Society and London Companies, who obtained the confiscated estates of Catholics, and hold them in trust for the purpose of education, the twelve thousand Catholic citizens of Derry do not supply *even one scholar* to this liberally endowed institution.

The head masters of all these schools were, in 1858, members of what was then called the *United Church*, and all, with the exception of those in the Catholic districts of Wexford and Ross Carbery, were clergymen, some of whom, as in Ballymena, had also charge of a parish. No Roman Catholic held any position whatever on the staff of these schools.

Summing up the statements of the several parliamentary Committees and Royal Commissions, which have inquired into the diocesan free schools, we find they report that:—

(1) The Diocesan Free Schools are, from their constitution, open to scholars of all religious denominations.

(2) The Lord Lieutenant or the Protestant Ordinary, to whom, under the Act (12 Eliz. c. 1), belongs the nomination of the master, may appoint a person of any religious denomination to the charge of any of these schools, the restriction as to Englishmen, or those of English birth in Ireland, having, long since, been abandoned as impracticable.

(3) There is no legal right to enforce on the scholars any particular religious instruction, as a condition of admission.

(4) The right of a reasonable number of scholars to free classical education is clear, though set at nought by the masters, for their own profit.

Yet, notwithstanding these repeated declarations, there is no Catholic teacher on the staff, which is entirely Protestant, and, with two exceptions, clerical.

The muster of scholars in the 12 Elizabethan academies in 1858 was 304, the average *daily attendance* being only 240—or 20 boys in each school. Of this whole contingent to the Diocesan Free Schools of Ireland, the religious classification was—

		Scholars.	Per Cent.
Episcopalians	232 ⎫		
Presbyterians of all denominations	22 ⎬	266	87·5
Methodists	7 ⎥		
Quakers	5 ⎭		
Catholics		38	12·5
		304	100.

Five of the 12 schools had no Catholic on the rolls; one had three; one five, and another six boys; while 22, or over half the number of Catholics on the rolls, were in the two schools of Ross Carbery, a small village in the south-west of Cork, and Elphin, a small town in Roscommon—both of them localities almost entirely Catholic.

These details, wearisome and almost contemptible as they may appear to many, must possess great interest for any one honestly desirous of understanding the problem of Irish education. They give help of an invaluable kind—the light of experience—showing what to avoid in framing a scheme of Intermediate Education for Ireland; for they are the results of an experiment continued through three centuries, from 1570 down to the present day.

The leading features of this class of schools may now be noticed. The Diocesan Free Schools were given to Ireland to fill the void caused by the destruction of the Catholic educational foundations whose endowment had been confiscated. The tax for the support of the masters imposed by the statute of Elizabeth on the incomes of the intruded bishops and incumbents, and the right of nomination, vested partly in the crown and partly in some of the bishops, afford the clearest proof that with a transfer from the Catholic clergy of the ecclesiastical revenues, the Protestant clergy were required, by statute, to bear, at least fiscally, some of the educational burdens which had more directly been borne by the ancient Church. This view pervades alike the legislation with regard to diocesan schools and their whole history. Combating the pretensions of the clergy to special claims for free admission of their sons into these schools, the Endowed Schools Commissioners, in their report, 1858, p. 37, say:—

"We do not recognise that the payment of the diocesan school tax by the clergy gives them claims to direct benefits from the schools in priority to other inhabitants, as the tax was intended to be a charge on their income for the benefit of the inhabitants of the district generally".

Thus, after precisely three hundred years' operation, we find the statute of 1570 producing the abortive results indicated. The Protestant Church established by Elizabeth was disestablished in 1869, because it had failed in fulfilling the chief conditions supposed to attach to the Church of the nation. One of those conditions was education. Their incomes were granted to the Protestant clergy upon several trusts for the benefit of the people. Among these trusts was the duty of providing and supporting thirty-four free Latin grammar schools in Ireland. For three hundred years the bishops and the clergy of the Established Church have, as shown, appropriated to their private use revenues to which they had no title, have violated solemn trusts upon which their incomes had been assigned to them, and have denied to the nation institutions to which it had not only a moral and equitable claim, but a right secured to it by statutory enactment. It is quite beside the question to say that the systematic neglect by the Protestant clergy of a solemn moral duty as well as legal obligation, has been condoned by the acquiescence, or rather tacit connivance, of the Government of this country, which, during all this long period of three centuries, has not only not enforced the law, but has not made even an honest attempt to do so. Just as it is no defence for this same neglect of the Protestant clergy and connivance of the Government, to say, that had those grammar schools been set up and endowed out of the tax on the clergy of the Established Church, they would not have been attended by Roman Catholics, owing to the certainty of interference with their religion. Such reasoning does not touch the substance of the matter. Here is a lien, or charge, for educational purposes on the ecclesiastical property of the kingdom, transferred with that property, in the sixteenth century, to an intruded clergy. For three centuries this clergy has evaded the terms under which, by statute, they held the property, and have diverted to their own private use vast sums which should have been devoted to the education of the people.

That the view now expressed is perfectly justified may be understood from the evidence of the Secretary to the Commissioners of Education, Dr. Kyle, before the Endowed Schools Commission in 1855.—(See *Endowed Schools Commission, Ireland*, 1858. Evidence, Q. 21,369.)

"It appears that the following district Diocesan Schools, for which salaries were appointed by the Lord Lieutenant—namely,

Cashel, £100; Ardfert and Aghadoe, £80; Waterford and Lismore, £90; Clonfert and Kilmacduagh, £40; and Killala and Achonry, £50; making in the aggregate £360—have not been in operation for upwards of twenty years; and that Cloyne, with a salary of £100, has not been in operation for five years; and that Wicklow, with a salary of £100, has not been in operation for sixteen years. These salaries have never been raised or paid, and thus *a sum of £9,000 has, within twenty years, been illegally withdrawn from the purposes of education*".

These endowments, derived under the statute of 1570, and settled by warrant of the Lord Lieutenant and privy council, as well as those from several other dioceses, have continued,[*] even since 1858, to be "illegally withdrawn from the purposes of education", being retained by the bishops and incumbents.

When the Irish Church Bill of 1869 was under consideration, this element did not enter into the "equities" of the measure. The Church body, as a whole, was granted compensation for life interests, without, however, any investigation of its just liabilities for the support of the thirty-four diocesan free schools of Queen Elizabeth. This was unfair. The income of the Irish Protestant Church had imposed upon it, during the last three hundred years, an equitable and statutable charge for the becoming support of those diocesan schools. This charge still continues to be imposed upon the existing incomes of the present incumbents, for the recent Act of Disestablishment has not relieved them of it. The surplus funds of the Disestablished Church—estimated, 1st March, 1869, by Mr. Gladstone, at from seven to eight million pounds sterling—the allocation of which has yet to be settled by Parliament, clearly bears as one of its first incumbrances the amount of compensation due to

[*] Except the endowment of £40 from Clonfert and Kilmacduagh, which has been applied to the school at Elphin since 1862.

the country for the vast sums which, during those three hundred years, have been diverted from the legal purposes of education, and appropriated to their own use by the Protestant bishops and clergy. When the statesman comes to deal with the "equities" of the Irish Education question, the Diocesan Free Schools of 1570 are sure to obtain deserved prominence. In her Grammar Schools, as in her preaching of the Gospel, the Irish people repudiated the mission of the Church Establishment, while in the one case, as in the other, the clergy of that Establishment appropriated the revenue which belonged to the accepted ministers and teachers of the people.

CHAPTER III.

THE DIOCESAN FREE SCHOOLS OF QUEEN ELIZABETH (CONTINUED).

Recapitulation of the provisions of the Act, 12th Elizabeth, cap. i., and of subsequent legislation on Diocesan Schools. Number of legally distinct dioceses; each ought to have a school; the full number never existed; only 12 in 1857; consequences of this contraction of number. The Bishops and Clergy of the late Established Church held their preferments and benefices subject to the condition of maintaining Diocesan Schools; the Church Act of 1869 did not release them. If all the schools were in full operation, the masters' salaries would amount to upwards of £5,000 a-year; amount of actual diocesan charge in 1858; total amount leviable at that period.

Besides the present annual contribution of Bishops and Clergy, a large sum for arrears must be taken into account. Examples to show character and extent of these arrears; arrears due by the Dioceses of Dublin and "Glandelagh" for a school in Wicklow; arrears due by the Dioceses of Cashel and Emly and of Waterford and Lismore for schools for those dioceses; arrears due for a school for the Dioceses of Ardfert and Aghadoe; arrears due from the Dioceses of Clonfert and Kilmacduagh for a school for those dioceses; union of endowment for this school in 1862 to that of Elphin; arrears on account of a Diocesan School from the Dioceses of Achonry and Killala; union of this endowment in 1857 to that of Tuam; arrears due on account of the Diocesan Schools for the Diocese of Cloyne at Mallow. A complete list of arrears not given; only a few of the more striking cases of arrears cited as examples; amount of these arrears due since 1824; this sum due to the people of Ireland for purposes of Intermediate Education; legal proceedings should be instituted by Attorney-General to compel payment of these arrears; some of the cases of arrears referred to easy of redress, thus, arrears due by the Right Rev. Dr. Daly, Bishop of Cashel; by the Most Rev. Dr. Trench, Archbishop of Dublin; by the Right Rev. Dr. Graves, Bishop of Limerick; total amount of arrears due by these three prelates; the Bishops and clergy have no more right to retain the arrears, than they would have not to pay income-tax or rent.

Besides the arrears of the last forty-seven years, there are the arrears from 1570 to 1824; the rate of accumulation in the latter period not less than in the former. Evidence that the

Diocesan Schools were scarcely in operation before 1695; the Diocese of Kilmore never had a Diocesan School; in 1800 there were twelve dioceses which did not contribute to a school; even now there are ten dioceses which do not contribute; annual charge for each diocese down to 1824, £32 10s.; amount of arrears from 1570 to the year 1824; gross amount of arrears to the present time; part of arrear still recoverable; the remainder fairly chargeable on property of the late Established Church.
Recapitulation of the revenues of the Diocesan Schools.

In the preceding chapter we have given a brief history of the Diocesan Schools—the first step made towards reconstructing Intermediate Schools after all Endowments had been wrested from Catholics for the establishment of Protestantism. As some matters connected with those schools must be taken largely into account in the future re-adjustment of Intermediate Education, we find it necessary to discuss them more in detail than was convenient in the preceding chapter. Before doing so, let us briefly recapitulate what the Act 12th of Elizabeth, chap. i., provided, and what subsequent legislation and inquiries have established regarding Diocesan Schools. As to the first, it was enacted that, thenceforth, there was to be a free school in every diocese in Ireland, the schoolmaster to be an Englishman or of English birth. The Lord Lieutenant and Council were to appoint the master's salary, *of which one-third* was to be paid by the ordinary, and *two-thirds* by the other ecclesiastical persons in each diocese; and " all churches, parsonages, vicarages, and other ecclesiastical livings, which had come by any means to the Queen or her predecessors" were to be charged with this payment, " *in whose hands soever they should be*". As to the second, successive enactments authorized the grand juries to make presentments for the repairs of those schools, and even for their erection; and as a fact, in five counties liberal aid was contributed out of the county funds for building school-houses. Several Royal Commissions and Parliamentary Committees have declared that those schools are open to scholars of all religious denominations.

As the legal arrangements connected with the Irish Protestant Church have always recognised 34 distinct dioceses (although two or more might be united under one bishop), it follows that there ought to be now in existence in Ireland 34 free Diocesan Grammar Schools, maintained by the bishops and clergy of the Protestant Episcopal Church. But the full number of these schools seems to have never existed; and gradually they became fewer, until in 1857 there were only 12 of them in operation. This contraction of number from 34 to 12 involved two serious consequences. In the first place, the bishops and clergy of the late Established Church retained in their own hands the moneys which, by law, they ought to have paid for the support of the Diocesan Schools that should have been in active operation. In the second place, the schools designed by the legislature for the whole people were monopolised by a small section, not exceeding one-tenth of the community.

Ever since 1570—that is to say, for the last 300 years—the bishops and clergy of the Irish Protestant Church have held their ecclesiastical preferments and revenues, subject to the condition of maintaining those Diocesan Schools. The Irish Church Act of 1869 did not release them from those obligations. They are at this hour just as much bound to provide for the maintenance of those schools as they were at any time since 1570. The powers of the Lord Lieutenant as to fixing the salaries and appointing the masters remain precisely as they were. To put the matter more plainly—under the several Acts referring to those Diocesan Schools the Lord Lieutenant has the power of fixing what he considers an adequate salary for the master of a Free Grammar School in every one of the 34 dioceses in Ireland, to be paid by the Protestant bishop and clergy. Further, with certain exceptions, the Lord Lieutenant has the right of appointing the masters to those schools. Now, supposing these powers to be honestly exercised, with a view to the interests of the entire people of Ireland, the aggregate amount of the salaries of 34 efficient masters of Grammar Schools would amount to a considerable sum. Assigning the average salary at the moderate estimate of 150*l*. a school, the total sum would exceed 5,000*l*. a year. We submit that, had the acts regarding those institutions been honestly carried out—were they even at this moment enforced with any sort of decent regard for the rights and feelings of the people of Ireland— the bishops and clergy of the Protestant Episcopal Church would now be contributing that amount towards the intermediate education of Irish youth Is 150*l*. a moderate salary for a competent master of a Public Free Grammar School? If it is, then the actual incomes of the Protestant bishops and clergy are chargeable to the extent of 5,000*l*. a year for the support of Intermediate Schools.

The Endowed Schools Commission of 1858 reported the amount of the actual diocesan charge for the fifteen existing schools at 1,384*l*. 12*s*. 3*d*. To this should be added 286*l*. 3*s*., amount of diocesan charge fixed by the Lord Lieutenant's warrant for four schools that have no existence; thus making the total amount at this moment leviable for Diocesan Schools off the Irish Protestant ecclesiastical incomes 1,670*l*, 15*s*. 3*d*. It is evident that this sum, amounting to about 88*l*. per school, and 49*l*.

per diocese, was fixed with reference to a system of schools intended for a minority of the population, and not for the whole people. But, were the Diocesan Schools as numerous and comprehensive as their founders intended, it is plain that our estimate of 5,000*l.* might be impeached rather for insufficiency than for excess. Therefore, we repeat, were the Irish Executive to honestly use the powers which it actually possesses, with regard to Diocesan Schools, the Protestant Episcopal Church would be called upon for an annual contribution of at least 5,000*l.* towards a proper system of Intermediate Instruction.

But all this regards the *present* annual contribution to be levied off the existing ecclesiastical incomes, under the 12th of Elizabeth. In addition to this, a large sum must be taken into account, being the accumulation of the moneys which ought to have been paid towards the maintenance of Diocesan Schools by the bishops and holders of ecclesiastical benefices in Ireland, and were not so paid, but were retained by them. What this mass of arrears, which have been accumulating during the last three hundred years, may amount to, we do not undertake to estimate. But that we are justified in saying that they amount to a " large sum", will be admitted by any one acquainted with even an outline of the case. We will refer to one or two sample facts, as instances and witnesses. They shall be taken, not from any remote time, but from our own days.

On April 17th, 1824, a notice appeared in the *Dublin Gazette* that his Excellency the Lord Lieutenant in Council, in pursuance of the powers conferred on him by the Acts dealing with the Diocesan Schools, had appointed a salary of 100*l.* for the master of a school to be established in Wicklow, the amount to be made up by the Archbishop of Dublin and his clergy, in the proportion of 55*l.* for the diocese of Dublin, and 45*l.* for that of " Glandelagh". A master was appointed, whose pupils varied in number from four to fifteen, and who received the salary of 100*l.* till his death in 1834. *Since then there has been no master of the Wicklow school.* The appointment is in the hands of the Protestant Archbishop. This personage is therefore responsible for the omission and its consequences. That is to say, there is now owing from the Archbishop of Dublin and the clergy of Dublin and "Glandelagh" *an arrear of* 100*l. a year for* 37 *years, amounting to* 3,700*l.* And, we repeat, the Archbishop and clergy hold their preferments and benefices on the condition of paying this money.

Again, a similar notice appeared in the same number of the *Gazette,* appointing 100*l.* salary for the master of a Diocesan School, to be established for the diocese of Cashel and Emly, and 90*l.* salary for the master of a Diocesan School, to be established for the dioceses of Waterford and Lismore. *Neither of these schools has ever been established.* That is to say, there are now owing from those dioceses *arrears of* 100*l.,* and 90*l. a year, respectively, for* 47 *years, amounting together to* 8,930*l.*

Again, the same *Gazette* contained a notice appointing 80*l.* salary for the master of a Diocesan School for Ardfert and Aghadoe (Kerry). This school has never been established; so that an arrear of 80*l.* for 47 years is now due from those dioceses, amounting altogether to 3,760*l.*

A similar notice, of the same date, appointed 40*l.* salary for the master of a Diocesan School for Clonfert and Kilmacduagh. No school was, however, established for those dioceses. In 1862 the endowment was, by warrant, dated 5th November, 1862, united to that from the Diocese of Elphin; and the combined endowments were directed to be applied to a District school for the three dioceses to be held at Elphin. There is, therefore, owing from Clonfert and Kilmacduagh an arrear for the thirty-eight years from 1824 to 1862, amounting to 1,520*l.*

Again, a similar notice, of the same date, appointed 50*l.* salary for the master of a Diocesan School for Achonry and Killala. But no school was established, nor master appointed, down to 1857, when those dioceses were united with Tuam into a school district, to have a common Diocesan School at Tuam. An arrear is, therefore, now due from Achonry and Killala of 50*l.* for the 33 years from 1824 to 1857, amounting altogether to 1,650*l.*

The mastership of the Cloyne (Mallow) Diocesan School was vacant from 1849 to 1857, so that an arrear of 100*l.* a year for those eight years, or 800*l.*, is now due from that diocese.

It is hardly necessary to say that we do not propose to give a complete list of the arrears owing, even since 1824, on account of the Diocesan Schools. We have only taken those cases and items which appear on the face of the returns, and are most striking. It is highly probable that many other cases of at least partial arrear would be disclosed upon an investigation. But we shall confine ourselves to those glaring cases which we have found open, so to say, to the gaze of the world.

The following table shows the amount of the arrears above enumerated:—

Diocese.	Annual Amount of Diocesan charge for support of a Diocesan School	No. of Years of Arrear.	Total Amount of Arrears.
Dublin and Glandelagh	£100	37	£3,700
Cashel and Emly	100	47	4,700
Waterford and Lismore	90	47	4,230
Ardfert and Aghadoe	80	47	3,760
Clonfert and Kilmacduagh	40	38	1,520
Achonry and Killala	50	33	1,650
Cloyne	100	8	800

We thus find that the evident arrears of charges on ecclesiastical persons for the maintenance of Diocesan Schools, which have accumulated since 1824, amount, without taking interest into account, to 20,360*l.* And these arrears, be it remembered, have accumulated on the very low charges established by the notice in the *Gazette* of April 17th, 1824.

We submit that every penny of this sum of 20,360*l.* is owing to the people of Ireland for the purposes of Intermediate Education. We cannot repeat too often that the Bishops and the Clergy of the Protestant Church have always held their preferments and benefices on the condition of paying this money; their title to the former was dependent on their performance of the latter. If ever there was a case in which the legal maxim, *nullum tempus occurrit regi*, was fairly applicable, it is this. It is not long since the administrative world was edified and quickened by the legal proceedings connected with what was harshly called the "Edmund's Scandal". There was a question of requiring a gentleman to surrender an accumulation of fees which he had been appropriating during many years, in the belief, as he alleged, that they were his lawful perquisites. All the machinery of the law was put in force, and the most stringent measures resorted to, to compel the surrender of this accumulation. Surely the case of those diocesan charges for Intermediate Education is far clearer and more urgent. Why should not steps be taken to require the ecclesiastical persons concerned to give up moneys to which they have no shadow of a claim? Why should not the Attorney General, if necessary, move in the matter? We are being always taunted with the poverty of our country, and the many claims it consequently makes on the public exchequer. Is our Government then so bitterly ironical as to ask us to acquiesce in this misappropriation of over 20,360*l.*?

One or two of the cases referred to are especially easy of redress. Thus the annual amount which, under the Lord Lieutenant's warrant, the Bishop of Cashel and Emly is bound to contribute towards the support of a Diocesan School for those united dioceses, is 33*l.* 6*s.* 8*d.*; and towards the support of a Diocesan School for Waterford and Lismore, 30*l.* That is—the sum of the contributions which he is already bound to pay annually is 63*l.* 6*s.* 8*d.* Now the Right Rev. Robert Daly has been Bishop of Cashel since 1843. During the twenty-eight years which have since elapsed, he was bound to contribute annually 63*l.* 6*s.* 8*d.* towards the maintenance of Diocesan Schools within his episcopal territory. No such schools have existed during all the time of his episcopate; the arrears of this charge which have accumulated in his hands amount, therefore, to 1,773*l.* 6*s.* 8*d.*

Similarly, the Most Rev. Dr. Trench, as Archbishop of Dublin, has in his hands an accumulation of seven years' arrears of contributions to a Diocesan School amounting to 233*l.* 6*s.* 8*d.*

The Right Rev. Dr. Graves, of Limerick, has in his hands an accumulation of five years' arrears of contributions to a Diocesan School for Ardfert and Aghadoe, amounting to 133*l*. 6*s*. 8*d*.

May not the people of Ireland fairly expect that these three prelates of the Disestablished Church shall be invited to surrender accumulations, amounting to 2,140*l*., which they have no more title to retain than they would have to retain rent or income tax? And if they are not so invited, may not men be excused, if they are bewildered as to the meaning of the phrase "*Religious Equality*"?

Besides this sum of 20,360*l*., recoverable from living persons, or the representatives of persons lately deceased, there are the arrears of the sums which, during the period between 1570 and 1824, ought to have been contributed by the Protestant bishops and holders of church benefices, for the maintenance of Diocesan Schools, and were not paid by them. If, during the forty-seven years which have gone by since 1824, over 20,000*l*. of arrears have accumulated, may we not fairly assume that in the preceding 254 years, when equal attention was not paid to matters connected with education and finance, the rate of accumulation was not less? The epoch of the scandalous transactions connected with the Cavan Royal School, which will be referred to in our next chapter, was not likely to be more squeamish than our own times. The Commissioners of Irish Education Inquiry, in their Fifth Report, 18th May, 1827, give us to understand that up to 1661, the Act 12 of Eliz. had really not been carried into effect: in fact, the "Board of Education in Ireland", appointed in 1809, had not been able to find any trace of those schools previous to the Restoration. Nay, the preamble to the Act 7 Will. III., c. 5, implies that the Act of Elizabeth had not been carried into effect, at least up to its date, 1695. It would also appear, from the

Report of 1827, that the wealthy diocese of Kilmore never had a Diocesan School, and that even in 1809 there were *twelve* dioceses which did not contribute a farthing towards a school. We shall cease to be surprised at this, when we remember that at this moment there are *ten* dioceses which do not, even in name, contribute a fraction for this object.

Of course it is not possible for us to say, even approximately, what the gross amount of the arrears for those 254 years may be. This is a matter of long and tedious account, and, in some instances, of legal inquiry. We may, however, make some sort of rough estimate from the data we have just referred to.

For reasons which we cannot here go into, but which are referred to in the Fifth Report of the Education Commissioners, just cited, we may set down the average annual charge for each diocese at 32*l.* 10*s.* for all the time down to 1824. This will give for the 91 years to the Restoration (1570–1661), during which no Diocesan Schools existed, an annual sum for the 34 dioceses of 1,105*l.*, making for the 91 years a gross arrear amounting to 100,555*l.* We may next take an annual sum of 390*l.* for the twelve dioceses which had not contributed anything according to the Report of 1809—a state of things which continued even on paper down to 1824. This will amount, for the 168 years subsequent to the Restoration (1661–1824), to 63,570*l.*

If, further, we take into account the 34 years from 1661 to 1695, during which it would appear from the preamble to the Act 7 Will. III., c. 5, those schools continued to be non-existent, we shall have a further annual amount of 715*l.* for the other 22 dioceses, making a total arrear for them, on the 34 years, of 24,310*l.*

Thus the arrears owing on account of contributions

which the Protestant Bishops and Clergy were bound by law to make towards the support of Diocesan Schools, and which they did not pay, stand as follows :—

Amount owing for 91 years, from 1570 to 1861 ...	£100,555
Amount owing from 1661 to 1824 for twelve dioceses	63,570
Amount owing for the other 22 dioceses from 1661 to 1695	24,310
Amount ascertained to be owing since 1824, according to Notice in *Dublin Gazette* of April 17, 1824	20,360
Total	£208,795

The last sum may, in part at least, as we have shown above, be recovered from persons still living. The remainder is fairly chargeable on the gross property of the late Established Church—estimated by Mr. Gladstone, when introducing the Bill of 1869, at sixteen millions—which is now vested in the hands of the Church Commissioners. That property was held subject to the charge of maintaining the Diocesan Schools as a primary burden. Therefore the accumulated arrears payable on foot of that charge must, in equity, be liquidated out of it.

The funds connected with the Diocesan Schools stand, therefore, thus:—

The annual amount now chargeable on all the dioceses under the Lord Lieutenant's warrant is 1,670*l*. 15*s*. 3*d*. Were the schools to be put on an efficient footing, and were they to be extended so as to afford anything like suitable provision for the education of the country at large, and not, as now, of a fraction of the Protestant minority, this annual amount should be increased to at least 5,000*l*. The power to order this increase is at the discretion of the Lord Lieutenant.

64 DIOCESAN FREE SCHOOLS OF ELIZABETH.

There is an accumulated arrear (partly recoverable from living persons) of 20,360*l.*, owing for contributions which ought to have been paid towards the support of those schools since 1824.

There is another accumulated arrear chargeable on the gross Church property in the hands of the Church Temporalities Commissioners, amounting to 188,435*l.*

That is to say:—For the purpose of reconstructing the system of Intermediate Education in Ireland, there is available an actual fund connected with Diocesan Schools of 1,670*l.* 15*s.* 3*d.* (or, under proper arrangements, of 5,000*l.* a year), besides a capital sum of accumulated arrears amounting to 208,795*l.*, the interest upon which, at 5 per cent., would be nearly 11,000*l.* a year. In other words, were a new system of Intermediate Education in Ireland started, there ought to be available for the purpose of its support an annual income of nearly 16,000*l.*, derived from funds exclusively connected with the Diocesan Schools of the 12th of Elizabeth.

CHAPTER IV.

ROYAL FREE SCHOOLS OF JAMES THE FIRST—THE PLANTATION OF ULSTER.

Submission of O'Neill and O'Donnell; James the First disappoints the hopes of Irish Catholics; appoints Protestant Bishops to several Sees; the sham-plot and the "Flight of the Earls"; attainder of Tyrone and Tyrconnell; confiscation of six Ulster counties.

Order in council in 1608 establishing Royal Free Schools; allotment of land for their maintenance. Objects of Royal Schools, political and religious. Appointment of masters to the several schools. Extent of confiscated land granted to them; list of schools; lapsed endowments; the property of the disestablished Church liable for the value of one of those lapsed endowments; another intercepted by the Irish Society. Patronage of the Royal Schools.

Legislation concerning Royal Schools, and inquiries into their condition and management: Report of Commissioners of Education Inquiry of 1791; frauds of masters; case of Rev. James Cottingham, D.D.; free scholars. Commissioners of Irish Inquiry of 1807 report a continuance of abuses; value of endowments and number of scholars in 1812. Appointment of "Commissioners of Education in Ireland" in 1813, to take charge of those and certain other endowed schools; changes effected by this Commission. Scholarships founded in Enniskillen Royal School. Exhibitions or scholarships in Trinity College in connection with the Royal Schools,—their annual value. Endowed Schools Commission of 1858; condition of schools according to the Commissioners' Report. Table of endowment of Royal Schools; table showing expenditure; table of the income and expenditure for 1867. Tables showing accommodation for day-boys, and for boarders, and fees charged. Free scholars. Number of scholars, and their religious denomination. Analysis of these tables.

The establishment of Protestantism and "the English habite and order", one of the main objects of the Plantation of Ulster. Royal Schools have failed to secure the objects for which they were established; their history marked by fraud, malversation of funds, and abandonment of duty. Commissions and Inquiries have not secured their efficient management.

Summary of the results of the Royal Schools. Conclusions.

The foundation of " The College of the Holy and Undivided Trinity" and of the University of Dublin, in 1591, by Queen Elizabeth, completed, within forty-five years, the series of Protestant educational institutions in Ireland. The English Parish School Act of Henry the Eighth provided Primary education; the Act of Elizabeth, in 1570, provided Diocesan or Grammar Schools for Intermediate education; and the Charter of 1591 established Collegiate education, with University privileges. Although this last foundation is now noticed in chronological order, it will be found, as we observed in the preceding chapter, more convenient to postpone the consideration of university education until the several classes of institutions for intermediate instruction shall have been dealt with. Such schools are the tributaries or feeders of universities, and ought, therefore, to be considered before them. We shall now, accordingly, proceed to describe the great Royal Schools of the Ulster Plantation.

Although Elizabeth had heard of the defeat of the Irish arms before her death, the capitulation of Hugh O'Neill was not signed until after that event, so that James the First, on his accession in 1603, inherited a conquest achieved under his predecessor. O'Neill and O'Donnell submitted, visited the court of James, accepted English titles, and returned home to see Tyrone and Tyrconnell parcelled out into shires. The first of the Stuarts was not long on the throne when the Irish expectation that he would not alone tolerate, but encourage the faith of his mother and his ancestors, was disappointed. He, at once, made appointments to the sees of Derry, Raphoe, and Clogher, introducing, for the first time, alien prelates into those dioceses. The Confiscation and Plantation of Ulster were a foregone conclusion; the sham plot, the anonymous letter found in the Council Chamber in 1607, and the "flight of the earls" a few months afterwards, although startling and important events in themselves, were mere incidents in that strange drama. Acts of attainder against the

Earls and their " accomplices" were passed, and special commissions having hanged as many of the " traitors" as were available, inquisitions were held concerning the forfeitures. The finding was, as a matter of course, that " Hugh, sometime Earl of Tyrone, Roderick, sometime Earl of Tyrconnell, Sir Cahir O'Dogherty, and others, did enter into rebellion, and at the time of the said entering into rebellion were seized in their demesne, as of fee, of, etc.", a finding which entailed a forfeiture of their own estates, but which the Attorney-General of that day—Sir John Davies—contrived to extend to all the free-holders owing fealty to them according to Irish law. A project for planting the escheated lands was laid before the Privy Council. Although the " great scopes and extent of land in the several counties of Armagh, Tyrowen, Coleraine, Donegal, Fermanagh, and Cavan", " available to the purposes of the planters", which are enumerated in the Privy Council's project, amount to only 394,811 acres, the unforfeited estates, church lands, bogs, mountains, woods, lakes, and " other unprofitable scopes", being in terms excluded, the whole of the six counties were in the end practically confiscated, as a great part of the counties of Antrim and Down had been on the attainder of Shane O'Neill.

In 1608, King James made an order in council that one free school, at least, should be established in each of the six confiscated counties. The following year a commission was issued, in which instructions were given to mark the boundaries of the lands allotted for the endowment of those schools. As in the case of the parish schools of Henry the Eighth and the diocesan free schools of Elizabeth, the avowed object in the foundation of the royal free schools of James the First was two-fold, political and religious. " To stir up and recall the province of Ulster from superstition, rebellion, calamity, and poverty, to the true religion of Christ, and to obedience, strength, and prosperity": these were the specific ends of their foundation, as stated by the king, nearly all whose letters patent and charters explicitly set forth the same double object— "for the good education of the youth of the realm of Ireland in literature and knowledge of true religion; to the end that they may learn their duty towards God and true obedience towards us".

The setting out of the lands and the selection of sites for schools, as well as the legal arrangements concerning the patronage of the appointment of masters, and the trusteeship of the school estates, occupied a few years; so that the earliest appointment of master to the first free school, that of Mountjoy, now Dungannon, was not made until 13th May, 1614; to Enniskillen school, 3rd September, 1618; and to Cavan school, 12th February, 1620-1. On the accession of Charles the First, in 1625, the work of establishing these foundations was resumed, and charters were issued founding the Royal Schools of Carysfort, county of Wicklow, and Banagher, King's County, 1629, and Clogher, county of Tyrone, in 1632; while the first record of an appointment to the Royal Free School in Donegal, now Raphoe, county of Donegal, is in letters patent of Charles the Second, dated 26th May, 1663.

The landed endowments given by James for Church and school purposes, out of the six confiscated Ulster counties, amounted to one hundred thousand acres. The Royal Free Schools are: Armagh, Dungannon, Cavan, Enniskillen, and Raphoe, in Ulster; Banagher, in King's County; and Carysfort, in Wicklow; this last being only an English or primary school. Besides these seven, two other endowments, namely, those of Clogher, in Tyrone, and of Londonderry, are not in operation. The Endowed Schools Commissioners of 1858, noticing these two lapsed endowments, state that the parcel of 100 acres of land, "about the identity of which there is no reasonable doubt", which Charles the First authorised to be appropriated "for the establishment of a school at or near Clogher", passed, together with the property of that see, "into the management and control of the Ecclesiastical Commissioners"; and they give it as their opinion, "that the income which the Ecclesiastical Commissioners receive from the lands ascertained to have been intended for the free school, should be made over to the Clogher school and secured to it as a permanent endowment" (*Report*, pp. 58, 59). The Commissioners of Church Temporalities in Ireland, appointed by the Disestablishment Act of 1869, have succeeded to all the liabilities of the former Ecclesiastical Commissioners, as well as to the legal possession of all the property of the disestablished Church. There is, therefore, an equitable claim for the purposes of Intermediate education against these Commissioners, to the extent of the value of those hundred acres of land intended for the Clogher school. The Londonderry endowment of two townlands containing three hundred acres, intended by James the First for a school in that county, was intercepted and appropriated by the Irish Society, who allege that their duty is fulfilled by endowing the Foyle College or Londonderry diocesan school (*End. Schools Report*, p. 60), already mentioned in a previous chapter. As in the case of Clogher, the endowment is in the hands of a public body, and, therefore, can be made available.

The patronage of all the royal schools is vested in the crown, with the exception of those of Armagh and

Dungannon, the appointment of master to the former since 1684, and to the latter since 1682, having been made by the Protestant Archbishop of Armagh. The claim on the part of the Protestant Primate to make these appointments has long been questioned, and was discussed, at considerable length, by the Commissioners of Education Inquiry, in 1791, and also by the Endowed Schools Commission, in 1858.

Like the Diocesan Schools, the Royal Schools were the subject of repeated legislation and public inquiry. The first of the statutes referring to them was the Act 14th and 15th Charles II., c. 10, of 1662, authorising a division of the endowments of any one of the royal schools, into two or more, for the support of new foundations; and also granting power to change the sites of the schools. The former permission has never been availed of; but, under the latter, Mountnorris school was removed to Armagh, Mountjoy to Dungannon, and Donegal to Raphoe. Subsequent Acts were passed—in 1725, 12 Geo. I., c. 9, regarding leases of the school estates; in 1727, 1st George II., c. 15, enabling the master to charge the endowment with cost of repairs and building; in 1771-2, 11 and 12 George III., c. 17, authorising fines to be taken on the renewal of the leases, the amount of such fines to be expended on building and repairs, the reserved rent not, however, to fall below three-fourths of the true value of the lands; and in 1822, 3 George IV., c. 79, permitting the application of the surplus funds of any one of the schools to the improvement and maintenance of the others.

The Commissioners of Education Inquiry, in 1791, reported very fully on the Royal Schools. The frauds committed by the masters, to whom in fact the original grants or patents were made, and who leased the school lands to members of their own families, just as the bishops did with the Church lands, were frequent and extensive. It will be sufficient to refer to the case of Cavan school, of which the Commissioners of 1790 say:

"The Rev. James Cottingham, D.D., was appointed by the King's letters patent, in the year 1755, to be master of this [Cavan] school, in the room of the Rev. James Moore, to whom Dr. Cottingham gave £2,000 for his resignation, with the knowledge, as he stated to us, of Primate Stone, then a Lord Justice. Dr. Cottingham let the lands to a friend in trust for himself, reserving £90 yearly to the schoolmaster for the time being, and sold the school to the Rev. Mark Kerr, who was appointed by patent to succeed him, for £5,000. Kerr resigned in favour of White, his usher, for £1,500. White died in four years, and Dr. Cottingham procured himself to be again appointed schoolmaster, merely, as he acknowledged, from an apprehension that the lease abovementioned, which he had made to the prejudice of the charity, might be broken, if another person should be appointed schoolmaster, and with an avowed intention of not keeping the school himself. This traffic on great charitable foundations, which might be rendered highly useful to the community, is too shameful to need any comment"—(*End. Sch. Com.*, 1858, vol. ii., p. 347).

The report of 1791 also states that from 1777 the Banagher schoolmaster had not a single scholar, although he had the sole use and benefit of "204 acres of profitable ground", besides the glebe house for a residence; that the schoolmaster at Raphoe "had done no duty" since 1785, although the lands belonging to the school produced to him yearly £335 14s. 5d. Of the master of Carysfort school, appointed in 1784, the report says:—" Mr. Bailey has never kept a school, nor done any duty as a schoolmaster, nor does he even reside in the town". The Commissioners recommend that these schoolmasters should be proceeded against by the Attorney-General, or dismissed by the Crown. The school at Armagh was the only one reported to be in a satisfactory condition. The Commissioners were of opinion "that large salaries to schoolmasters are generally ruinous to schools, and that moderate salaries, not exceeding £100 yearly, ought to be appointed for each schoolmaster on these foundations" (*ibid*).

With regard to free scholars, the Commissioners of 1791 found that, of the six Royal schools in operation, two had none, two had five in each, and the other two, 12 and 16 respectively, or 38 free scholars out of a total of 211. They recommended that each schoolmaster "should be obliged to receive a certain number of day, scholars gratuitously, not exceeding 20 in each school'.

The Commissioners of Irish Education Inquiry, of 1807, report a continuance of gross abuses in the Royal Schools. They complain that no proceedings had been taken against the master of Cavan school, though recommended by the commission of 1791, and that for years the late master had been incapable of attending to his duties. Banagher, which had had no school for 14 years before the inquiry of 1791, had none in 1807; while 77 acres of the endowment had been lost by the encroachment of neighbouring proprietors and the negligence of the masters. An absentee and sinecure schoolmaster held Carysfort in 1791; a reverend pluralist, a baronet and an absentee, was schoolmaster in 1807. In the face of the recommendation of the commissioners of 1791, that proceedings should be taken against the then schoolmaster, the Crown, in 1806, appointed the Rev. Sir Thomas Foster, Bart., to this small English or primary school, although he held two Church livings, and neither attended to the duties of the school in person nor resided in Carysfort. The commissioners of 1807-12 observe in reference to these great abuses:—

"We trust that no instance will occur in future of any persons being appointed to be masters of public schools, or being suffered to continue in these situations, unless they reside and discharge the duties thereof in person".

The fourteenth or last report of this commission (1812) states that the aggregate endowments of the Royal Schools were then £5,000 per annum, and the number of scholars about 360, very few of whom received free instruction.

As was stated in the chapter on diocesan free schools, a special body, styled "the Commissioners of Education in Ireland", was appointed in 1813 to take charge of the Royal and some other endowed schools, with power to enter into possession of the school-estates, except where leases were subsisting. This limitation excluded them from the possession of the Armagh and Dungannon estates till 1832. Among the changes produced by the action of the commission, we may mention the following: "Armagh school has, since 1849, been obliged to receive ten free day-boys, children of tenants on the school-estate paying not less than £20 a-year rent, or of inhabitants of the city of Armagh, dwelling in houses rated to the poor of not less than £10 annual value—restrictions considered by the Endowed Schools Commission of 1858 to be indefensible. No steps, however, have been taken to secure the admission of free scholars into any of the other royal schools. Scholarships were founded in Enniskillen in 1831, and exhibitions in Trinity College in connection with the Armagh School in 1828, and with the schools at Armagh, Dungannon, and Enniskillen, in 1834.

The establishment of a limited number of scholarships on the foundation, with an allowance of £20 a-year towards education, maintenance, and clothing, is peculiar to Enniskillen. The scholarships or exhibitions in Trinity College, founded in connection with the Royal Schools, and endowed out of their funds, are very important. They consist of 30 exhibitions, called Royal Scholarships, for students who shall enter the University of Dublin from the Royal Schools of Armagh, Dungannon, Enniskillen, or Cavan—viz., five scholarships of £50 per annum each for Armagh school; five of £50 and five of £30 per annum for each of the schools of Dungannon and Enniskillen; and five of £25 per annum each for Cavan school; or 15 exhibitions of £50 each, 10 of £30 each, and five of £25 each; total, 30 exhibitions of £1,175 per annum. The exhibitions are confined to students of the respective schools named. They may be held for five years from the time of election, so as to enable the holders to go through their full university course. The exhibitioners are permitted to wear velvet caps, and take academic rank after the university scholars.

The select committee of the House of Commons on Foundation Schools (1835–38) had the Royal Schools under consideration, but the inquiries and report of the Endowed Schools' Commission of 1858 give much more recent information. The four great Schools of Armagh, Dungannon, Enniskillen, and Raphoe are reported to be efficient as to their course of instruction, and satisfactory (save Raphoe) as to the state of their school-rooms and dormitories. Of 311 scholars only 37 were free. The Commissioners of Education are censured for permitting the masters to restrict the boon of a free education to so small a number. The Cavan school is reported to be inefficient and unsatisfactory in every respect; the Banagher school to be in bad repair, and the instruction not satisfactory; the Raphoe school-house to be in want of repair and deficient in accommodation; while the Carysfort (English) school, six miles from Rathdrum, County Wicklow, had only 41 scholars, children of small farmers and labourers in the vicinity.

The following table, showing the extent of land with which each school is endowed, the annual value of the school premises, and the net income derived from the lands, is compiled from the report of the Endowed Schools' Commissioners, 1858, pp. 62, 124:—

TABLE I.—ENDOWMENT OF ROYAL SCHOOLS.

Locality of Royal School.	Acreage.			Annual Value of School Premises.			Net Annual Income from Land.		
	A.	R.	P.	£	s.	D.	£	s.	D.
Armagh	1529	1	31	255	0	0	1265	17	9
Cavan	923	1	26	256	3	10	473	15	8
Dungannon	3890	3	12	141	9	0	1404	1	1
Enniskillen	5566	0	2	316	15	10	1949	10	4
Raphoe	8825	3	35	113	13	0	462	4	4
Banagher	599	0	17	—			191	11	7
Carysfort	590	1	25	12	7	10	119	1	4
Total	21925	0	28	1095	9	6	5866	2	1

The following table shows the distribution of this income in salaries of masters, exhibitions to scholars, and miscellaneous purposes:

TABLE II.—DISTRIBUTION OF INCOME, ETC.

Locality of Royal School.	Distribution of Income.				Surplus Income for various Purposes.		
	Salary.		School Scholarships.	Exhibitions in Trinity College.			
	Masters.	Assistants.					
	£	£	£	£	£	s.	D.
Armagh	400	150	—	250	465	17	9
Cavan	100	100	—	125	148	15	8
Dungannon	400	200	—	400	404	1	1
Enniskillen	500	350	80	400	619	10	4
Raphoe	100	100	—	—	262	4	4
Banagher	100	—	—	—	91	11	7
Carysfort	55	—	—	—	—		
Total	1655	900	80	1,175	1992	0	9

This area of 21,925 acres then produced in 1857 but the small net income of £5,866, or an average of 5s. 4d. an acre, owing to frauds in leasing and fining, perpetrated by former masters. The following return of income and expenditure, submitted to the Royal Commissioners on Primary Education (*Rept.*, etc., vol. 3, p. 669), October, 1868, by Dr. W. Kyle, Secretary to the Commissioners of Education, who are charged with the Royal and Diocesan Schools, supplies information ten years later:

TABLE III.—INCOME AND EXPENDITURE FOR 1867.

Royal School.	Year ended 31st December, 1867.		
	Income.	Expenditure.	Balance.
	£ s. D.	£ s. D.	£ s. D.
Armagh	1602 9 10	1148 18 9	453 11 1
Cavan	569 13 8	343 1 5	226 12 3
Dungannon	1823 4 11	1794 15 3	28 9 8
Enniskillen	2284 14 1	1814 15 3	469 18 10
Raphoe	300 2 8	397 13 3	97 10 7*
Banagher	182 2 0	161 3 0	20 19 0
Carysfort	135 10 11	101 0 4	34 10 7
Total	6897 18 1	5761 7 3	1136 10 10

This return shows a considerable increase in income, but a still greater increase in expenditure, between 1857–1867, leaving a smaller balance at the latter date.

The extent of accommodation for day-boys and boarders, the number of scholars, the average daily attendance, the number of each religious denomination, and the rates of fees, may be seen (omitting Carysfort, which is a primary school) from the following tables:

* This item represents a deficit, and must, consequently, be deducted from the sum of the other items, which represent surplus, in order to obtain the net total given at foot.

TABLE IV.—ACCOMMODATION AND FEES.

Royal School.	Accommodates		Annual Rates.		Free on Roll.
	Schoolroom.	Dormitories	Boarders.	Day Pupils.	
			£ £	£ £	
1 Armagh	140	72	60	10	14
2 Cavan	102	38	20 to 34	3 to 6	2
3 Dungannon	147	45	30 to 50	4 to 10	13
4 Enniskillen	114	64	42 to 44	4 to 8	13
5 Raphoe	50	38	52 10s.	10 10s.	4
6 Banagher	98	25	36	8 8s.	1
Total	651	282			47

TABLE V.—NUMBER AND RELIGIOUS DENOMINATION OF SCHOLARS IN THE YEAR.

Royal School.	Episcopalian,	Rom. Cath.	Presbyterian.	Others.	Total	Average daily attendance.
Armagh	49	—	7	—	56	No report.
Cavan	34	—	—	—	34	26
Dungannon	57	—	4	4	65	56
Enniskillen	69	1	—	—	70	65
Raphoe	45	2	8	—	55	50
Banagher	31	—	—	—	31	30
Total	285	3	19	4	311	227

School-room accommodation is provided for 651, and dormitories for 282 boys; yet the actual daily average attendance (setting Armagh down at 50) is only 277 boys, or about 42 per cent. of the number of boys for whom there is sufficient school-room accommodation.

Three of the six schools may be said to have no free scholars, of whom there are among all the schools only 47, or 15 per cent. Assuming the attendance to have been the same in 1867 as in 1857, the annual expenditure for each scholar at Enniskillen is nearly £28, and it is little less at Dungannon. With reference to the religious denomination of the boys, Cavan and Banagher had Episcopalians only; Armagh and Dungannon had each a few Dissenters; Ennniskillen had within the year *one solitary Roman Catholic;* while Raphoe could boast of reckoning *two* Roman Catholics amongst its scholars. Thus, of the whole muster of 311 scholars among all the Royal Schools for a year, 285 belonged to the Protestant Episcopal Church, or nearly 92 per cent. of the whole; 23, or 7 per cent., were Presbyterians or members of other Dissenting bodies; and 3, or less than *one* per cent., were Roman Catholics.

Such are the results of the great scheme of James the First. One of the main objects of the Plantation or Settlement of Ulster was the making provision for the religious and educational wants of the people, by setting apart 100,000 acres out of the confiscated estates for the endowment of the Church and the establishment of schools; thus securing, as it was hoped for ever, the triumph of Protestantism and "the English habite and order", throughout the province. The intruded and alien Church, the possessor of this magnificent endowment, having hopelessly failed, has been disestablished. The Royal Schools have also utterly failed to secure the objects, political, religious, and educational, for which they were founded by James the First and Charles the First. Theirs, indeed, has been a melancholy, or rather, a shamelesss history, marked at every stage of their career by fraud, malversation of funds, and private plunder, by a profligate abandonment of duty on the part of those who were charged with their management, and by a neglect and indifference on the part of the Government, amounting, at least constructively, to an acquiescence in notorious abuses. From Primate Stone and the Cavan case to the appointment of a reverend pluralist, a baronet, to the charge of the primary school at Carysfort, jobbery and misconduct abound. The same language may be applied to the Royal Schools which was used by Dr. W. C. Kyle, the Secretary to the Commissioners of Education, when describing the condition of the diocesan free schools in his evidence on the 24th October, 1868, before the Royal Commission on Primary Education (Q. 15,467), " *the whole system of diocesan schools is perfectly and completely rotten*"; and (Q. 15,469) " *we know little more about them than the person who is walking in the street*". And yet the Education Commissioners, for whom he thus speaks, are charged by statute with the direction of both diocesan and Royal schools. The labours of Royal Commissions and the action of Parliament have alike been unable to secure for them efficient management, and to stimulate them into a fruitful vitality. They have, indeed, been a source of wealth to adventurous and unscrupulous schoolmasters, but they have not educated the people for whose improvement they were ostensibly founded, while a remnant only of their rich endowments now remains to the nation. They were intended by King James the First to play a great part in stirring up the province of Ulster, and recalling it "from superstition to the true religion of Christ". Have they fulfilled this mission? Catholics form 80 per cent. of the population of Cavan, notwithstanding its Royal School; 75 per cent. of the population of Donegal, notwithstanding its Royal

School; 56 per cent. of the population of Tyrone, notwithstanding its Royal School; 56 per cent. of the population of Fermanagh, notwithstanding its Royal School; 48 per cent. of the population of Armagh, notwithstanding its Royal School; and 40 per cent. of the population of Londonderry, notwithstanding its endowment for a Royal School merged into a diocesan college. The six plantation counties with their Royal Schools, which have been in operation for nearly 250 years, contain more than 60 per cent. Catholics, and the five schools, with 20,735 acres of land, school sites valued at £1,083, and a net income from land of £5,555 a-year, had among them all, *three* Catholic scholars, out of a Catholic population, in these six counties, of 672,753 persons!

So stand in 1871 the results of the Royal Free Schools, the great foundations of James the First, which were to have reclaimed the North to Protestantism and "good manners". These are simple facts which require no deep statecraft to be comprehended. They are thoroughly understood by the people of Ulster. Surely, they ought to have a great influence in determining the principles by which our rulers will be guided when drawing up their plan for a redistribution of the educational endowments of Ireland.

CHAPTER V.

SCHOOLS OF THE IRISH SOCIETY OF THE NEW PLANTATION.

James the First invites the Corporation of London to undertake the Plantation of Ireland; subscriptions of the London Guilds for the purpose; incorporation of twelve of those guilds, now known as the Irish Society; lands, etc., allocated to the Society; objects of the Society as set forth in the Charter; repeated charges of violation of trusts by the Society.
Position and functions of the Irish Society as laid down by Lord Chancellor Cottenham in 1836. Income of the Society; expenditure in 1867; one-third of the trust fund expended in management. Classes of Primary Schools to which the Society makes grants. Under the Act of 1570 there ought to have been a Diocesan Free School in Derry before the "Settlement"; intention of James the First to have a Royal School in each of the six confiscated counties; misappropriation of the lands allocated for the purpose of the Derry School; Irish Society ordered to find out the seven hundred acres of land; failure of the Society to do so; their property sequestrated for this and other causes in 1625.
A school built by a London tailor in 1617 made a Diocesan School; twenty marks annually subscribed to it by Irish Society; subscription afterwards gradually increased; contribution of bishop and clergy; erection in 1814 of present schoolhouse under a special Act of Parliament; subscriptions of other London Companies; two county presentments grant two thousand pounds towards the building of the school; the school now known as Foyle College; exceptional character of this school; extent of its endowments. Teacher nominated by the agent of the Society; the Society contemplated making the College altogether their own; extraordinary character of this proposal. The Academical Institution at Coleraine. Annual grant to Magee College. Model School established in Derry receives fifty pounds a year from the Society for prizes.

82 SCHOOLS OF THE IRISH SOCIETY.

Position of the Irish Society anomalous; their pretensions always opposed by Corporation of Derry; Commission of Inquiry into the Corporation of London in 1854 recommend dissolution of Society; recommendation of the Endowed Schools Commission of 1858; opinion of the Primary Education Commissioners, 1868, that the whole of the net funds of the Society should be devoted to education; value of the property of the Irish Society. All the educational and other institutions in the hands of, or aided by the Society are Protestant monopolies; Catholic schools alone receive no aid. Have the ends which James the First had in granting the confiscated estates to the Irish Society been fulfilled? Reason why the case of the Irish Society has been specially dwelt upon. No people could become so degraded as to allow such injustice to continue. The revenue of the Society used to pay fees and travelling expenses to governors, and for election contests. The lands and other property of the Society given for the same purposes as that of the Disestablished Church; the Society, like the Church, having failed in its objects, should likewise be disestablished.

The Plantation of Ulster produced more educational institutions than the Royal Schools, which we considered in our last chapter. One of the six confiscated counties—Coleraine, now Londonderry—was exceptionally settled by a peculiar class of undertakers. Anxious to secure the subscriptions and the sympathies of the City of London in favour of his Ulster scheme, King James invited the Lord Mayor and the Corporation to a conference, when the arguments were submitted known as "Motives and Reasons to Induce the City of London to undertake the Plantation in the North of Ireland". The glowing picture given of the natural beauties, the industrial resources, commercial attractions, and tempting field for investment, the complete subjugation of the "savage natives" already partially effected, and the befitting enterprise which it afforded for the civic magnates of the metropolis, all touched the cupidity of the wealthy aldermen and common councilmen, so that they lent themselves with little hesitation to share with the king the cares and the expenses, but in reality the profits, of the settlement of Ulster. A Court of Common Council was convened on the 1st of August, 1609, at which it was agreed that four wise, grave, and discreet citizens should be sent to Ireland to view the state of the proposed Plantation and report to the Court. The Committee on their return reported favourably of the project, and an agreement was accordingly entered into between the Government and the Common Council, by which "it was agreed by the City, that the sum of £20,000 should be levied; whereof £15,000 was to be expended on the intended plantation, and £5,000 for the clearance of private men's interests in the things demanded". Ultimately, however, the sums disbursed amounted to £40,000, which was raised by the twelve principal companies or guilds of London tradesmen, with each of which were joined a number of inferior companies. Thus, for a sum of about £40,000, a principality passed over to the mercers, grocers, drapers, fishmongers, goldsmiths, skinners, merchant tailors, haberdashers, salters, ironmongers, vintners, and clothworkers, who, on the 29th of March, 1613, were incorporated by charter as " The Society of the Governors and Assistants in London of the New Plantation in Ulster within the Realm of Ireland". The whole of the estates included in the agreement in the County of Coleraine or Derry-Columcille—a name changed into that of Londonderry, after the new proprietors—was parcelled out in equal shares between the twelve London guilds or companies above mentioned, who had contributed in equal shares the £40,000. The City of Derry, with 4,000 plantation acres of adjacent land and some bog and mountain, and the town of Coleraine, with 3,000 acres of the surrounding land, were not however included in the division. These, together with the valuable fisheries of the Bann, and the Foyle, the slob-land, the advowsons of several church livings and various other properties, the value of which we shall see presently, were reserved for the common corporate body—the Irish Society, consisting of one governor, one deputy to the governor, and twenty assistants elected by the Common Council of London, and of whom the recorder of London and five aldermen should be members.

To this Society and the guilds or companies above mentioned fell the duty of " planting" this fine county from the Bann to the Foyle, and providing for the several objects of the settlement, including, of course, " loyalty, religion, and education", as set forth in the Charter of the Society, the preamble of which is as follows:—

" Whereas the Province of Ulster, in our realm of Ireland, for many years now past, hath grossly erred from the true religion of Christ and Divine Grace, and hath abounded with superstition, insomuch that, for a long time, it hath not only been harassed, torn, and wasted by private and domestic broils, but also by foreign arms; we, deeply and heartily commiserating the wretched state of the said province, have esteemed it to be a work worthy of a Christian Prince and of our Royal functions, to stir up and recall the same province from superstition, rebellion, calamity, and poverty, which heretofore have horribly raged therein, to religious obedience, strength, and prosperity".

As it is not our business to enter into the general operation or history of these undertakers, suffice it to state that, on repeated charges of violation of their usts, the property of the Irish Society was frequently sequestrated—*e.g.*, in 1625, 1628, and 1632; that in 1635 they were fined £70,000; that in 1637 the Lord Chancellor and judges annulled the patent of James, and Londonderry was again seized into the King's hands; that it was only in 1641, under pressure of the great rising of the North, that the sentence was reversed and the charter restored; and that from that date to the present time, litigation, inquiries, and complaints have been unceasing.

The exact position and functions of the Irish Society were set forth by the late Lord Chancellor of England, Cottenham, in the suit of the Skinners' Company against the Irish Society, in 1836. He lays down that the latter have no beneficial interest in the property, of which they are mere trustees. He says:

"These trusts are still continuing. They have still to provide for the Protestant religion, the Protestant establishment of that district; and, with the establishment of religion in that district, they have also to superintend and take care of that which is closely and intimately connected with religion, and is part of it—the education of the inhabitants of the district".—(12 *Clarke and Finnelly's Reports*, page 481; *Report of Prim. Ed. Com.*, 1868, p. 498).

The ordinary income of the Irish Society was returned by Mr. Richard Williamson, their surveyor and architect, in his evidence before the Primary School Commission, 1868, as about £14,000 a-year (Q. 21,016). According to a statement handed in to the Commissioners by him, the gross income for 1867 amounted to £21,059, but this included a balance of £1,454 from the preceding year and various extra receipts; so that Mr. Williamson's statement of the annual amount is, probably, correct. The expenditure for 1867, according to the same statement, may be represented as follows (*Evidence*, Q. 21,015, Table A, p. 943):—

Permanent Payments, Crown Rents, etc. ...	£1344	17	4
Payments to Corporation, Mayor, etc., of Derry	1200	0	0
Purchase of Property in Derry and Coleraine ...	2575	9	3
Balance carried forward to the Account of 1868	2011	18	2
Management and Incidental Expenses ...	7293	12	4½
Public Improvements, Buildings, etc. ...	3742	18	8
Charitable Donations	635	18	5
Donations to Schools	2255	2	5
	£21,059	16	7½

From this statement it appears that about one-third of the large income of more than £21,000, for the year 1867, held in trust, according to the highest legal authority, for the promotion of religious education, has been swallowed up in " managing" the trust.

Independent of the portion of the income of the Irish Society employed in the purchase of building sites, and in the building and repair of schoolhouses, they subscribe to over 100 schools sums of from £5 to £20 a year each. These schools are of almost every kind and character, *Catholic alone excepted*. The majority of them are National Schools; others are Protestant Parochial or Church Education Society's Schools; some are under Erasmus Smith's Board; a large number are for Presbyterians of various kinds; a few are Wesleyan or Methodist Schools; others are Sabbath Schools; some Industrial or Ragged Schools, or schools for deaf mutes; others Orphanages. Every sort of Primary School *not Catholic* finds a place on their roll. According to Mr. Williamson's estimate, the grants of the Society in 1867 to schools of all kinds amount, as we have seen, to £2,255, apart from the very large outlay on buildings. Of this sum

£1,070 were given to Primary and Sunday Schools, and £1,185 to Intermediate Schools.

The grants of the Irish Society to Grammar or Intermediate Schools, though not numerous, are very important. The Act of Queen Elizabeth, 1570, founding Diocesan Free Schools, preceded the Plantation scheme by more than forty years, so that under that statute a school should have been in operation in Derry long before the Settlement was proposed, and still longer before the Irish Society was incorporated in 1613. James the First intended, according to the terms set forth in the Plantation scheme, to have at least one Royal Free School in each of the six forfeited counties, and for this purpose allotted 700 acres—(the Endowed Schools' Commission says, through mistake, 300 acres)—for the maintenance of the Free School of Derry, " being the most notable place of the north of Ireland". It appears from the following passage out of Bishop Downham's Visitation Book of the Diocese of Derry, about 1622, that even at that early date those lands had been already in some way misappropriated, so that they could no longer be identified :—

" As touching schools, it is well known that his Majesty intended a convenient proportion of lands, as well for Londonderry as for Dungannon or Donegal; yet both these have fair proportions allotted to them for the maintenance of schooles; but the lands intended for the schooles of Derry *have been swallowed up*, I know not by whom; but the general surveyor is the likeliest to know what is become of them. Notwithstanding, there is a fair schoolhouse built at Londonderry, by Matthias Springham, merchant taylor of London, and the city of London hath assigned a yearly stipend of 20 marks to be given to the schoolmaster; but our gracious King's grant is suppressed".

In 1624, the Mayor, Commonalty, and Citizens of

Derry, in a petition to his Majesty's High Commissioners for Irish Causes, reiterate the same claim:

"It hath been credibly reported that his Majestye in his pious and princely care of the yt plantacion, did appoint 700 acres of land for the maintenance of a free schoole in the said citty, which land hath bin, and yet is, by some undue means (as we conceive), detained, though the like guiftes unto other places are freely and quietly enjoyed".

The Privy Council in England ordered the Common Council of London to find out the 700 acres of land, and apply them to the use for which they had been allotted, to which order the latter answered (2nd June, 1624), that they were not aware in whose possession such lands were; whereupon commissioners were appointed by the King, who again ordered the lands to be given, failing which, upon this and other grounds, the whole of the property of the Irish Society was sequestrated in September, 1625. The 300 acres of land referred to by the Endowed Schools' Commission of 1858, were the endowment which the Commissioners appointed by the Society in 1616 to inquire into the state of the Plantation, suggested as a substitute for the 700 acres originally granted by the King.

The school built in 1617 by the private generosity of a London tradesman, became the Diocesan School of Derry. The Irish Society first subscribed 20 marks (£13 6s. 8d.) annually to its support, subsequently increasing the contribution from time to time. The bishop and clergy, under 12 Eliz., chap. 1, also contributed, as has been stated above in chap. II., p. 45, on the Diocesan Free Schools. A special Act of Parliament, 49 George III., c. 59, was obtained in 1809, under which the present handsome and commodious school-house was erected in 1814, at a cost of about £13,000. Several of the London Companies subscribed to the building fund, as did also the Protestant bishop, while there were two county presentments, one in 1811 and another in 1815, granting £2,000 towards the erection of the school, which is known as " Foyle College", or the Derry Diocesan Free Grammar School, a foundation altogether exceptional among the Grammar and Intermediate Schools of Ireland.

The endowments of this College are considerable. Besides paying the salaries of the teachers of a new commercial school opened in connection with the College, in August, 1868, the Irish Society contributes £500 a-year to it. This £500 includes £350, salaries for one principal and two assistant masters, and £150 for five exhibitions of £30 each in Trinity College, Dublin, for scholars from this College.

The contribution of the bishop and clergy to the Foyle College, as the Diocesan Free School, is £92 per annum, and the Mercers' Company gives annually £50; so that, apart from the salaries of the masters in the new commercial department (probably £150), there is an annual endowment of £642, three acres and a half of land, and school premises of the annual value of £377; or a total of £1,000 a-year. The absolute power of nomination of the masters is exercised by the agent of the Irish Society (*Ev. End. School Com.*, Q. 10,947). Mr. Williamson, the Surveyor and Architect of the Society, in his evidence before the Royal Commission on Primary Education, 1868, states (Q. 21,067) that " the Society, further, had it in contemplation, or rather have it under consideration, to make Foyle College altogether their own school; to undertake the maintenance of the buildings, and all the other duties connected with the ownership of the school, in the same way as they do now for the Coleraine Primary School. That will involve a considerable expenditure". Considering that the county contributed £2,000 towards the erection of the house; that the corporation gave, for many years, annual grants to the support of the school; that the Irish Church Commission is liable for £92 6s. 2d., heretofore paid by the bishop and clergy under the Act of 1570; and that the Society defrauded the public of 700 acres of land, allotted by King James for its endowment, this is a most extraordinary proposition on the part of the Honourable the Irish Society.

The only other Grammar School aided by the Society is the Academical Institution, Coleraine, upon the erection of which they have recently expended £5,000 thus providing accommodation for 500 boys. As the Institution was not completed at the close of 1868, when the society's surveyor gave his evidence before the Primary Schools' Commission, he was unable to state the amount of its endowment; but he observed that already, in the Coleraine district of their property, they annually expended on schools alone £697 10s. (Q. 21,165).

The Magee Presbyterian College, Derry, founded in 1865, endowed chiefly out of a bequest from Mrs. Magee, and designed mainly for the education of young men proceeding to the Presbyterian ministry, also enjoys considerable grants from the Irish Society. Their offer of 20 acres of land, as a site, having been declined, they subscribed £1,000 towards the erection of the College, and they gave an annual endowment of £500, namely—£250 for a chair of Natural Philosophy and another sum of £250 towards the general expenses of the College (*Royal Comm. Primary Ed.*, 1868. Evid. page 945, Return A).

Although Londonderry has Foyle College, one of the best endowed intermediate Schools for Protestants in Ireland, a National Model School, which must of necessity become practically a Protestant institution, has been also erected there at an expense of £8,895, and is maintained at an annual cost of, on an average, more than £1,600. This school, notwithstanding that it receives a handsome sum from the Commissioners of Education for premiums, shares the bounty of the Irish Society, which gives it £50 a-year for " the Society's Prizes".

The circumstances under which the London Companies obtained possession of an entire Irish county are remarkable. From almost the date of their charter to the present moment, their unnatural and arrogant pretensions have been persistently opposed, and by none more warmly than the Corporation of Derry and the people of the county generally. The frequent sequestrations of the property of the Society, the annulling of their charter, renewed in 1641, only in view of the great Rising of the North, and the continued opposition to the whole action of the London Companies, prove that their position in Ireland cannot be defended, and ought not to be continued. The Lord Chancellor of England laid down in 1836 the exact functions of the Society. A Commission of Inquiry into the Corporation of London in 1854, recommended that the Irish Society be dissolved, its charter repealed by act of parliament, and its property vested in a new set of trustees, whose number and character should be defined in the act. The Endowed Schools' Commission recommended in 1858, that "immediate steps be taken in order that all the funds devoted to education under the charter of the Irish Society should assume a definite form, and be placed under a system of official management, and that the scattered funds of the society should be secured for, and concentrated in a limited number of, efficient endowed schools on this foundation in the county of Derry".

Referring to Lord Cottenham's decision, that the Irish Society are mere trustees for the maintenance of religion and education, the Royal Commissioners on Primary Education, 1868, in their Special Report on Model Schools, justly observe (vol. 1, part ii., p. 771), " since religion is otherwise supported, the whole of the large surplus of about £12,000 a-year, which remains after feeing most irregularly the trustees, and paying the annually elected officers, should be available for that object which seems most to bear the character of a continuing and unfulfilled trust, viz., the education of the district". The property of the Society, though a portion of the lands is let in perpetuity, is of great value, the fisheries alone bringing upwards of £4,000 a-year. The Society's surveyor returned, as we have stated, the ordinary income at £14,000. This large income is obtained from estates more than one-half of the population on which are Catholics; and yet not one penny is given towards the building or support of any Catholic institution. The Catholic occupiers of land in the county had to pay their share of the county presentments of £2,000 for the erection of Foyle College, and yet this institution is a monopoly in the hands of the Irish Society, and has not even one Catholic on its staff or among its scholars. The Magee College, for the exclusive education of Presbyterians, has an endowment from the Society of £500 a-year. The Academical Institution or Grammar School, Coleraine, erected by the Society at a cost of £5,000, and maintained by it, is also a Protestant monopoly. The Derry Model School has £50 for "the Society's Prizes", and Trinity College annually receives from the Society £150 for five exhibitions for the students of Foyle College. More than one hundred primary schools and benevolent institutions of every religious denomination and of every variety—*Catholic alone excepted*—share the Society's bounty; and this not only on their own estates in Londonderry, but also in the counties of Antrim, Tyrone, and Donegal. Nor should it be forgotten, that besides annual contributions for education, amounting to £2,255, all given to Protestant Colleges and Schools, the Society has given large sums towards the building of Protestant churches and meeting-houses, the maintenance of their ministers, and the support of various institutions connected with the Protestant religion.

Bearing in mind all these facts, must not every thinking man ask himself:—Have the ends which James the First had in view when he handed over those estates to the Irish Society, been secured by this unvarying promotion of the religion and interests of the colonists, to the exclusion of everything dear to the native majority, out of whose forefathers' lands the Society is endowed?

We have dwelt on the case of the Irish Society, not alone because of the number or the value of its educational endowments, but also because of the remarkable illustration thus afforded of the action of the British Government in the matter of education in Ireland. Not even the Penal Laws could degrade a people so low, or so stamp out of them the sentiments of manhood, as to render Ulster Catholics quiescent under such unjust and cruel treatment. These twenty-six London Common Councilmen—Governor, Deputy-Governor, and twenty-four Assistant Governors—drew, in 1867, £643 for their attendance at forty meetings, and £557 for the annual visitation expenses to Derry of some of their members, while they quarter their nominees in the many lucrative positions on their Irish property. It is alleged that the Society spent £3,000 out of their funds on an election contest at Coleraine, in which a London Alderman was candidate (Roy. Com. Prim. Ed., Ireland. Evid. Q. 21,030); and the minutes of the Society are cited (Q. 21,031) in proof of the active part taken to influence Parliamentary elections in Londonderry and Coleraine. The experiment to convert Irish people to the "*true religion*", tried for 335 years, has failed, and the great Corporation, the Irish Church, founded in 1535—nearly 80 years before the Irish Society—has been disestablished and disendowed, to the repentant cry of the Empire, "Cut it down, why cumbereth it the gronnd?" The remnant of the ancient revenues of the Catholic Church has been again taken possession of by the State. The lands and other property granted to the Irish Society were given for the promotion of religion and education, and are therefore analogous to the endowments of the Disestablished Church: the Society, like that Church, having failed in its mission, justice requires that it be dissolved, and its property vested in some Board like the Church Temporalities Commission. The property so vested should—as recommended by the Select Committee of the House of Commons in 1854—be sold; for it is not possible that the duties of landlords, involving a great personal responsibility, can be discharged by an absentee corporation established in London. Such a body is wholly unfit to have the management of so important and valuable an estate as an entire Irish county, including an ancient city and an important borough.

CHAPTER VI.

SCHOOLS AND OTHER FOUNDATIONS OF THE GOVERNORS OF ERASMUS SMITH.

Erasmus Smith acquires some of the Irish confiscated estates; makes provision by Indenture of 1657 for five Grammar Schools; objects of the foundation; his proposal to give all his Irish estates accepted; charter of 1669 appointing thirty-two Governors; only three schools proposed in the charter; free scholars; course of instruction; other advantages to be given to free scholars. The teaching of Protestantism prescribed in the Charter. The schools failures even in the lifetime of the founder, as shown by a letter of his. The infamous statute of William the Third having failed in driving Catholics to the Protestant schools, the Protestant masters employed Catholic assistant-masters to induce them to attend. The act of Anne of 1709 passed to prevent the evasion of the law; Protestant bishops enforced this statute; rules of the Governors of Erasmus Smith's Schools of 1712 in aid of the same object; withdrawal of eighty-five "Popish" boys in one day from the Galway School, when it was attempted to enforce the "rules"; complaint of the master, and discretionary power given to the Archbishop of Tuam on the subject; the masters of Erasmus Smith's Schools active agents in enforcing Penal Laws.

Income exceeded expenditure in 1709; petition of Samuel Smith, son of founder, to apply surplus to found and support a mathematical school in Dublin; suggestion approved of, but not carried out; new school in Dublin, perhaps, a tardy fulfilment of it; Act of 1723 establishing professorships, fellowships, and exhibitions in Trinity College, Dublin, ratifying agreement for the support of twenty boys in Blue Coat Hospital, and for the establishment of "English" or Primary Schools; Governors pay £130 a-year to Christ's Hospital in London under the Charter of Charles the Second; constitution of Board of Governors.

Extent and character of the estates.

Teaching staff of Grammar Schools—three of the four headmasters clergymen; table of the value of school premises, accommodation for day-boys, and boarders, and amount of salaries of masters; table of attendance and religious denomination of scholars; number of primary schools under Governors, and attendance at them; distribution of these schools according to province, as contrasted with the income of the estates of the Governors in the respective provinces.

University Exhibitions.—The foundation of Primary Schools a diversion of funds not only from the proper localities, but from the objects of the founder. The University foundations more or less legitimate; original value of the Exhibitions in Trinity College; changes in 1861; original value bore a certain relation to value of estates: present value bears no relation thereto; their value should have increased with the change in the value of money.

University Professorships. Power given to Governors by Act of 1723 to apply surplus funds for the benefit of Trinity College. Grants made in virtue of this power.

Annual expenditure upon each class of endowments; surplus of £20,000 in bank in 1868; net income not easily determined; estimate of it made by Endowed Schools' Commissioners in 1858; amount devoted to purely educational purposes; Primary Schools absorb half the whole income; the Erasmus Smith's estates public property. Opinion on the subject of Education Commissioners of 1791; the dissolution of existing corporation recommended. Suggestion as to application of income; opinion of the Primary Education Commissioners on the subject.

Among the persons who at the close of the war of 1641 obtained estates in return for "adventure *bona fide* paid for lands forfeited in Ireland," was one Erasmus Smith, whose name has acquired considerable prominence in connection with Irish education. He was originally a common trooper in one of Cromwell's regiments; but having in some way acquired wealth he became an alderman of the City of London. Anxious to promote the education of the people remaining, or newly settled, on the estates which he acquired, he, by an indenture dated 3rd December, 1657, named eighteen persons, six of them Protestant ministers, as trustees, to carry out a scheme of education for this purpose. In this indenture Erasmus Smith made provision out of the confiscated Irish estates allotted to him for the payment of £300 a year towards the erection and support of five school-houses, "for the teaching of grammar and the original tongues, and to write, read, and cast accompts"—of which one was to be in the town of Sligo; one upon his lands in the barony of Clanwilliam, in the county of Tipperary; one upon his lands in the barony of Dunluce, in the county of Antrim; "and one where his lands that are deficient (which is £2,700) shall be fixed". The trustees were to "obtain license from his Highness the Lord Protector, for incorporating themselves in succession", for the object set forth.

Amongst the conditions specified in the Indenture, the following may be noticed as bearing directly on our present object:—

"And that such other tenants on the lands, their children, as shall be made fit for the University or Trinity College, near Dublin, shall have towards their maintenance £10 a year a piece, for the first four years, after their entrance, and not longer; and for want of such, for the relief of such other poor scholars, as the said trustees, or seven of them, shall hold fit to receive the same'.

The founder clearly sets forth the object he had in view:—

"Whereas, most of the sins which in former times have reigned in this nation have proceeded chiefly of lacke of bringing up of the youth of this realm either in publique or private schooles, whereby, through good discipline, they might be principled in literature and good manners, and so learn to loathe those haynous and manifold offences which when they come to years, they daily perpetrate and commit: Now this Indenture witnesseth, that the said Erasmus Smith, for the great and ardent desire which he hath that the poor children inhabiting upon any part of the land of Ireland, as hereafter is expressed, should be brought up in the fear of God, and good literature, and to speak the English tongue, and for other good ends, in and by these presents hereafter declared, hath hereby bargained to the said parties and their heirs", etc.

The claim of the Puritan "Adventurer" to the forfeited lands met with opposition under the Restoration; and, no settlement having been finally made at the date of the Indenture above mentioned, Erasmus Smith made a virtue of necessity, and agreed, if opposition were withdrawn, to give all the forfeited Irish estates then in his possession for the endowment of schools. This proposal having been received with favour, a Charter was granted in the year 1669, giving the visitation and government of the schools to a Board of thirty-two Governors, with power to elect their successors, reserving, however, to Erasmus Smith during his lifetime the right to make laws under his hand and seal for the direction of the schools. By the Indenture these schools were to be five in number, but in order that a more liberal maintenance might be appointed for the schoolmasters, he proposed in the Charter to establish only three—Tipperary, Galway, and Drogheda, of which the two first only were on his estates. All the tenants' children living on the lands, and twenty poor children living within two miles of each school, were to be taught, *free of charge*, Latin, Greek, and Hebrew, *to fit them for the University*, if their parents should desire it, or writing and ciphering to prepare them for trades or other employments. The poor children, besides receiving free instruction, were to be clothed whilst at school, and to get pensions if proceeding to the University; while provision was also made for those bound apprentices. The masters were also to be at liberty to receive, on payment of reasonable fees, other scholars, who were to follow the prescribed course of instruction.

The Charter prescribed that the masters should catechise the scholars in Archbishop Ussher's Catechism; and it is provided in the "Lawes and Directions" given under the hand and seal of the founder, and made binding by the Charter, that the schoolmaster shall publicly read the Scriptures, and duly catechise the children in the same catechism. Catholic children were thus absolutely excluded from the schools. In a letter addressed to the Governors, dated London, 6th June, 1682, thirteen years after the granting of the Charter, Erasmus Smith refers to these provisions of the Charter and of the rules and byelaws, and explicitly states his object was to promote Protestantism. He says:—

"My end in founding the three schools was, to propagate the Protestant faith according to the Scriptures, avoiding all superstition, as the Charter, and the bye-lawes, and the rules established doe direct. Therefore it is the command of his Majesty to catechise the children out of Primate Ussher's [catechism], and expound the same unto them, which I humbly desire may be observed upon the penalty of theire [*i.e.* the masters'] places".

From the following passage in the same letter we have evidence that even in the lifetime of the founder these schools were failures, and that then, as now, the Irish people refused to accept education at the price of their religion:—

"My Lords, my designe is not to reflect upon any, only I give my judgment why those schools are so consumptive, which was, and is, and will be (if not prevented), the many Popish schooles, theire neighbours, which, as succers, doe starve the tree. If parents will exclude theire children because prayers, catechismes, and exposition is comm[.]anded, I cannot help it; for, to remove that barre, is to make them Seminaries of Popery. Therefore I beseech you to command him [the schoolmaster] that shall be presented and approved by your honours to observe them that decline those duties and expel them, which will oblecge, my lords and gentlemen, your most humble servant,

ERASMUS SMITH".

Erasmus Smith died in 1691. In 1694, three years after his death, the infamous statute of William III. (7 Wm. III. c. 4) was passed, which enacted " That no person, whatsoever, of the Popish religion shall publicly teach school, or instruct youth in learning, or in private houses teach or instruct youth in learning, within this realm, from henceforth, except only the children or others under the guardianship of the master or mistress of such private house or family, upon pain of twenty pounds, and also being committed to prison, without bail or mainprize, for the space of three months for every such offence". And, in order the more effectually to debar Catholics from receiving education in Catholic schools, they were prohibited to go abroad for that purpose, or to send their children abroad, or pay for them while there, under pain of forfeiture of all civil rights, goods, and lands for life. These penalties appear to have been ineffectual in preventing Catholics from teaching; and the schools of Erasmus Smith and other Protestant foundations continuing very "consumptive", the Protestant masters, in order to induce Catholics to fill their empty schools, employed Catholic assistant-masters and ushers. To prevent this evasion of the law a more stringent Act than that of William III. was passed in 1708 (8 Anne, c. 3), which provided that whatever person of the Popish religion " shall publickly teach school, or shall instruct youth in learning in any private house within this realm, or shall be entertained to instruct youth in learning as usher, under-master", or assistant, by any Protestant schoolmaster, was to be punished by imprisonment for the first offence, and to be held guilty of high treason for the second. Prosecutions under this act were vigorously carried out under the direction of the Protestant Bishops. The Governors of Erasmus

Smith's Schools, in order to aid in this iniquitous crusade, issued on the 12th July, 1712, four rules to prevent youths educated in their Free Schools from turning Papists. These rules, which were to be hung up in every school and duly enforced upon all, were as follows:—

"1st—That prayers be read morning and evening in each of the said schools by the master or usher out of the liturgy by law established, at which every youth shall be obliged to attend.

"2nd—That every youth educated in the said schools shall be instructed by the master or usher in Doctor Mann's *Catechism*, and upon Sundays be publickly examined in the same in the church.

"3rd—That every person educated in the said schools shall duly attend the publick service in the parish church where each school is situated every Lord's Day, and such other time as the master or usher shall appoint; and upon neglect thereof, after due admonishment, to be expelled the said schools.

"4th—That every person so educated, when he is sufficiently instructed in the aforesaid catechism, shall be brought by the master or usher to the bishop to be confirmed".

When the Master in the Galway school attempted to carry out these rules, 85 "*Popish*" scholars left *in one day*, 70 of whom paid for their schooling. The Master complained of this to the Governors, and prayed that they should either relax the stringency of the rules, or increase his salary, in compensation for this serious loss. This incident proves, on the one hand, the desire of Catholics for education in defiance of the penal laws—seeking it even in Protestant schools as long as they could do so without sacrificing their religion—and, on the other hand, the laxity of observance of the rules of the Founder and Governors, both as to the exclusion of Catholic boys, and the enforcement of Protestant formularies in the schools. The Governors referred the matter to the Protestant

Archbishop of Tuam, giving him discretionary power to deal with the master.

A return made by Walter Taylor, Warden of Galway, to an order of the Irish House of Lords, in 1731, shows that the masters of Erasmus Smith's Schools were active agents in enforcing the Penal Laws, and did not disdain even to act the part of common informers. The Warden says:—

"I am also to acquaint your lordships that some time ago, on the information of Mr. Garnett, Master of the Free School, I gave him my warrant against one Gregory French, whom he alleged to be a Popish Schoolmaster, and to keep a Lattin School, and having called upon Mr. Garnett to know what he had done in the said warrant, he said French had dropped the school".

As early as 1709 the rents of the school estates exceeded the expenditure upon the schools set up by the Founder, and a surplus rapidly accumulated. In that year, Samuel Smith, son of Erasmus Smith, presented a petition to the House of Commons praying that part of the surplus should be applied to the foundation and support of a Mathematical School in Dublin. The suggestion was approved of by the Governors, but was never carried out, unless indeed the new and handsome school just opened in Harcourt Street, Dublin, where the offices of the Governors are now fixed, be a tardy fulfilment of this idea.

The surplus continuing rapidly to increase, part of it was applied, in 1720, to found a number of Exhibitions in Trinity College, Dublin, and in 1723 an Act of Parliament (10 Geo. I.) was obtained sanctioning this application of the funds, and further authorizing the endowment of two Lecturerships and three Fellowships in that institution, and the application of the surplus to various purposes—educational and charitable. The whole foundation now underwent a radical change. Besides the establishment of Lecturerships and Fellowships, the number of exhibitions in Trinity College was increased; and buildings were provided there, at a cost of £942, for the accommodation of the holders of those exhibitions, with free chambers, in addition to free education. An agreement with the Blue Coat Hospital, Dublin, for the support in that institution of twenty boys from the schools was ratified. Permission was also given, among other things, for the establishment of " English" or Primary Schools.

As the result of the Act, an endowment, originally intended for the foundation and support of Intermediate or Grammar Schools, was diverted in great part to the purpose of primary education; for while the " English" or Primary Schools have increased to 144, only one additional Grammar School, that of Ennis, founded in 1773, was added to the original schools established under the Charter of 1669. The " English" School at Nenagh was, however, for some time used as a Grammar School. The new school in Harcourt Street raises the number of Grammar Schools now on the foundation to five—the number contemplated in the Indenture of 1657.

Besides the grant to the Blue Coat Hospital, Dublin, for the support of 20 boys from the Erasmus Smith's Schools above mentioned—the Governors make an annual payment, under the Charter of Charles II., of £100 to Christ's Hospital, London, a payment which has been now made for 200 years.

The Board of Governors, in great part a self-electing body, consists of 34 members, of whom seven are *ex-officio*—viz., the Protestant Primate, the Protestant Archbishop of Dublin, the Lord Chancellor, the Chief Justices of the Queen's Bench and Common

Pleas, the Lord Chief Baron, and the Provost of Trinity College, Dublin—and 27 other members, among whom are three Protestant Bishops and six Protestant clergymen, the rest being Peers, Judges, and Commoners of position. Vacancies among the members who are not *ex-officio* are filled up by the members of the Board itself. The offices of Lord Chancellor, Chief Justice of the Common Pleas, and Lord Chief Baron, being at present held by Catholics, there are consequently just now three Catholics *ex-officio* Governors: all the others, *ex-officio* and co-opted, are members of the Dis-established Church.

The Estates constituting the landed endowments are made up as follows:—

4,345A. 2R. 19P., statute measure, along the Waterford and Limerick Railway, in the county of Limerick—the Pallas station, about fourteen miles from the city of Limerick, being on the property;

3,037A. 2R. 28P., in detached parcels, in the county of Tipperary, some of them adjoining the town of Tipperary;

2,617A. 2R. 21P., in the county of the town of Galway, part of the present town being built on the estate;

767A. 2R. 32P., and a fee farm rent of £93 3s. 1d., in the county of Westmeath;

284A. 0R. 7P., and a large tract of mountain, in the county of Sligo;

A fee farm rent of £23 1s. 6½d., out of about 300 acres of land in the Queen's County;

Or, in all, 11,050A. 2R. 27P., exclusive of the two rent charges and the mountain land in the county of Sligo.

The total rental in 1854 was £9,219 0s. 6d., including receivers' fees, but exclusive of the tolls of Pallas Fair, and quarry and turf bank rents on the Limerick estate, which produced in 1854,

£188 11s. 11½d, and which the agent expected, would produce from £100 to £200 more in future. With the exception of the tract of mountain near Sligo, these estates are all well situated, and consist, for the most part, of rich agricultural land, town parks, or building ground. With the exception of lands situated within counties of cities and counties of towns, the Governors cannot by their Charter, grant any leases for a longer term than 21 years, and are bound to reserve "the highest yearly rent or more, which any tenant or occupier of the lands did pay, at any time within the space of seven years next before the making of any such lease"; hence these estates, if at any time sold, would be sure to bring their full value. In 1854 the Limerick, Tipperary, and Galway estates, exclusive of the portion within the city of Galway, were let at moderate rents very little exceeding Griffiths' valuation of the land.

Without reckoning the School in Harcourt Street, Dublin, which we do not take into account, as it was established so recently, there are, as we have said before, four Grammar Schools upon this foundation— Drogheda, Galway, and Tipperary, founded in 1659, and Ennis in 1773. All the head-masters of these schools are graduates of the University of Dublin, and three of them clergymen of the Protestant Episcopal Church. The teaching staff is considerable for the number of scholars, there being two assistants in Drogheda, five in Ennis, two in Galway, and three in Tipperary. The following table gives the annual value of the school premises of these grammar schools, the accommodation provided in them for day boys and boarders, and the salaries paid by the Governors to the master, according to the Endowed Schools Commission in 1858:—

TABLE SHOWING VALUE OF SCHOOL PREMISES, ACCOMMODATION, AND MASTER'S SALARY IN EACH OF THE FOUR GRAMMAR SCHOOLS ON ERASMUS SMITH'S FOUNDATION.

Name of School.	Annual value of School Premises.	Accommodation for		Salaries paid by Governors to Masters.
		Day-Boys.	Boarders.	
	£ s. d.			£
Drogheda	64 6 8	275	27	190
Galway	282 18 0	120	50	190
Tipperary	273 7 0	144	56	100
Ennis	86 4 5	88	37	277
Total	706 16 1	627	170	757

Since the report of the Endowed School Commissioners, these salaries have been somewhat increased.

The following table gives the attendance in 1858 at these schools:—

TABLE SHOWING ATTENDANCE OF SCHOLARS AT EACH OF THE FOUR GRAMMAR SCHOOLS ON ERASMUS SMITH'S FOUNDATION.

Name of School.	Present Daily.	No. on Rolls.				Free.
		Episcopal Protestants.	Others.	Catholics.	Total.	
Drogheda	53	59	—	2	61	6
Galway	20	17	—	3	20	8
Tipperary	—	8	1	12	21	7
Ennis	43	52	—	6	58	9
Total	116	136	1	23	160	30

Thus, after two hundred years' operation only 160

boys are on the rolls of schools having accommodation for 797. These schools are called free, yet of 160 boys on the rolls only 33, or 19 per cent., receive free instruction. Catholics are excluded by the Charter, the bye-laws, rules, and the "Lawes and Directions" of Erasmus Smith; yet, if the 23 on the rolls were omitted, the meagre muster-roll would be reduced to 137.

Although primary schools formed no part of the scheme of the founder, the Governors returned the number of primary schoolrooms in connection with them in May 1868, as 146, of which 81 were in Ulster, where the Governors have no estates, and only 23 in Connaught and Munster, where the great bulk of the estates are situated (*Rep. Prim. Ed. Com.*, p. 486). The Police Returns made to the Primary Education Commissioners for the 25th June, 1868, give the number of distinct schools as 107, of which only nine were in Munster, which contributes £5,712 of the annual endowments, six in Connaught, which contributes £2,976; thirty-four in Leinster, which contributes only £535; *and 58 in Ulster, which contributes nothing!*

Erasmus Smith intended the schools of his foundation in the first place for the tenants on his estates, and next, for such poor scholars as lived in the neighbourhood of the schools. Yet we have seen that a considerable part of the endowments derived from confiscated estates in Munster and Connaught, where Protestants were scarce, and Catholics obstinate, has been bestowed upon the already richly endowed province of Ulster. And as the Royal Schools and other Grammar Schools supplied most of the wants of the Northern Protestants, as regards Intermediate education, the bounty of the Governors took the form of primary schools—thus, not only diverting the endowments of Erasmus Smith from the localities he intended to benefit, but from the very object itself which he had in view.

But although the Governors lost sight of the founder's object, by establishing Primary Schools broadcast, especially in a district which had no shadow of claim for such a display of their bounty, we must in justice admit that in another and most important matter they have to a certain extent followed his views and ideas. He and they alike thoroughly understood that, while the Intermediate School and the University College, are wholly different institutions, they are most closely linked together, the school being the nursery of the University College, and the latter the necessary complement of the former. Indeed, so desirous have the Governors been to secure the close connection of their schools with the University, that they are open to the charge of having gone beyond their legitimate functions by devoting to purely University purposes funds, the proper application of which should always have exclusive reference to the improvement of the schools under their own care.

We have already seen that in the Indenture of 1657, Erasmus Smith proposed to grant burses or exhibitions of £10 each to "such other tenants on the lands, or their children, as shall be made fit for the University or Trinity College", for their maintenance while there for the first four years after their entrance. Under the Act of 1723 twenty exhibitions of the value of £7 7s. 8d. (£8 Irish currency), and fifteen of the value of £5 10s. 9d (£6 Irish) were established in Trinity College for the scholars of the four grammar schools. The 35 students holdings these exhibitions were to receive, as we have already said, free chambers and free education. The number of these exhibitions has remained unchanged, but their values have been modified from time to time, especially in 1861. According to the arrangements then made, while the number and value of the original exhibitions were to continue as when first established in 1724, " Supplemental Exhibitions" of £32 12s. 4d., and £17 12s. 4d. respectively were founded, to be annually allotted, on a competitive examination, among freshmen students who had entered the University from one of the four grammar schools, and were holders of one of the original exhibitions of £7 7s. 8d. But whereas the original exhibitions are tenable for seven years, the " Supplemental Exhibitions" are tenable for five years only. In addition, the most meritorious candidate at such competitive examination shall be entitled, upon the recommendation of the Board of Trinity College, to receive from the governors a further sum of £10 per annum, thus raising the total amount of his exhibition money to £50 a-year. The Erasmus Smith's Exhibitions in Trinity College stand, therefore, thus:—

Twenty original ("statutory") first-class exhibitions of £7 7s. 8d. each, tenable for *seven* years;

Fifteen do. second-class, of £5 10s 9d. each, tenable also for *seven* years;

Five " Supplemental Exhibitions" of £32 12s. 4d each, tenable for *five* years;

Five do. of £17 12s. 4d. each, tenable for *five* years;

And five special exhibitions of £10 each, tenable for *five* years;

Thus making, supposing all to be in operation, a total exhibition fund of £531 17s. 11d. a-year.

Before we leave this subject of Erasmus Smith's Exhibitions in Trinity College, we should observe that while the exhibitions, as originally founded, bore a certain proportion to the value of the estates, this proportion has utterly disappeared in the case of the present exhibitions. Remembering also what was the value of money a century and a-half ago, we can at once understand that £6 or £8 would then have been a substantial aid to an industrious student—a quality which can scarcely be attributed to the paltry grants which are now dignified with the name of exhibitions. Had the governors fairly fulfilled their duty to the schools, the exhibitions would have increased in number and grown in amount with the increasing value of their estates. But instead of doing this, they spent a small portion of their annually increasing income in founding, with stinted salaries, professorships in the university, while they squandered the large residue in calling into existence a number of primary schools, and erecting school houses, even the sites of many of which can now hardly be identified.

Erasmus Smith's bounty was not confined to the scholars of his schools. In 1671 he gave £30 a-year for the maintenance of a Hebrew lecturer in Trinity College. In 1720 the Governors gave £70 a-year for the support of two lecturers, one on Oratory and History, the other on Natural and Experimental Philosophy; and £100 a-year for founding and supporting three new Fellowships in the same College. These foundations were sanctioned by the Act of 1723, so that they really date from 1724. In 1762 three new Professorships were founded in Trinity College by the Governors—namely, one of Mathematics, one of History, and one of Oriental languages; the former Professorship of Oratory and History being made one of Oratory only, and since 1855, of Oratory and English Literature. In the year 1763 an additional annual sum of £65 was given by the governors for the purpose of raising the salary of the Professor of Natural Philosophy to £100 a-year, thus putting him on an equality with the holders of the chairs established the preceding year.

The Act of 1723 seems to have been specially drawn up in the interest of Trinity College. The last section enacts as to the disposal of any surplus funds that may accrue out of the estates as follows:— "Then, and in such case, it shall and may be lawful to and for the governors of the said schools for the time being, from time to time, and for ever hereafter, to apply and dispose of the residue and surplus of the said yearly rents for and towards some public work, or use, in the said College". Before the passing of this Act, but as the result of the negociations which led to the passing of it, " the Governors gave in 1720 the sum of £942 2s. 9d., for erecting lodgings for 32 exhibitioners", and £144 3s. " for lodgings for the Chemist". The building for the exhibitioners having been partly destroyed by fire, the sum of £580 was granted in 1726 to rebuild it, the College undertaking in consideration of the grant to give free chambers for 35 students, the total number of Erasmus Smith's exhibitioners. From the evidence before the Endowed Schools Commission in 1855, it would seem that the privilege was not taken advantage of, and was even unknown to the Governors and officers of the Erasmus Smith's Board, although one at least of the Governors was Senior Fellow of Trinity College! Among the donations mentioned in the list of benefactors published in the " The Dublin University Calendar", is the following:—" 1776, by the said Governors, the sum of £200 per annum to be disposed of in premiums for the encouragement of composition". No trace of this grant is to be found in any of the documents or evidence of the Endowed Schools Commission. Perhaps, like the privilege of the exhibitioners, it has been forgotten! The year before this grant was made, namely, 1775, the Governors gave £2,500 to build a theatre, now known as the Examination Hall of Trinity College. In 1802 the Governors purchased for the College the library of M. Greffier Fagel, Pensionary of Holland, which had been removed from the latter country to London, in 1794, on the occasion of the French invasion of the Netherlands. This library contained 20,000 volumes, and cost £10,000.

The annual expenditure upon the three classes of educational institutions — primary, intermediate, and university — on the foundation of Erasmus Smith (including the rent-charge to Christ's Hospital, London, and the expenses of management, but exclusive of receivers' fees), as collected from the evidence of the Registrar, Eustace Thorpe, Esq., before the Royal Commission on Endowed Schools in 1858, may be thus approximately stated in general terms :—

Four Grammar Schools	£1,200
Professorships and Fellowships in Trinity College	600
Exhibitions in ditto (supposing all to be in operation)	532
Blue Coat Hospital, Dublin	700
Christ's Hospital, London	100
146 "English" or Primary Schools (reduced in July, 1868, to 144)	4,500
Administration, etc.	900
Total Annual Expenditure	£8,532

In 1868 there was an accumulation in the bank amounting to £20,000, arising partly from surplus revenue (*R. Com. Prim. Ed.*, Ev. QQ. 12,790—12,793-8), and partly from the sale of land to railway companies, whose lines pass through the Governors' estates. The interest of this sum is another source of income which must be added to the gross rent already given. We have been unable to discover with any approach to accuracy the net income of the Governors after paying rent-charges, receiver's fees, etc. The Endowed Schools Commissioners, in their report in 1858, estimated it at 8,162*l*. 6*s*. 2*d*., of which they considered 7,462*l*. 6*s*. 2*d*. was available for educational purposes. According to the above approximate estimate, the amount devoted to such purposes, including exhibitions in Trinity College, is 6,932*l*. The estates, if well managed, ought easily to produce a net income of at least 10,000*l*. per annum. Thus it appears that, while these large estates of nearly 12,000 acres, exclusive of mountain, were mainly intended by the founder to maintain three or five grammar schools, the support of these now forms a very secondary item, scarcely exceeding *one-seventh* of the expenditure. One hundred and forty-four primary schools, very few of which are on the estates, absorb one-half of the whole income, while a sum nearly as large as that devoted to the original object of the founder is annually added to the surplus lying idle in the bank.

Such is a brief, and therefore necessarily imperfect sketch of this great foundation, which is known by the name of Erasmus Smith. It is impossible to look upon it as, in any sense, a private endowment. From what we have already stated, it is more than doubtful whether even the estates constituting the endowment which passed to the Governors under the Charter, in 1669, were ever considered to be the private property of Erasmus Smith. But even if we admit that he was not a mere trustee, like the Irish Society, the changes which have been effected in the objects and mode of administering the trust funds, and the way in which those changes have been brought about, have made the foundation a public one. This was the opinion of the Commissioners of Irish Education of 1791. They observe in their report, which is quoted by the Endowed School Commission of 1854:—" The schools of Erasmus Smith, though originating in the intentions of a private individual, yet, from the repeated interposition of the Legislature and of the Crown, may be now considered as public institutions" (*End. Sch. Com.* 1858, vol. ii., p. 351). The existing corporation ought to be dissolved, and the estates transferred to the same commission which would be entrusted with the funds of all similar foundations. The driblets of grants now given to Primary Schools, many of them connected with the Church Education Society, and the greater number of them unconnected with the estates, should be discontinued. These schools can in future be provided for out of the State grants, which will be open to schools of this class if the recommendations of the Royal Commissioners on Primary Education are carried out. They very properly observe in their Report that:

"The national system now provides all parts of Ireland with the means of primary instruction, open to all denominations among the pupils. Secondary instruction is still deficient. It is precisely this secondary education which Erasmus Smith's endowment was designed to supply; and we think that the trust funds may be devoted to this purpose with great advantage" (*Rep.*, p. 492).

CHAPTER VII.

VARIOUS OTHER ENDOWED GRAMMAR SCHOOLS.

Endowments for Intermediate Education already described; other schools of the same class; most of these may be regarded as public institutions; some may be private; the latter mentioned to show extent of provision for education of Protestants, and how much remains to be done for Catholics; educational equality can only be attained by making reparation for past injustice.

Richard Boyle, Earl of Cork, and the schools founded by him.

Bandon School: nature of original endowment; school assisted by Corporation; in a satisfactory state in 1858; amount of original endowment, supplemented by Duke of Devonshire; master denies that he is bound to receive free scholars.

Charleville School: particulars of endowment unknown; schoolhouse in ruins in 1791; in the same state in 1858; salary of master.

Lismore School: founded in 1610; endowment of £20 a-year for a free school by will of Earl of Cork in 1642; value of school premises; salary paid by Duke of Devonshire; Report of Endowed Schools' Commissioners of 1858.

Youghal Collegiate School: original endowment; directions of James the First with reference to it, not carried out; Report of Endowed Schools' Commissioners of 1858.

Lifford School: endowed in 1619 by Sir Richard Hansard; terms of endowment; reports of successive Commissions; made an English School by the Earl of Erne in 1840; opinion of the Bishop of Derry that it ought to be an English, and not a Grammar School, contrary to that of several Commissions.

Kilkenny College: foundation by Duke of Ormonde in 1684; nature and object of original endowment: appointment of masters passed to Trinity College on the failure of the male heirs of founder; school-house in ruins in 1783; rebuilt by means of a grant from the Irish Parliament; no inspection of school by Trinity College; school managed at discretion of master; Report as to attendance and inspection unfavourable in 1857; this is the most important of the schools of this class; not now a private foundation; claims of the citizens of Kilkenny.

Clonmel Classical School: foundation in 1685 by Michael and Stephen Moore; terms of endowment; trustees; frauds on the trust; law-suit of a master of the school to set aside a fraudulent lease; injury sustained by school; report of Commissioners of 1812; effect on it of opening of Clonmel Model

School; state of school in 1857; views of Endowed Schools' Commissioners on the patronage of the school, etc.; school almost inoperative; value of endowment; foundation lost to town; school notorious for its seduction of Catholic boys from their faith.

Navan and Ballyroan Schools: the foundation of Alderman John Preston of Dublin; nature of trusts; misapplication of endowment; report of Commissioners, etc., thereon; law-suit carried on for ninety-nine years regularly; the endowment; disgraceful state of schools in 1857, according to Report of Endowed Schools' Commissioners; value of endowment; opinion of last-named Commissioners on mismanagement; suggestion made by them to apply the funds to found a Grammar School at Maryborough; grant to these schools of thirty acres of the commons of Navan by Corporation of town in 1776.

Midleton School: the foundation of the Countess of Orkney in 1696; nature and abuse of endowment; unsuccessful attempt made to recover estates; has two exhibitions in Trinity College, Dublin.

Carrickmacross School: founded in 1711 by Viscount Weymouth; extent of endowment; school-house for fifty boarders and house for master built by founder; boys from the barony of Farney entitled to free admission; master considers the admission of free scholars optional; visitors of school; they never visit.

Eyrecourt School: originated in a bequest; Report of Endowed Schools' Commissioners in 1858; originally intended to be a primary school.

Schools connected with Municipalities.

Waterford Grammar School: founded at a very early period; £50 a-year and free house allowed by Corporation in 1791: a small Scholarship in Trinity College attached to school; salary discontinued by Corporation in 1840, and master ejected; master succeeded in establishing a life interest in the salary; state of school in 1858; school given up on the death of the master; recommendation of Endowed Schools' Commissioners; not agreeable to citizens of Waterford; house rented to Catholic Bishop, who has established a school, but receives no aid from the corporation; exhibition in Trinity College not filled.

New Ross School: founded in 1713 by John Ivory; value of endowment; trustees; now managed by Town Commissioners; a Catholic master appointed, but endowment not yet received.

Dundalk Grammar School: founded in 1727; value of endowment, and by whom made; salary now paid by the Earl of Roden.

Kinsale School: founded in 1767 by Edward Southwell; value of endowment; teacher appointed by Town Commissioners; in 1791 the corporation gave £20 a-year to the school; this sum not paid for some time previous to 1858, and not included

among the endowments by Commissioners of Endowed Schools; the master has a house and garden.
Bandon School might be included amongst municipal schools.
The designation "Schools of Private Foundation" given to the sixteen schools noticed in this chapter, inappropriate; reasons why most of these schools may be regarded as public schools.
Tables showing date of foundation, endowments, number of scholars, etc., of the sixteen schools; analysis of Tables.
One of the objects of the founders of the Diocesan, Royal, and other schools described in previous chapters, to provide students for Trinity College; the foundations now noticed intimately connected with Trinity College.
These Grammar Schools have failed as educational institutions; and still more so in their object of Protestantizing the country; as the disestablishment of the Church has given religious equality, educational equality, its complement, should now be secured.

In the preceding chapters we have considered the endowments for the various classes of Intermediate Schools, by which successive sovereigns of England sought, either directly by legislation and by acts of the royal prerogative, or through the agency of others, "to extirpate superstition and to spread the English order and habite" in Ireland. The Diocesan Schools of Queen Elizabeth, the Royal Schools, founded by King James I., the schools of the Irish Society, and Erasmus Smith's schools, under the board incorporated by King Charles II., were foundations for middle-class education spread over the country, giving support to the University created by queen Elizabeth, and enabling it, as their founders desired and anticipated, to assert the dominion of Protestant and English ideas over the minds and souls of the Catholic people of this country. In addition to these institutions—all integral portions of one great homogeneous scheme of education, at the head of which is Trinity College—the seventeenth century saw established several other Endowed Schools, the chief of which we now propose to review. Some of these institutions are closely akin to those we have already considered, having been founded in furtherance of the same views of the " settlement" of the country which gave rise to the schools of the Irish Society, and of Erasmus Smith. Those foundations are really public property. They were established simply to carry out the public policy of the Government of the day, and should now follow the public reversal of that policy. Some schools of this class are admittedly public, because founded by, or maintained out of municipal funds or public revenues. Others again, although ostensibly created by private munificence, were really endowed out of the confiscated estates, and have virtually become the property of the nation through change of circumstances, and especially by the frequent interposition of the legislature. There may, however, be some of those institutions, which were originally purely private endowments, intended for the education of Protestants only, and still devoted to that object. As to these we would be the last to interfere with the rights of our Protestant fellow-countrymen; and if we mention those private endowments, we do so with the view that all may see how ample is the provision for education which Protestants enjoy, and how much remains to be done for Catholics before they can be said to possess educational equality with their privileged fellow-countrymen. Any legislation which attempts to remove the educational grievances of the Catholics of Ireland, must make reparation for the past, and take into account the baneful action of the iniquitous Penal Code, which, for so long a period, rendered impossible the foundation or maintenance of Catholic schools.

Early in the seventeenth century several of the intruded settlers, imitating the example of the sovereigns, betook themselves to the work of educating and evangelizing the Irish Catholics, even by founding Grammar Schools. Among these, one of the first in order of time, and one of the most remarkable in other respects, was the personage who is commonly known as the Great Earl of Cork.

Richard Boyle, of a Herefordshire family, first landed in Dublin, almost a penniless adventurer, in 1588, when he was about 22 years of age. After various vicissitudes of fortune, he ingratiated himself into the favour of Queen Elizabeth, who appointed him Clerk of the Council to the notorious Sir George Carew, then President of Munster. Sir Walter Raleigh, who had obtained 12,000 acres of the confiscated estates in Waterford and Cork, but, on account of the distracted state of the kingdom, derived no income from them, sold this vast territory to Boyle for a nominal sum. Carew having been promoted to be Lord Deputy, Boyle's fortunes rapidly rose. In 1603 he received the honour of knighthood; in 1612 he was sworn a Privy Councillor; in 1616 he was created Lord Boyle, Baron of Youghal; in 1620 Viscount Dungarvan and Earl of Cork. King Charles I. wrote to Falkland, Lord Deputy, under date 30th November, 1627, directing him to confer on the earl's second son, then only eight years of age, the dignity of baron and viscount; and, recapitulating the father's virtues, the King enumerates, in the preamble to the Patent, amongst others:—

" Building towns, and fortifying them with fair walls, and *filling them with English colonies; building churches, and reducing the people to civil obedience; in establishing religion, extirpating superstition* . . . to the plentiful increase of riches and civility by planting and continually supporting leaders and other men, experienced in arms, from England, to the number of fifteen hundred, and to the perpetual security and defence of those parts; and all this he did at his own expense, and by his own industry", etc.

From this we can understand the relation of the Earl of Cork to educational foundations on his Irish estates. He reigned like a prince in his castle of Lismore, and during his lifetime saw three of his sons created peers. At the battle of Liscarrol, or Knocknanos, in 1642, four of his sons fought against the Confederate Catholics, and the eldest was slain on the field. His was a Plantation over the broad lands of Desmond, analogous to that which was going on at the same time in Ulster. The London guilds of tradesmen, Richard Boyle, Erasmus Smith, and all the leading adventurers, had a common object, and they used similar means to attain it. The sword and the school were equally employed "to reduce the people to civil obedience and to establish religion". The Earl of Cork established on the estates which he acquired the Grammar Schools of Bandon, Charleville, Lismore, and Youghal, commencing his assistance to them so early as 1610, and by his will in 1642, creating in favour of each of them a rent-charge of £20 a-year for a master, and £10 a-year for an usher.

We shall now briefly describe each of the schools coming within the scope of this Chapter, commencing with those of the Earl of Cork.

BANDON.—Besides an endowment for the master and usher, the Earl of Cork gave directions in his will, for the building at Bandon of a school-house, to be kept in repair by his heirs, specifying that the house and rent-charge were for a free school. This school was at a later period assisted by the Corporation, who, for many years, gave a sum of £20 to the master. The school was reported by the Endowed School Commissioners in 1858 to be in a satisfactory state; and while the original endowment amounts to only £27 13s. 10d. British currency, the Duke of

Devonshire, the representative of the founder, gives an annual salary to the master of £40, besides a house and land valued at £64 a year. But notwithstanding the specific object stated in the founder's will, the master denied that he was bound to admit any free scholars; and, as a fact there were none.

CHARLEVILLE.—The Endowed School Commissioners report that the particulars of this endowment are unknown, the original deed of foundation having been lost. It is probable that no such deed ever existed, and that, like its sister institutions, the school depended for its support, first on the bounty, and then on the will of the Earl of Cork. The Commissioners of 1791 report that the ruins of a large school-house then existed, indicating that the establishment had been formerly conducted on an extensive scale. The Endowed Schools Commissioners also found, in 1856, "the school-house in ruins, and the state of the education very unsatisfactory". The master received in (1858) £36 18s. 5d. annual salary. The land in his possession was valued at £1.

LISMORE.—The Commissioners of Education in their report (9th March, 1812) state that this school was founded in 1610. By his will (1642) the Earl of Cork charged his heirs for ever with a payment of £20 per annum to the schoolmaster of "*the free school*" by him "lately erected at Lismore", and directing them to keep the school in good repair. The estimated annual value of the school premises is £20 10s.; the master's salary in 1858 was £30, paid by the Duke of Devonshire, in addition to a free residence worth £20 a-year. The Endowed Schools' Commissioners report of this school as follows (page 118):—

"It is referred to in the appendix to the report of the Commissioners of 1791. . . . . . The school then appeared to be in a flourishing condition, attended by twenty-seven boarders, eight day boys, and *five free pupils*.

"The present condition (in 1858) is very different. Our Assistant Commissioner reports there are now no free scholars, nor have there been any since 1851. The master, however, is paid his salary by the Duke of Devonshire, who also allows him a house rent free, and keeps it in repair. The school-house is beautifully situated, and kept in good order. . . . It is said that the master aspired to have the school (*a free one by the terms of the foundation*) attended by members of the highest classes alone, and actually discouraged the attendance of the middle and lower classes. The master, *as in most free schools*, does not admit the right of any one to nominate free pupils, and he retains the entire endowment for himself, though £10 of it is intended for an usher.

"The annual returns made by the master of this school to the Commissioners of Education must have shown to them the declining state of the school, and the ultimate discontinuance of the attendance of pupils. The Commissioners are responsible, as visitors of the school, for having taken no step............ Vigilance at an earlier period on their part would also have prevented the master from converting a free school into a private one, and denying the right of free pupils to be admitted".

YOUGHAL COLLEGIATE SCHOOL was, as we observed above, assisted in 1610 by the Earl of Cork, who gave it a school-house and thirty pounds a-year. It "attracted the favourable notice of King James I., who, in 1613, directed the Lord Deputy to promote the success of the institution, by granting a charter of incorporation, and a license to hold lands, notwithstanding the mortmain laws. These directions, however, would appear not to have been complied with"—(*End. Sch. Com. Report*, p. 116).

The school is specially designated "the Free School of Youghal", by the Earl of Cork, in his will in 1642, by which he charged his heirs to pay 20*l*. annually for the master, and 10*l*. for the usher. The Endowed

Schools Commissioners report that notwithstanding the terms of the endowment, there were in 1856 no free scholars, and the master denied that he was bound to admit any. The estimated value of the school premises was, in 1858, 23*l*. 6*s*. The salary paid to the master by the Duke of Devonshire (representative of the Earl of Cork) was 27*l*. 13*s*. 10*d*., equivalent to 30*l*., Irish currency; the master had also a free residence, of the annual value of 20*l*. Thirty-one scholars were in attendance, all day-boys, and all very young.

LIFFORD SCHOOL, in the county of Donegal, comes next in order of time, having been endowed in 1619 by the will of Sir Richard Hansard, " who left 30*l*. a-year for the support of a master, and 20*l*. for an usher, for instruction in learning at a free school at Lifford, where *all the children* in the parish of Clonleigh were to be entitled to a *gratuitous education*". Yet the Commissioners of 1791 reported there were no free pupils in this school. The Commissioners of 1807–12 state, that while both the master and usher received their salaries, " the business of the school was in reality conducted by a third person, at a salary of 6*l*., who taught writing and arithmetic only to some children of the town". The Commissioners accordingly observed that " the intention of the founder to establish a classical school at Lifford was not carried into effect". The constant tale of " inefficiency" and " unsatisfactory condition", told by successive Commissions, continued down to 1841. Soon after that date the Earl of Erne, " exercising the right of nomination of the Bishop of Derry, converted the establishment into an English school"; and so it has continued to the present time, the Bishop of Derry, according to the Endowed Schools Commission (*Report*, page 113), considering " that under the terms of the will it ought to be an English school and not a grammar school"—rather an off-hand assumption, and quite contrary to the opinions of all the Commissions which had taken cognizance of the school.

KILKENNY COLLEGE.—By deed, bearing date 18th March, 1684, the Duke of Ormonde granted a large mansion, with nearly ten acres of land adjoining, for a grammar school, and charged the tithes of certain rectories to the extent of £129 4s. 7½d., "for repairs of school, and for resident master (to be a member of the Established Church and an A.M.), and for an usher to instruct, free, children in grantor's service, and certain others, and at half the usual fees of remarkable schools in Dublin, children of the city of Kilkenny fit to enter on grammar learning, in religion, Latin, Greek, Hebrew, oratory, and poetry; school to be visited annually by the Bishop of Ossory and the Provost of Trinity College, Dublin, on last Thursday of July". The male issue of the founder having failed, the appointment of masters became almost from the first vested in the Board of Trinity College. "When Dr. Ellison was appointed master in 1783, he found the schoolhouse in ruins, but succeeded, after several applications, in obtaining a grant of £5,064, from the Irish Parliament for building a new one. With this grant the present spacious schoolhouse, capable of containing about 50 boarders, was erected". (*End. Sch. Com.* 1858, *Rep.*, page 112).

The master of the school stated to the Endowed Schools Commissioners in 1855, that "during the fourteen years he had kept the school, there had been no inspection or visitation either on the part of the Provost of Trinity College or of the Commissioners of Education", who, under the Act of 1813, have superintendence over the school. The bishop's visitation was, according to the master, confined to "looking over the house and place". The Assistant-Commissioner reports:—" The statutes relating to the visitation of the school have been completely disregarded, *no visitation having taken place for perhaps a century.* The master has received no directions whatever as to the government of the school, and has made acquaintance with the statutes simply as matter of curious research in Ledwich's *Antiquities of Ireland;* while the studies of an important public institution, having positive rules for its management, are as much at the discretion of the master as those of any private school". The Commissioners report (page 112) " the condition of the school as very unsatisfactory as regards both attendance and inspection", and that " the rules of the foundation are completely set at nought".

None of the grammar schools of the class which we are at present considering are of equal importance with this institution. The historic fame of the city of Kilkenny, and the number of eminent men educated in the college, invest it with a special interest. Remembering that the Irish Parliament gave £5,064 towards it, and that the present school premises have been wholly built out of funds provided by the nation, we cannot imagine how any one can pretend to look upon Kilkenny College as anything else than a public school. Besides, the fact that Trinity College, the head of the existing Protestant educational arrangements of the country, stands towards it in the founder's place, effectually takes it out of the category of private schools. The citizens of Kilkenny have certainly a claim that their rights shall be considered with reference to an endowment which was intended to afford " grammar learning" to their children " at half the usual fees".

CLONMEL CLASSICAL SCHOOL was founded in 1685, by Michael Moore and his son Stephen, of Barna, near Clonmel, and endowed with 683 acres of land and a site, vested in trustees, for the erection and support of a Grammar School, where the children of Protestant Freemen of Clonmel should be taught gratis. The deed of grant provided that the founders or their heirs, the Duke of Ormonde, who had endowed Kilkenny College the year before, and the Mayor of Clonmel for the time being, or any two of them, should have power to appoint or remove the schoolmaster at pleasure. Like most of those schools, this noble charity was soon the victim of fraud and individual rapacity. It was found in 1791 that the lands, then worth 370*l.* a-year, had been leased at 200*l.* a-year at the instance of the Earl of Mountcashel, heir to the founders. The Earl also appointed a relative of his own nominal master at a salary of 120*l.* a-year, for which he did no duty, and gave the residue of 80*l.* to Rev. Mr. Carey, who had charge of the school. There were then thirty-one scholars, ten of them boarders, and only two free pupils. The estate and town having been transferred to Mr. Bagwell, Mr. Carey, at his own expense, commenced a Chancery suit to set aside the fraudulent lease, which the court eventually did set aside; but the validity of a sub-lease at 400*l.* a-year, which did not expire for many years afterwards, was upheld. In the meantime the litigation and pecuniary expense had withdrawn the master from his duties, to the great injury of his school. The Royal Commission of 1807–12 found 21 day scholars, only one of whom was free, and no boarder. This is one of the few cases in which a visitation was held under the Commissioners of Education of 1813; but, notwithstanding the very unsatisfactory state in which the visitors found the affairs of the school, no remedies were provided. The opening in 1849 of the Clonmel National Model School, just beside it, withdrew nearly all the few boys attending the endowed school; and the Commissioners of 1858 report most unfavourably of the condition of the institution. The attendance was stated to be 27 day scholars, 10 of them being free. The course of classical instruction was elementary. The school-house, admirably planned and especially suited for boarders, had had none for many years. The master was a Protestant clergyman, appointed by the Earl of Mountcashel, who, conjointly with the Marquis of Ormonde, claims the patronage, and the Endowed Schools Commissioners, 1858, in their report (page 111), thus epitomise their views of the foundation, then 173 years in operation:

"The state of this school indicates that patronage in private hands ought not to be separated from the local connexion which is a check upon its proper exercise. The compassion of the inhabitants, visitors, and commissioners appears to us greatly misplaced—it would have been much better to have dismissed the master at once, and thus prevented his imprudence from depriving an important town of an efficient school for some years, and we think that steps ought now to be taken for his removal".

The school has since declined from bad to worse, being virtually inoperative; and the benefit of the fine house and premises, the annual value of which is set down at 139l, and 683 acres of land, underlet at 425l. a-year, is lost to the inhabitants of Clonmel. Like too many of these foundations, this school, when in active operation, was notorious for the number of poor Catholic boys whom it seduced from their faith.

NAVAN AND BALLYROAN SCHOOLS.—In 1686 Alderman John Preston, of the city of Dublin, granted

1,737 acres of land, upon trusts, one of which was to pay a salary of 35*l.* to a Protestant master to teach at Navan, and another to pay 52*l.* on the like terms to a master at Ballyroan, Queen's County. This endowment was misapplied, and the abuses connected with it were fully set forth before the Committee of Inquiry of the House of Lords, in 1764, into abused charities, before the Education Commissioners of 1791, and before the Royal Commissioners of 1807-12. In consequence of those abuses a special clause was introduced into the act of 1813 (53 Geo. III., c. 107, s. 14), vesting the estate in the Commissioners of Education established under that statute. A suit which lasted 99 years respecting this charity was commenced in 1734, and was concluded in 1833, the law costs for the first 74 years having amounted to 3,000*l.* The Endowed Schools Commission of 1858 report most unfavourably of both schools, Navan and Ballyroan, and censure the Commissioners of Education for their neglect of the interests of the charity, the latter school not having been inspected by them for ten years. Ballyroan school, annual value of premises 23*l.* 17*s.* 5*d.*, the master of which had 92*l.* 6*s.* 2*d.* a-year, and a house worth 12*l.* with an assistant having 55*l.* 7*s.* 8*d.* a-year and a cottage worth 5*l.*, or a total income of 164*l.* 13*s.* 10*d.*, is reported as "*in a disgraceful condition, attended by only two day pupils, out of three on the roll, and their education is very much neglected*" (*Report*, p. 108). The report on the Navan school is no better. House in a bad situation; staff and salaries as in Ballyroan; "no boarders; *three* boys present out of five on the roll, of whom four were free, and all belonging to the United Church. One of the three boys present, who was preparing for Trinity College, seemed very well taught; but the others, who had but lately joined the school, knew less than the average of boys in the National Schools". Before suggesting that the whole annual endowments of 564*l*. 16*s*. 1*d*., school premises included, should be applied to the support of a Grammar School in Maryborough, the nearest town to the charity estate, the Endowed Schools' Commissioners say: " It thus appears as if some fatality attended these schools or the localities in which they were situated, for on no schools has a greater amount of inquiry been bestowed, and in the case of no schools have more expensive and protracted legal proceedings been adopted, and yet there are none to be found in a more unsatisfactory state".

An important fact connected with this foundation appears in the proceedings of the same Commission (*Evidence*, 12,865). " The Corporation of Navan, in 1776, made a grant under their seal of 30 acres of the Commons of Navan to the school, on which it was proposed that a school-house should be erected out of the savings of the endowment. The loss of those savings, and other instances of misconduct and mismanagement of the funds, may well account for this grant never having been actually fulfilled, and being still withheld".

After this quotation it is unnecessary to add a word of comment, to point out that those schools have passed from the domain of private endowments, and must be reckoned among those of a public character.

MIDLETON SCHOOL.—The Countess of Orkney granted, in 1696, over 2,000 acres of land for the foundation of a Free Grammar School at Midleton in the County of Cork, with exhibitions in the University of Dublin. The endowments of this school were shamefully abused, the land having been let on leases, renewable for ever, with small fines, at a rent of

200*l.*, the property now being worth fully 2,000*l.* a year. An attempt was unsuccessfully made in 1828 by the Commissioners of Education to break the leases. The Endowed Schools Commissioners of 1858 report unfavourably of this school. There are two exhibitions in Trinity College connected with it, one for 30*l.*, the other for 20*l.* The subjects of examination, etc., are the same as for the Royal Schools.

CARRICKMACROSS SCHOOL "was endowed in 1711 by Viscount Weymouth, who granted a rent of 70*l.* for the support of a Grammar School, the proceeds to be devoted to the repairs of the school-house and the payment of the master. The Commissioners of 1791 state that a few years previously a schoolhouse, capable of containing fifty boarders, and a dwelling-house for the master, had been built by Viscount Weymouth". Although "the founder conferred the right of free admission on all persons from the barony of Farney, nevertheless the master considers it altogether optional with himself whether or not he is to receive free pupils, and exercises the discretion with which he conceives himself invested, by admitting a very small number"—(*End. Sch. Com. Rep.*, page 109). The number of "Free Pupils" in 1856 was TWO.

By the deed of foundation, the Protestant Primate, the Vice-Chancellor of the University of Dublin, the Protestant Bishop of Clogher, and the Provost of Trinity College, were appointed visitors of this school, established in an almost exclusively Catholic district. They, or any two of them, were required to visit annually. The Endowed Schools Commissioners report "*that they never visit*".

EYRECOURT SCHOOL, in the county of Galway, owes its origin to a bequest, in 1730, of 700*l.* for the founding of a *charity school* at Eyrecourt for the maintenance and education of *poor children* of the parish of Donanaghta. The Endowed Schools Commission, 1858, reports (page 112), "That no efficient steps were taken for carrying out these directions. Instead of being a school for the poor, and therefore giving an education adapted to their wants, it was from the commencement made a classical school". Of course, none of the scholars were free. There was "one boy in 1857 learning Greek and Latin, and his proficiency in those departments was as low as that of the others in English, which could scarcely be more unsatisfactory than it is". The Commission further states " that the mode of procuring masters is, that each one purchases the good-will of his predecessor".

The preceding are all the Grammar Schools which owe their existence to the bounty of private individuals—an origin which, as we shall afterwards have occasion to observe, by no means implies that the schools themselves are to be regarded as private institutions. We have next to speak of a group of schools which, being connected with the municipalities, possess undoubtedly a public character.

The WATERFORD SCHOOL is both the oldest and the most important of this group. It must have been founded at a very early period, since the municipal books contain, so far back as 1669, minutes relating to the appointment of masters. The Commissioners of 1791 reported that the corporation paid 50$l.$ (Irish) a year, and allowed a free house to the master; and that 30 pupils—ten of them boarders—attended, none being free. Attached to this school, there is a small scholarship in Trinity College of 15$l.$ (Irish), tenable for seven years, founded in 1787 by the Rev. William Downes. After the passing of the Municipal Reform Act of 1840, the corporation passed a resolution to discontinue the salary, and ejected the schoolmaster; but he succeeded in establishing, by legal proceedings, his right to the salary during his life, the question as to the permanency of the endowment remaining undecided. The Endowed Schools Commissioners of 1858 report that they found the school in active operation, 61 boys being present—six of them boarders, and none free. Of the 69 on the roll, 50 were Episcopalian Protestants, and 19 Dissenters of various kinds. The corporation then paid the master, who was a Protestant clergyman, 45*l*. 3*s*. 1*d*. a-year, and allowed him 18*l*. 9*s*. 2*d*. for premiums for the scholars. Shortly after the date of the Endowed Schools Commissioners' report, the master, Rev. Dr. Price, died; the school was given up, and the schoolhouse returned into the hands of the corporation. The Commissioners of 1858 had recommended that the diocesan endowments of the dioceses of Waterford, Lismore, Cashel, and Emly, which had been long dormant, should be united to the municipal endowment, and applied to a mixed school. The citizens of Waterford were most unwilling that this recommendation should be carried out. The school-house was falling into a very dilapidated condition, when the Catholic Bishop, having taken the premises from the corporation at a rent fully equal to their value, if not in excess of it, the school was re-opened under his sanction. A large sum was spent from private resources in re-fitting the house, which is a very old one, and in furnishing it so as to render it available for school purposes; and a thriving Catholic school soon sprang up, and continues to flourish We understand that within the last three or four years the corporation has reduced the rent of the premises, which are in a very decayed part of the city; but it neither pays the salary to the master nor gives any other assistance to the school. Of course the exhibition in Trinity College remains unfilled.

NEW ROSS SCHOOL is neither so ancient nor extensive as the Grammar School at Waterford. In 1713 John Ivory granted to trustees the premises of an old Augustinian abbey for a Free Grammar School in which four Protestant boys should be entitled to gratuitous education. The direction of the foundation is vested in the trustees and the Corporation and Vicar of New Ross. At present the Town Commissioners manage it. The premises are valued at 32*l*. 7*s*. 5*d*., and the endowment from house property at 20*l*., which is reported as rapidly declining in value. A Catholic master was appointed to the charge of the school in 1868 by the Town Commissioners, by whom he was put in possession of the school premises; but we understand that the tenant who holds the house property, on which is charged the small annual endowment of 20*l*., refuses to pay that sum.

DUNDALK GRAMMAR SCHOOL was endowed in 1727, the estimated annual value of the school premises being 64*l*. 2*s*. 6*d*., and an income from land of 46*l*. 3*s*. 1*d*. With respect to the circumstances connected with the foundation of this school, there is a conflict of statement. The Endowed Schools Commissioners, 1858, say (*Report*, page 111):—

" It is alleged on the one hand that the endowment was made by the Earl of Limerick in 1725, in consideration of certain commons of Dundalk, on which he had some claim, being given up to him by the Corporation. It is alleged, on the other hand, that the claim was not well founded, but that the Corporation, being under the influence of the Earl of Limerick, too readily yielded to it".

Elsewhere (Vol. iii. page 181), the following passage occurs:—

"It is very commonly believed in the locality [Dundalk] that the premises comprised in the deed of 1725 were the actual *bona fide* property of the Corporation, and that the Earl of Limerick, at a time when that body were in complete subservience to him, induced them to part with their estate in consideration of the paltry endowment of 50*l.* a-year. The property in question is now very valuable, and worth many hundreds per annum. It must be admitted that the deed of conveyance above mentioned wears a very suspicious appearance, though it may be impossible at this distance of time to impeach its validity. In the Reports of 1807-12, p. 285, it is stated that the schoolhouse was built by the Corporation of Dundalk, and an acre of land granted by them for the use of the master, and that the annuity of 50*l.* per annum was granted in consequence of a compact entered into between the late Earl of Clanbrassil and the Corporation, the latter having given the former a part of certain commons near their town, which was their property, upon condition that the Earl of Clanbrassil would endow this school with 50*l.* a-year, and oblige the master to educate the sons of the freemen of the Corporation for half a guinea per quarter each. The Report further states, that in 1809 there were fourteen boys in the school who had availed themselves of the privilege of the grant in favour of the sons of freemen, and paid two guineas a-year each for their education".

The Earl of Roden, the present representative of the Earl of Limerick, pays a salary of 46*l.* 2*s.* 6*d.* to the master, who has also a house and garden valued at 50*l.* a year.

KINSALE SCHOOL was founded in 1767, by Edward Southwell, subsequently Lord de Clifford. It has school premises valued at 41*l.* 2*s.*, and a rent-charge of 27*l.* 13*s.* 10*d.* given by the founder, in consideration of the "friendship and generosity of the Corporation" in transferring to him the right of presentation to a certain benefice. The present Town Commissioners exercise the right of appointing the master, and pay him the amount of the rent-charge as a salary. The Commissioners of 1791 report that the school was then assisted by the Corporation to the extent of 20*l*. a year, and they reckon this sum among the endowments of the school. The Commissioners of 1858 observe that the report of 1791 omitted to state whether this municipal subsidy was secured. It appears not to have been paid, for some time at least, previous to 1858; and it is not reckoned by the Endowed Schools Commissioners among the endowments, although no explanation is given of the omission. In addition to his salary, the master has a house and garden valued at 30*l*. The condition of the school is reported by the Endowed Schools Commissioners as unsatisfactory.

BANDON SCHOOLS, already mentioned among the foundations of the Earl of Cork, having received during many years an annual grant of 20*l*. from the Corporation of the town, might, perhaps, be properly included in the category of Municipal Schools.

We have now reviewed the sixteen grammar schools (in operation) which the Endowed Schools Commissioners of 1858 designated " Schools of Private Foundation". This designation is most inappropriate, if thereby it is meant to be suggested that those schools are for the benefit of private interests only, holding the same place as schools of private adventure, and, equally with them, exempt from public control or legislative interference. The designation is also inaccurate, if intended to mark the origin of all those schools. Even putting out of sight that Lord Cork held in Munster, in the early part of the seventeenth century, the same position which the London Companies occupied in Ulster at the same period—or, rather, indeed, a position much more important, embodying the political, social, and military power of England; we may ask, by what sophistry schools founded by Corporations can be designated " private foundations"? Was it an unconscious leaning to the pretensions to a monopoly of educational endowments on the part of the Protestant Ascendency of the day, that led the Commissioners to adopt so ill-suited but significant a name? Had they said that *some* of those schools were established by "*Private Founders*", their language would have been less equivocal and more accurate.

Of those sixteen Grammar Schools, *eight* are in Munster, *five* in Leinster, *two* in Ulster, and *one* in Connaught. The Earl of Cork founded four of those in Munster—Lismore, Youghal, Charleville, and Bandon, the last of these having been aided by the Corporation of that town. If the fact of a school having been founded by a private person, makes it for all time and under all circumstances a private foundation, then Winchester School, and New College, Oxford, are private foundations. In this sense only can Lord Cork's schools be regarded as private foundations; they are really no more private schools than those of Erasmus Smith or the Irish Society. Waterford and Kinsale are unquestionably corporate foundations; while, as regards Clonmel, it must not be forgotten that the founders, by appointing the mayor of the town one of the trustees, would seem to have gone far towards making the school a municipal, that is a public, institution. Midleton is the only Munster Grammar School which can pretend to be private. Of the five Grammar Schools in Leinster, whatever may be said of Ballyroan, neither Navan nor New Ross can be fairly looked upon as private schools, inasmuch as the Corporation of Navan voted, as we have seen, a large landed endowment to the former, while the Town Commissioners of New Ross administer the latter. Kilkenny was aided by large grants from the Irish parliament, and special privileges were secured to the children of citizens. Dundalk must be deemed a corporate foundation. The two Ulster Schools, Carrickmacross and Lifford, were little needed in a province already enjoying opulent foundations in the Royal and Diocesan Schools; but neither the former, to which all persons from the barony of Farney have a right of free admission, nor the latter, " where all children in the parish of Clonleigh are entitled to a gratuitous education", can be designated "private" schools. Connaught, excluded from all advantages, has a solitary Grammar School, with an acre of land, premises valued at $19l.$, and $15l.$ per annum, the annual interest from some trust funds. This school was intended by the founder to be a *Primary* and not a *Grammar* School; but in any case, having in view the terms of his will, it cannot justly be said to be a Private School. No false delicacy should restrain us from asserting the nation's right to control endowments that came originally, directly or indirectly, out of the national estate, or which were granted for purposes of public education; just as, we hope, no pressure of injustice, or weariness of waiting for that equality which has been so often promised to us and is still so long deferred, should ever tempt us to covet what plainly belongs to our Protestant fellow-countrymen.

The following tables, compiled from the Report of the Endowed Schools' Commission, give a clear idea of the main facts connected with the Sixteen Grammar Schools of what are called " Private Foundation" in Ireland:—

TABLE I.—ENDOWMENTS.

Locality of School	Date of foundation.	Endowment.		
		Acreage, etc.	Annual value of School Premises	Annual income from land or other endowments.
			£ s. d.	£ s. d.
Bandon	⎡1610⎤	Rent-charge.	...	27 13 0
Charleville	⎱ and ⎰	Do.	4 8 0	36 18 0
Lismore		Do.	20 10 0	30 0 0
Youghal	⎣1642⎦	Do.	23 6 0	27 13 0
Lifford	1619	Do.	9 10 0	46 3 0
Waterford	1669	Annuity.	...	78 9 0
		A. R. P.		
Kilkenny	1684	9 3 32	161 17 0	129 4 0
Clonmel	1685	683 2 11	139 0 0	425 0 0
Navan	1686	760 0 5	...	309 1 0
Ballyroan		591 1 15	23 17 0	231 16 0
Midleton	1696	2005 0 0	61 10 0	203 10 0
Carrickmacross	1711	Rent-charge	65 18 0	70 0 0
New Ross	1713	Houses.	32 7 0	20 0 0
Dundalk	1725	1a. 2r. 19p. and Rent-charge.	64 2 0	46 3 0
Eyrecourt	1730	1a. 0r. 0p.	19 0 0	15 0 0
Kinsale	1767	Rent-charge.	41 2 0	27 13 0
		A. R. P.		
Total	...	4052 2 2	666 10 0	1724 9 0

ENDOWED GRAMMAR SCHOOLS.

TABLE II.—NUMBER OF SCHOLARS ON ROLL.

Locality of School.	Protestant.	Catholic.	Total.	Number of Free Scholars.
Bandon	25	—	25	—
Charleville	—	4	4	—
Lismore	—	—	—	—
Youghal	20	11	31	—
Lifford	—	—	—	—
Waterford	69	—	69	—
Kilkenny	47	—	47	—
Clonmel	27	—	27	10
Navan	5	—	5	4
Ballyroan	2	1	3	2
Midleton	23	—	23	6
Carrickmacross	23	3	26	2
New Ross	19	—	19	5
Dundalk	—	—	—	—
Eyrecourt	6	4	10	—
Kinsale	5	4	9	—
Total	271	27	298	32

From the first of these tables, we see that eleven of these schools were established within the half century from 1642 to 1696; that is, during the period in which the double conquest and confiscation of the southern half of the island was effected, under the Parliamentary generals and in the Williamite wars. It was the same period which witnessed the substantive establishment of the royal schools, the plantation of Ulster, and the great endowment of Erasmus Smith.

According to the foregoing tables, the school premises of these foundations are estimated at the annual value of over 666*l.* The extent of land in their endowments is 4,052a. 2r. 2p., and the net annual income, 1,724*l.*, or a total annual income of nearly

2,400*l.* estimated value. There is accommodation in fifteen of the schools for 1,106 day boys, and in eleven for 285 boarders; while in thirteen of them there were only 313 boys on the roll when visited by the Endowed Schools' Commissioners. Of these thirteen schools, seven had no Catholic scholar, one had a solitary Catholic name on its roll, another had three, three had four, and one school, Youghal, had eleven Catholic boys. We have returns of the religion of only 298 of the scholars. Of these 240, or 80·5 per cent. were Episcopalian Protestants; 27, or 9 per cent., Catholics; 9, or 3 per cent., Presbyterians, and 22, or 7·5 per cent., other Protestant Dissenters. Only eight of the schools in operation had free pupils, the aggregate being 32, or about 10 per cent. of those on the rolls. The state of instruction is reported, in 1858, as " very satisfactory" in Carrickmacross; " satisfactory" in Waterford, Clonmel, Youghal, and Bandon; " unsatisfactory" in some respects in Kilkenny and Dundalk; and " unsatisfactory", or very much so, in Navan, Ballyroan, New Ross, Charleville, Kinsale, Midleton, and Eyrecourt. Such, in brief, are the results of these foundations after an operation of over 200 years.

As in the case of the Diocesan Schools, the Royal Free Schools, the Irish Society, and the Schools of Erasmus Smith, one of the main designs of the several founders of the groups of Grammar Schools of which we have treated in this chapter, was to secure a supply of students for Trinity College. The deed of foundation of Carrickmacross School, intended, as we have already said, for the admission of all persons in the Catholic barony of Farney, county of Monaghan, appoints, as visitors of the school, the Protestant Primate, the Vice-Chancellor of the University of Dublin, the Protestant

Bishop of Clogher, and the Provost of Trinity College. The nomination of the masters of the College of Kilkenny, eminently the most important of all those foundations, has devolved upon Trinity College in the failure of heirs male of the Duke of Ormonde. The Countess of Orkney, by the same deed by which she founded Midleton School, set apart $50l.$ a-year for exhibitions in Trinity College. Dr. Downes attached a scholarship in Trinity College to Waterford School. Among the Commissioners of Education appointed under the act of 1813 for the regulation of these and others of the Endowed Schools, there are several *ex-officio* members officially connected with the University of Dublin, viz., the Archbishop of Dublin, one of its visitors; the Provost of Trinity College, the member for the University for the time being. Thus we see how closely Trinity College is connected with these foundations.

These Grammar Schools, viewed as a whole, have lamentably failed, even as educational institutions; failed still more signally in the object, which nearly all their founders had chiefly in view, " to establish (the Protestant) religion, and to extirpate superstition". They have failed, like the Disestablished Church, to which they were so closely allied. She was the mistress; they were her handmaids. Let us hope that the political wisdom which has taken her down from her preëminence, and destroyed ecclesiastical ascendency in Ireland, will bestow on the Catholics of this country the great boon of educational equality.

CHAPTER VIII.

THE CHARTER SCHOOLS AND THE INCORPORATED SOCIETY.

Public educational institutions of the last three centuries founded by aliens. History of Primate Boulter; his scheme of schools; his letter on the subject to the Bishop of London; the Society founded for the purpose enjoyed Parliamentary grants for 100 years. This Society already referred to; our present purpose as regards it. Amount of Parliamentary grants; other sources of the Society's income; the endowments of two kinds—special and general; chief endowments of each class. Property in the hands of the Society when the public grants were withdrawn.

Objects of the Society as set forth in the Charter, to instruct the children "of poor Popish and other poor natives" in the English tongue and the principles of true religion and loyalty. Children of "Popish" parents only, admitted up to 1775; this practice formally sanctioned by a resolution; establishment of boarding schools; and of nurseries in 1757; Howard's account of the deplorable state of the schools in 1784; resolution of 1775 annulled in 1803; the clause in the Charter "other poor natives" then availed of.

The notorious name of "Protestant Chartered Schools" dropped when the State grants were withdrawn; the schools now known as those of the Incorporated Society. Constitution of this body; present operations of the Society as given to the Commission of Primary Education in 1869 by the Secretary; "Missionary" character of the schools openly avowed. Course of instruction in the schools as described in official returns. Some of the foundation boys after their course of four years at a boarding school, go to the Society's "Training Commercial and Scientific institution" at Santry. Character of that institution; sums allowed for its support. Table showing the number of free and paying boarders, and of day scholars, in each of the boarding schools. Two boarding schools on the foundation of the Earl of Ranelagh; the Pococke Institution, the Celbridge Girls' School, and the Farra School founded by private persons. Distribution of the day schools of the Society; the Aungier Street School, Dublin. The Society does not undertake to teach classics, but superadds them when desired. Objects of the training at Santry; the boys of the latter institution successful at public examinations, and in Trinity College, Dublin; the Thackeray Exhibition founded there by the Society for the boys of their schools. Class in society to which the boys belong. Mode of appointing masters shows how well linked the Intermediate Schools and the University are. No official statement of expenditure by the Society later than that for 1854-55; table of expenditure on boarding and on day schools; 75 per cent. of expenditure made on account of boarding schools, and less than 4½ per cent. on day schools.

Contrast between present position and original design of the Society. Application of doctrine of *cy-près* administration of trust funds to justify present misapplication of funds; examination of this plea; funds devoted without judicial decision or the authority of Parliament; three ways in which the Society intended to benefit "poor Popish children"; repeated admissions of failure to make Catholic children Protestant; reasons assigned for the failure of the schools in carrying out the other objects. What the remedy for the failure should have been according to a true application of the *cy-près* doctrine; a different course adopted by the Society; this misapplication of funds made by a Society of which the Lord Chancellor, chief judges, and Attorney and Solicitor-General are *ex-officio* members! not one of these lawyers appears to have remonstrated; the sanction of their names lent to what they would eloquently denounce as fraud and robbery in the case of ordinary trustees. Duty of the Attorney and Solicitor-General to intervene in such a case; several of the legal functionaries enumerated Catholics, who might be expected to help in remedying those abuses; they owe this duty to their poorer brethren by whose aid they have risen. The Lord Mayor of Dublin an *ex-officio* member of the Society. Has he been summoned to the meetings? The Pococke Institution in Kilkenny; objects of its founder; interest which the citizens of Kilkenny possess in this institution. The third object of Society according to charter, namely, to spread the Protestant religion *established* in Ireland, now impracticable, there being no established religion, such a condition cannot now attach to the funds of the schools. Religious equality cannot exist while these funds continue to be misapplied as at present. The State should take into hands the control of those funds; Parliament might apply them for the purposes of a sound system of Intermediate Education.

It has been the fate of Ireland that, since the introduction of Protestantism, nearly all the educational foundations should originate with aliens in race and religion. Adam Loftus, Erasmus Smith, Richard

Boyle, and Hugh Boulter—four adventurers—founded every kind of educational institution, from the Charter School to the University.

In 1731, Primate Boulter, who, for several years had virtually in his hands the civil, as well as the ecclesiastical government of Ireland, got up a society for establishing a system of primary schools all over the country. Through his influence this society was incorporated in 1733 by a Royal Charter of King George II., from which circumstance the schools of the Society came to be designated "Charter Schools". Boulter had been chaplain to George I., whom he accompanied to Hanover in 1719; and having had the honour to teach his son (afterwards George II.) the English language, was promoted by him, in one year, to the Deanery of Christ Church and Bishopric of Bristol. Having filled that see for five years, he was appointed Archbishop of Armagh and Primate of all Ireland, mainly with a view to quell the popular excitement caused by Wood's patent, stimulated by the *Drapier's Letters*. Boulter's great panacea for the political and religious difficulties of the country was the project of the " Charter Schools". He exerted himself both in England and Ireland to promote the scheme, paid all the fees for passing the charter, was a large annual subscriber, and was prominent in founding the institution at Santry, near Dublin. Writing to the Bishop of London, 5th May, 1730, he prays his lordship to interest himself to promote the charter which he and the Society sought:—

"I can assure you the Papists here are so numerous that it highly concerns us in point of interest, as well as out of concern for the salvation of these poor creatures, who are our fellow-subjects, to try all possible means to bring them and theirs over to the true religion, and one of the most likely methods we can think of is, if possible, instructing and converting the young generation, for instead of converting those that are adults, we are daily losing many of our meaner people, who go off to Popery".

The Society, founded by Primate Boulter, enjoyed Parliamentary grants for a century, from its incorporation in 1733 to 1832, when the last grant, 5750*l*., was made.

We have already, in our first chapter (pages 30–33), referred to the original objects proposed to themselves by the founders, and to the general expenditure and failure in results of the Society. But what we were chiefly concerned with there was to exhibit, however imperfectly, the spirit which prevailed with regard to the education of Catholics during that dark period of the history of Ireland, as exemplified in the aims and working of this society and kindred institutions. We now propose to show that the original object—viz., the wholesale perversion of the Irish poor—having utterly failed, the large funds which still remain within the control of the Incorporated Society, have been diverted from the purposes for which they were destined by the original contributors; that Primary Education has, in the main, been abandoned, and Intermediate and Boarding Schools substituted; and that the people of Ireland, and especially the Catholics, have a clear equitable claim upon the large endowments, landed and funded, which remain.

The Parliamentary grants originally given were increased from time to time until they reached upwards of £40,000*l*. a year, at which amount they were continued from 1811 to 1819, decreasing to half that amount in 1826. The total grants in 90 years, up to the close of the session of 1823, were 1,027,715*l*., to which must be added nine years' further grants, ending in 1832. The tax on hawkers and peddlers, granted in 1745, which was also a Parliamentary subsidy, reached during several years over 2,000*l.* a-year. The "King's Bounty", from 1739 to 1793, was about 1,000*l.* a-year. The other sources of income were endowments, landed or pecuniary, and subscriptions in England and Ireland. The total disbursements to the close of 1823 amounted to 1,606,237*l.*, or on an average nearly 18,000*l.* a-year.

The endowments abovementioned are of two classes —one for special schools, the other for the general objects of the Society. To the former belong the estates bequeathed by the Earl of Ranelagh in 1708 for the schools of Athlone and Roscommon, and vested in the Society by Act of Parliament, 1 Geo. II., cap. 3); the bequest of the Rev. W. Wilson, 1740, for Farra School, in Westmeath; Bishop Pococke's bequest for the Kilkenny foundation of 1765; and the endowments of Celbridge schools, founded by the Conolly family, and transferred to the Society in 1809. To the latter class, or general endowments, belong Baron Vryhouven's bequest, 56,666*l.*, and the donation of an anonymous benefactor of 40,000*l*— both in the English funds. Several persons, as Mr. Rogerson, Dean Stewart, and Mrs. Anne Hamilton, left estates for the general purposes of the Society. It is obvious that the Charter School Society was entirely indebted for those endowments towards its general objects, to the supposed stability of its schools as public foundations, approved and supported by the King and Parliament.

When the state-grants ceased in 1833, a large property remained in the hands of the Society. The first official statement we have of this property is contained in the Report of the Endowed Schools Commissioners, 1858. According to the information obtained by that Commission, the total landed property held by the Society amounted to 17,230 acres. Of these the Ranelagh estates formed 9,729a. 0r. 13p. (not including the land attached to the school at Roscommon, amounting to 64a. 3r. 6p.); the Pococke estate, amounting to 1,147a. 2r. 5p.; and the general estate, to 6,288a. 2r and 22p. The gross income in 1865 of these estates was 7,934*l*. 1*s*. 4*d*.; and the net income, deducting charges of various kinds, 5,064*l*. 6*s*. 11*d*. The funded property produced a gross income of 3,000*l*., or a net income of 2,897*l*. 4*s*. 1*d*. Thus the gross income from all sources was 10,934*l*. 1*s*. 4.*d*; and the net income applicable in 1855 to the general purposes of the Society was 7,961*l*. 10*s*.

Some short notice of the changes which have occurred in the operations of the Society is now necessary. The Charter clearly and distinctly sets forth, that the scheme was designed for " the Popish natives, who have very little sense of religion, but what they implicitly take from their clergy, to whose guidance in such matters they seem wholly to give themselves up, and thereby are kept not only in gross ignorance, but also in great disaffection to our [King George the Second's] person and government, scarce any of them appearing to have been willing to abjure the Pretender to our throne". It is true, however, that in a subsequent passage it is added, " To the intent, therefore, that the children of the Popish and other poor natives of said kingdom of Ireland may be instructed in the English tongue and in the principles of true religion and loyalty in all succeeding generations". Notwithstanding this addition of the words "·other poor natives", scarcely any other children than those of Catholic parents, were admitted up to 1775. In that year a formal resolution was adopted, in conformity with the practice which had hitherto prevailed, " to admit none but the children of Papists, or such as were in danger of being bred up Papists". The original scheme contemplated day schools only. The Society soon found that the conversion through day schools of Catholic children living with their parents was impossible; thereupon it was determined to take them from their parents, and transplant them to boarding schools in remote localities. No Popish priest or relative nor any other Papist, nor any person unknown, was allowed to converse with the children, except in presence of the master or mistress. When it was found that the Catholic parents could not be induced to part with their children, nurseries were got up in 1757 to serve as feeders for the schools. In 1784 the benevolent Howard, the great reformer of prisons, visited the Charter Schools, and in his examination before the Select Committee of the Irish House of Commons, the celebrated philanthropist stated, " the children were sickly, pale, and such miserable objects, they were a disgrace to all society, and their reading had been neglected for the purpose of making them work for the masters". Failing to find Catholic children to enter the Charter Schools, the Board passed a resolution, 14th May, 1803, annulling the resolution of 1775, and resolved that the objects of the Society would be more effectually promoted if the children were admitted with " no other restriction than such as were imposed by the Charter". Thus, after an experience of seventy years, the Society, finding itself wholly defeated by the devoted attachment of the most destitute of the Catholic poor, who, unlike the English, had no Poor Law to fall back upon for relief, was driven to avail itself of the clause, " *and other poor natives*", in order to recruit with Protestant children the vacant boarding schools. For thirty years, Protestant as well as Catholic children were admitted, until the scheme utterly broke down, and the Parliamentary grants were withdrawn in 1833. The original objects for which the Charter Schools were ostensibly founded, lie outside our present purpose. We need not, therefore, enter into any detail of their results, further than to state that there is no form or shade of conceivable vice that did not abound in these infamous proselytising institutions.

The state-grant having been withdrawn on the recommendation of successive Royal Commissions, the Society dropped the name "*Protestant Charter Schools*", under which those schools had become so notorious, and they are now known simply as the schools of the "Incorporated Society". The Corporation is limited by the charter to 137 members, including 25 *ex officio*. The Lord Lieutenant is patron, the Protestant Primate is vice-patron, all the Protestant bishops, sôme of the dignitaries, and the chief judges being *ex officio* members. To a committee of 15, appointed every February, the Society delegates the executive administration of the foundation. The present operations of the Society are fully detailed by the secretary, Rev. John W. Hackett, in his evidence before the recent Primary Education Commission, 19th February, 1869, from which the following details, bearing on our purpose, are extracted:—

The Incorporated Society for promoting English Protestant Schools in Ireland has now nine boarding institutions, seven for boys and two for girls, and thirteen day schools, wholly or in part supported by them. About 1,000 children are under instruction in all the schools. Of these 234 are foundation scholars, who are boarded, clothed, and educated by the Society for a period of four years; and 257 pay-boarders, some of whom are received at reduced rates. All the others are day scholars. With the exception of 30 girls, nominated to the Celbridge Institution by Thomas Conolly, Esq., M.P., boarders are elected on the foundation by competitive examination, out of candidates from certain assigned counties or districts of counties. Such candidates must present a certificate from a Protestant clergyman, stating, in the case of boys, that they are not under twelve nor over sixteen years of age, and in the case of girls, they are between ten and fourteen; that they had during the last twelve months attended a school [named] where the Holy Scriptures are daily read by all the children who can read; and that their conduct was satisfactory; also a certificate of health from a medical practitioner. As to religion, there is no restriction, provided the candidate, Catholic or Protestant, has read the Scriptures, as stated, and is prepared to conform to the course of Protestant Episcopalian instruction and training in the Schools. Nor is it enough that the schools be *scriptural*, in reference to the candidates themselves: they must be so in reference to all the children attending them who can read, so that, as appears in evidence, the scholars of Church Education and all Protestant National Schools, that may happen to have even one Catholic scholar able to read, but who actually did not read the Scriptures daily, are on that account excluded from competition. As to area, the scholars of all the scriptural schools in fourteen entire counties, and of twenty-five districts of six other counties, embracing 618 ecclesiastical parishes, are entitled to compete. The proselytising aim of this arrangement is avowed by the secretary, who boasts that the Society has designedly extended the area of competition beyond the localities of the trust estates, so as to include districts where "religious inquiry" has been successfully prevailing under the Irish Church Mission Society amongst Roman Catholics. Mr. Hackett's words are:—

"Then we have enlarged the area. We have taken in districts where some inquiry was excited amongst Roman Catholics, as for instance in Kerry, and other Irish Society districts. We have thrown open the invitation to compete for places to the districts where religious inquiry has been successfully prevailing amongst Roman Catholics. We think that this is carrying out very much the original intention of the Charter". (Q. 25,984.)

To the literary programme in the competitive course, which is very fair, there are added certain portions of the Bible and the Church Catechism, with Scriptural references for the purpose of showing its doctrine to be in conformity with the word of God. The official returns describe the course in these boarding schools thus:

"The foregoing institutions afford a sound Scriptural and superior English, commercial, and mathematical education, calculated to fit young men for the offices of schoolmasters, accountants, assistants to civil engineers, and for commercial pursuits generally. The Thackeray Exhibition in Trinity College, Dublin, of the annual value of 30l., and tenable for four years, is open to the pupils of all the schools under the Incorporated Society.

"Each institution has the advantage of frequent visitation by the minister of the parish or other neighbouring clergyman, the paid officer (20l. a-year) of the Incorporated Society, by whom the pupils are regularly catechised and instructed in the Holy Scriptures.

"Boys are received as boarders, irrespective of locality, and without any preliminary literary examination. They enjoy all the educational advantages above referred to, and are comfortably dieted and lodged, washed for, and supplied with stationery and medical attendance at 20l. per annum.

"The masters are at liberty to provide instruction in classics, modern languages, drawing, etc., for pupils whose friends desire to afford them such advantages—the terms being subject to private arrangement.

"The several masters are permitted to receive parlour boarders—terms forty to forty-five guineas with extras". (*Royal Commission for Primary Education, Ireland, Vol. IV., pp.* 1316–18).

After the foundation-boys have passed their four years in the boarding-schools, a certain proportion of them are elected to the Society's Training, Commercial, and Scientific Institution, at Santry, near Dublin, there to remain for one or two years to continue and extend their studies. In this institution, which has been very successful, some twenty to twenty-four young men, candidate teachers, are maintained on the foundation. The Society generally allows the head master of each school 100*l.* a-year; a free house, and the land attached at a low rent; pays the salaries of assistants, all rent and taxes, and various allowances, servants included, with a view to enable the head master to take at a low pension a number of ordinary boarders, for whom ample accommodation is provided.

The following table gives the chief particulars connected with the Boarding Institutions of the Society:—

Table showing the number of free and paying boarders, and of day scholars in each of the Boarding Schools of the Incorporated Society.

Locality of School	Character of School	No. of Boarders		Day Scholars
		Free or on Foundation	Paying	
Santry (County of Dublin)	Boys	20	80	—
Celbridge (County of Kildare)	Girls	62	—	—
Pococke Institution (County of Kilkenny)	Boys	28	24	—
Dundalk (County of Louth)	Boys	44	56	16
Athlone (County of Roscommon)	Boys	20	45	14
Roscommon (Co. of Roscommon)	Girls	20	10	—
Primrose Grange (Co. of Sligo)	Boys	20	10	10
Newport (County of Tipperary)	Boys	—	20	10
Farra (County of Westmeath)	Boys	20	12	—
Total		234	257	50

There are two boarding institutions on the foundation of the Earl of Ranelagh, one at Athlone for boys, and one at Roscommon for girls. The Pococke Institution, at Linfield, Kilkenny designed to teach weaving and the Protestant religion to poor Popish natives, as also the Celbridge School for girls, and the Farra School, Westmeath, were founded by private persons. This last was originally established as an agricultural school.

The Day Schools of the Society are distributed as follows:—One in each of the following counties—Antrim, Donegal, Down, Meath (Trim), Queen's County, Roscommon (Athlone), and Wicklow (Arklow); four in Tipperary, and one in the City of Dublin (55 Aungier Street). They are all elementary, with the exception of the school in Aungier Street, which is intended for the benefit of middle-class boys not able to pay a large sum for education, and in which the fee is 4*l*. to 6*l*. a-year, French and German being included in the course. *(Prim. Ed. Com. Evid.* Q. 25,862), To this school a free place for a boarder in the Santry Institution is attached.

The Society declares that it does not undertake classical education at all (Hackett, *Evid.* Q. 25,793), although in some of the provincial schools the boys learn elementary classics; and in Santry " classics have been superadded where the boys expressed a desire for them". In Santry the scholars are prepared (1) for places in the civil service; and (2) as science teachers:

" They are qualified to obtain places perhaps in the Civil Service. They are largely sought for as science teachers in the grammar schools of England, and some are required for our own schools; more find their way into Trinity College, having obtained classical instruction in the school, and from their very superior scientific education, are enabled to obtain very high places in the University" Q. 25,791).

"The pupils are also qualified for the examinations held under the Royal Dublin Society, the Queen's Colleges, and the Science and Art Department, South Kensington, London . . . , Some of the pupils have been eminently successful in Trinity College—four have obtained Science Sizarships. To this high scientific prize the Incorporated Society grant per year an Exhibition of 30*l.*, to be held for four years, called the "Thackeray Exhibition", in commemoration of the service rendered to the Society's schools by the late Rev. Elias Thackeray". (Q. 25,793).

The Secretary, recounting the success of the Santry scholars in the examinations under the Science and Art Department in 1868-69, stated that Santry school ranked *third* among the schools of the United Kingdom which competed at that examination, a result which brought the master " nearly 300*l.*" (Q. 25,941).

Having thus shown that these establishments are really intermediate schools, let us now inquire what is the social class of their scholars. The Secretary, in answer to the question (*Evid.*, 25,869) " What class in society do these [Santry] boys belong to?" says:

"To classes of a mixed character. Some are the sons of clergymen, others the members of very respectable families of the gentry o limited means. Then, again, for the artizan class who wish to get their boys an advanced education, and at a very reduced rate, 20*l.*—they are dieted and educated for that. The expense of assistant masters is paid by our Society. Thus the master is enabled to take pupils at such a reduced rate, and afford them the advantages of board and instruction".

The mode of appointing the masters, as related (*Evid.*, 25,924) by the secretary, shows the intimate connection with Trinity College of these foundations, like all the Grammar Schools, and the manner in which the Schools and College act and react on each other:

"Our teachers are frequently appointed by the Committee of Fifteen, which consists of some of the Fellows of Trinity College. These masters are sometimes submitted to examination. They are more frequently those who have been brought up in connection with our own Society, and the Fellows of College, knowing them for years, are at once prepared to pronounce upon their competency to take charge of schools".

We have no official statement of the expenditure of the Incorporated Society later than that given in the Report of the Endowed Schools Commissioners for the year ended 31st March, 1855. The expenditure for that year upon the schools was as follows:—

EIGHT BOARDING INSTITUTIONS.

Teachers' and Officers' Salaries	£1,114 2 8
Dietary	1,742 15 4
Clothing	612 18 10
Allowances for Servants, Fuel, Soap and Candles	619 5 11
Books, Stationery, and other requisites	184 3 4
Incidental and Miscellaneous expenses	915 0 9
Ordinary Repairs	178 2 4
New Buildings and Improvements	1,315 17 3
Total	£6,682 6 5

ELEVEN DAY SCHOOL INSTITUTIONS.

Amount	£394 6 9
Total	£7,075 13 2

The aggregate expenditure that year, was 8,890*l*. 15*s*. 5*d*. The difference between this aggregate and the sum spent upon the Schools, amounting to 1815*l*. 2*s*. 3*d*., included 730*l*. 9*s*. 6*d*. for annuities to retired masters, mistresses, and officers of the Society, leaving 1,084*l*. 12*s*. 9*d*. for the cost of administration and miscellaneous expenses of various kinds. Seventy-five per cent. of the whole expenditure is thus given to the Boarding Institutions, and less than 4½ per cent. to the day schools. No change that has since taken place can materially alter the general relation of those items of expenditure.

So stands at this hour the great scheme of Primate Boulter and his English and Irish auxiliaries, after 140 years' operation, and an expenditure of little short of *two millions sterling*. Intended for the benefit of the poor Popish natives, whom it was to rear up in morality, religion, and English, its revenues have been diverted, for now nearly forty years, to the benefit of Protestant children exclusively. Designed by its author to promote the interests, both spiritual and temporal, of the very poorest classes professing one religion—and that the religion of the great majority of the population—its advantages are now monopolised by the middle classes and gentry, professing a different religion, and this not the religion of the majority. Primary education and industrial training in useful arts and trades, by which poor children might learn to earn an honest livelihood, were the original objects of the scheme. But they have given place to classics, modern languages, higher mathematics, physical science, preparation for sizarships and exhibitions in Trinity College. For the first 100 years of its existence the attempt was made to carry out the primary trusts for which the Society was founded. Abuses there were, no doubt, and hideous and revolting consequences followed; but still the effort was pertinaciously made to adhere to the original aims, although a gloomy experience proved how difficult, nay impossible, it was to obtain them. But since 1832 these efforts have been utterly abandoned, the trusts for which the Society exists have been without an exception ignored, and a scheme of education has been carried out which is in the most simple contradiction conceivable with the Charter.

The doctrine of the *cy-pres* administration of trust funds, so familiar to the Court of Chancery, has been appealed to, to give some colour to this flagrant appropriation for the intermediate education of Protestants, of endowments originally intended for the primary education of poor Catholics. We find the following in the report of the evidence given before the Primary Education Commission by the Rev. Mr. Hackett.

"25,981. *Rev. Mr. Cowie*—I should like to ask you whether you would consider it a harsh proceeding, if it were assumed your trusts had failed, and that therefore the Legislature could deal fairly with your funds?—I don't think we have failed in carrying out the trusts. . . . , ...

"29,995. *Master Brooke*—You have heard of the Chancery doctrine of administering a fund *cy pres*?—I have heard it, but I don't understand it technically.

"25,996. When circumstances make it impossible to carry out the intentions of a testator, the fund is administered as nearly as possible in accordance with these intentions. Which would be the more *cy pres* administration of these funds—the way in which your Society is at present administering them, or the way Mr. Cowie suggests?—Our system would, in my judgment".

It is then alleged that the doctrine of *cy pres* has been unhesitatingly acted upon in these proceedings. It must, however, be confessed that this has been done in a manner and spirit very remote from the benevolent ideas which first suggested that ingenious legal device. Let us see how the case exactly stands. The Incorporated Society finding themselves unable, through the opposition of Catholic parents, to carry out the intentions of their Charter by securing that improvement of the children of poor Popish natives, which was professedly the sole object of the Society's existence, have taken upon themselves, *without any judicial decision*, or *Parliamentary authorisation*, to divert their funds to a different purpose. They set about improving the Protestantism of Protestant children; and even in doing this, they are not solicitous that their bounty shall come only to the deserving poor.

Here is a Society founded expressly for the benefit of the children of *poor Popish natives*. On this plea they raised subscriptions in England, obtained legacies and gifts, procured a Charter and sundry Acts of Parliament, were assisted by the proceeds of a tax imposed by Parliament, and by an annual Parliamentary vote. In three ways the Society undertook to compass the benefit of the poor Popish children. First, by teaching them the English tongue, reading, writing, arithmetic, "and such other parts of learning as shall seem meet"; secondly, by bringing "them up in virtue and industry", and causing "them to be instructed in *husbandry and housewifery, or in trade or manufactures, or in such like manual occupation*"; thirdly, by instructing "them in the principles of the Protestant religion *established in our said kingdom*". The very last clause of the preamble of the charter recites that the operations of the Society are "to the intent that the children may be instructed in the English tongue, and in the principles of true religion and loyalty *in all succeeding generations*". It is admitted, or rather it was admitted on every occasion of inquiry into the operations of the Society, whether by Parliament or by Royal Commissioners—that the attempt to secure the conversion of the Popish children to Protestantism, on a scale at all commensurate with the great outlay, had failed. It was admitted that the reason the schools of the Society had not succeeded in their other objects was, that the promotion of those other objects had been utterly sacrificed in the anxiety to make them effective "instruments by which the children of the Roman Catholic peasantry were to be educated in the Protestant faith"; and that " as such they have, from the first institution of the Society, been the object of suspicion and aversion to the Roman Catholics".—(*Comm. Irish Education Inquiry,* 1825, *Report* page 89.) What was the remedy devised to escape from this dead lock? After an experience of 100 years it was found impossible to secure *one* of the objects of the Society, and it was also found that the vain effort to attain *this one impossible object* was jeopardising and nullifying *the other two.* The suggestion of common sense would have been to abandon the impossible object, and secure the two possible ones. The Society could not make Protestants of the poor Popish children, but it could make them good scholars and good husbandmen or artizans. We venture to say that an honest application of the *cy-pres* doctrine would give the same solution, and that if the question were fairly argued in an equity court, such would be the decision—at least if religious prejudice could be excluded from the argument, and the superstition of the essential "Protestantism of the Constitution" could be exorcised from the precincts of the judgment seat. But the Society determined to adopt in the administration of their funds no such course as a court of equity would have compelled ordinary trustees to follow. They gave up the poor Papists altogether, excluding them from the two beneficial objects of elementary education and industrial training, which the Charter intended them to reap from the application of the funds, because they would not take Protestantism into the bargain They did not transfer their benevolence to the poor only among Protestants; but—perhaps, because the funds were large and the Protestant recipients few—

they opened their doors to all alike, whether needy or in easy circumstances, and this was done, as we have already said, by the Society, on its own motion, of its own authority, without stating a case for the decision of the Court of Chancery, without petitioning Parliament to relieve them from the obligation of their solemn trusts. And this was done by a Society which numbers amongst its *ex-officio* members the Lord Chancellor, the Chief Justice of the Queen's Bench, the Chief Justice of the Common Pleas, the Master of the Rolls, the Chief Baron, the Attorney and Solicitor-General, and the First Sergeant, and which includes other lawyers also. If this marvellous application of the *cy-pres* doctrine—that funds held in trust for the benefit of Popish poor children may be diverted to the use of Protestant well-to-do children, because the obstinate Papists will persist in adhering to their own religion—if this singular doctrine had been clearly expounded and fully circulated, it is possible that the principle might have received a wider application, and the Irish Church might never have been disestablished.

We may well feel surprised that of all the eminent lawyers who were members of the Society, not one appears to have even gently remonstrated against the course which was adopted. They all lent the sanction of their names and their high official positions to a proceeding which, in the case of an ordinary trust, they would have been eloquent to denounce as a transparent fraud. But they were silent when a society, incorporated by Royal Charter, and lavishly endowed by a hundred years of Parliamentary bounty, confiscated for the benefit " of very respectable (Protestant) families of the gentry of limited means", funds destined for the education of poor Popish children. A private trustee who should have so acted, would have been denounced as a robber. A corporation however, which numbers amongst its *ex-officio* members the successive Attorneys and Solicitors General who have held office in Ireland down to the present hour, has been able to do this without reproof. It is the express duty of those high officers of Government to watch over the administration of public charities, to protect them from malversation, and, if necessary, to prosecute those who abuse them. In previous chapters we have referred to the recommendations of different Royal Commissions, urging the institution of proceedings against schoolmasters who had fraudulently dealt with the property of their schools. But how those individual cases sink into insignificance, when considered side by side with this gigantic confiscation, so unblushingly carried out by the Incorporated Society!

Among the legal personages who have been *ex-officio* members of the Society, there have been since 1835 several Catholics. One would have supposed that, even independently of the responsibility cast upon them by their official position, they would have resisted conduct so unfair to the poor children of their own faith. Year after year the banquet-hall of the Mansion-house in Dublin echoes a panegyric on the independence of the Irish Bench and Bar. How could that independence have been more nobly shown than by raising a voice to protect the rights and interests of poor and helpless Roman Catholic children? These eminent Catholic lawyers might have remembered what they owed to the poor Catholic people of the last century. Had those poor people yielded their faith to the solid temptations that were so invitingly held out to them, the question of Catholic Emancipation would not have been agitated, and Catholics could not have floated into wealth and position upon the tide of its success.

Dublin has not any particular interest in the proceedings of the Incorporated Society. At the same time, it ought not to be forgotten that the Lord Mayor is by the Charter one of its *ex-officio* members. Since Municipal Reform in 1841, there have been seventeen Catholic Lord Mayors. Has any one of them taken any part in the proceedings of the Society, or raised any discussion concerning the appropriation of the funds? Have the Catholic Lord Mayors been regularly summoned to the meetings of the Society? Has any one Lord Mayor ever attended those meetings? We cannot answer those questions.

Although the city of Dublin has not any special interest in the operations of the Society, we should have certainly thought that such is not the case with regard to the city of Kilkenny. Close to it stands one of the principal boarding institutions of the Society, which was founded and endowed by Bishop Pococke, "for the instruction of Papist boys in linen weaving and the principles of the Protestant religion". The training in linen weaving never seems to have been very vigorous. It has long since become quite obsolete. Nothing could more astonish the present master of the school than to be called upon to give up his classical instruction and his preparation for the "Science and Art" examinations, and to set about teaching "linen weaving". But if there has been nothing sacred about the "linen weaving", which was so dear to the heart of Bishop Pococke; if the rising tide of change has been allowed to sweep it away, and yet it is held that no substantial violation of his intentions has been thereby committed—why not allow the principles of the Protestant religion to go with the "linen weaving"? The founder left a splendid endowment for the training of poor Papist boys in "linen weaving" and Protestantism. Instead of this, the present master teaches classics and the South Kensington programme to Protestant boys who certainly do not come from the poorer classes. If this is not a violation of Bishop Pococke's intentions, we may fairly ask whether those intentions would not be equally carried out by teaching poor Catholic boys some useful arts, untainted by any interference with their religion? Who can doubt which of the two courses would commend itself most to the citizens of Kilkenny? If any one desires further reason why the citizens of Kilkenny should take an interest in Bishop Pococke's school, we may refer to the report of the Endowed Schools' Commissioners, 1858 (vol. III., page 142), which tells us that the Corporation of Kilkenny granted to this school twenty acres of land and an annuity of 27*l*. 17*s*. 10*d*.

We have referred at some length to the strange interpretation of the *cy pres* doctrine, by which it is sought to justify a monstrous misappropriation of a large public endowment. The argument does not originate with us. They have given occasion to it who, under cover of this doctrine, defend the proceedings of the Incorporated Society, in applying to the intermediate education of well-to-do Protestants, public funds intended for the education of poor Catholics. But there is another point connected with these great funds which is well worthy of consideration. The third object intended by the charter granted to the Incorporated Society was, as we have so often repeated, the instruction of the children in "the principles of the Protestant religion *established* in our said kingdom". It is on the failure of success with regard to this object that the Society grounds its deviation of the funds from Popish to Protestant children. But may it not be held that by the passing of the act of

1869 this object has no longer any legal existence? There is now no "Protestant religion" *established* in this kingdom. How then can children any longer be brought up in the principles of an *established* Protestant religion? We are dealing with funds which are an accumulation out of the proceeds of public taxes and Parliamentary grants extending over a period of 100 years. These funds are as much the national property as any public buildings erected under the authority of Parliament. One of the conditions which the legislature attached to the grant of these funds was, that they should be applied to the instruction of children in what was then the State religion. There is now no State religion in Ireland. Therefore, the condition has not only ceased to attach to those funds, but it cannot by any possibility be conceived to attach to them.

We will not here dwell upon the insult to Irish Catholics included in the fact, that the Queen's representative is the *ex-officio* president of a proselytizing society. But it is idle to tell the people of Ireland that religious equality has been secured by the act of 1869, if Parliamentary funds, intended for the benefit of poor Catholic children, are still allowed to be diverted to the benefit of Protestant children and for the promotion of Protestantism, and this by a Society, the President of which is the Lord Lieutenant. It is plain that the State ought immediately to resume its control over the administration of those funds, and rescue them from their present misapplication. The Commissioners of 1825 reported that the operations of the Incorporated Society "possess a character decidedly exclusive, and are never likely to undergo such modifications as could render them generally and extensively beneficial" (*Report*, page 89). Certainly, they are not less exclusive in 1871, than they were found to be in 1825. The Society ought therefore to be dissolved, and its funds handed over to a Commission, which will know how to administer them in a way that shall not be " an object of suspicion and aversion to the Roman Catholics", and so render them " generally and extensively beneficial". It is no longer possible to apply this money to those special purposes of Primary Education and industrial training for which it was originally intended. It is thus in the position of a derelict fund, fully at the disposal of Parliament for the promotion of education. There is no reason why Parliament may not apply it to the development of a new and sound system of Intermediate Education; inasmuch as those elementary schools which might have been legitimate objects of the Incorporated Society's care can in future be well provided for, if the recommendation of the recent Primary Education Commission be carried out.

CHAPTER IX.

MODEL SCHOOLS.—I. HISTORY.

The National Model Schools are Intermediate Schools.

The system of National Education designed exclusively for Primary Education, and avowedly for the Poor of Ireland, and to meet objections of Catholics against Kildare Place Society. The original scheme included a provision for training teachers; the teachers were to receive instruction in a Model School *sanctioned* by the Board : the latter provided with funds for establishing and maintaining such a school; only one such, and that in Dublin, contemplated in the original form of Mr. Stanley's letter. Changes in this letter suggested by the Board; these changes show that Mr. Stanley did not at first contemplate that the Board should itself establish the school, but only aid it. The altered scheme carried out in 1833; Model School in Marlborough Street opened in 1838; training of mistresses commenced in 1842. County Model Schools for preparatory training of candidate teachers mentioned in Report of 1835: charter incorporating National Board and giving the power "to erect, maintain and support" schools of their own. Hitherto, with the exception of the Training Schools, all schools erected with the aid of "building grants" were the property of local patrons and trustees; Charter enabling Board to erect Model Schools; this was a revival of the state primary school system which had fallen with the Charter Schools. Board refuse to give further building grants unless on condition of the school being vested in them; attempt to get possession of all the school property of Ireland. Queen's Colleges Act passed, and Charter of National Board granted within one month of each other; they must be viewed together as part of a common scheme of direct State Education, from the primary school to the university. Four Model Schools and three Queen's Colleges opened in 1849. The Model Schools come within our present scope only in so far as they are Intermediate Schools.

Scheme for establishing 32 District Model Schools drawn up in 1846; each school-house estimated to cost 800*l.*, and to accommodate 300 children; schools to be under direct control of Board; space to be provided for the future erection of middle class school-houses in connection with the Model Schools; limitation as to expense, accommodation, and the separation between primary and secondary education, soon abandoned. Cost and accommodation of some of the schools erected.

Local opposition of clergy and people to those schools when their

I. HISTORY. 167

true character began to be manifested. Successful opposition to establishment of Model School at Drogheda; unsuccesful attempt at Waterford; opposition increased from year to year. Grounds of this opposition stated in several documents. Schools parnlysed by the action of the Bishops; extravagant outlay upon schools shown by Parliamentary Returns; further extension stopped since 1866.
Difficulty of determining the proportion of the cost of erection and of maintenance which must be set down for the Model Schools in their function of Intermediate, as distinguished from those of Primary and Training Schools. Table showing date of opening, cost of erection and repairs, total cost to 1867, and cost in 1868, of each of the Model Schools. Explanation of table: expenditure on some schools, as given in published Reports of Board, less than that returned to Royal Commissioners on Primary Education; amount of this difference for one year in the case of four schools in Ulster; total cost of erection and repairs of all Model Schools exclusive of Agricultural Department and Central Training Institution. The persons trained for several years past chiefly pupil-teachers, monitors, and advanced boys from Model Schools; the training is no longer for the purpose of preparing teachers; Training Department merely supplies free scholarships to Model Schools; value of this scholarship.

It may, at first sight, seem outside our present purpose to discuss a department of the National system of Primary Education. But before we conclude we hope to show to the satisfaction of every impartial reader, that the Model Schools, founded and managed by the Commissioners of National Education, are, in truth, middle-class schools, and as such must have a place in any inquiry into the condition of intermediate education in Ireland.

The existing system, designed for the education of the *Poor* of Ireland, was devised and set forth forty years ago, in a memorable letter, dated 31st October, 1831, addressed to the Duke of Leinster, by the late Earl of Derby, then the Rt. Hon. E. G. Stanley, Chief Secretary for Ireland. The scheme was founded not only for *Primary Education* exclusively, but avowedly for the primary education of the *Poor* of Ireland. Even the preamble of the Royal Charter, dated 6th August, 1845, incorporating the National Board, contains the following declaration:—" Whereas, in order to promote the welfare, by providing for the Education of the *Poor* of Ireland, it is expedient that the Commissioners of National Education should be invested with the powers and privileges hereinafter contained". This instrument, including the preamble, is cited and retained in the amended Charter, dated 11th March, 1861. The National system, based on the results of Royal Commissions and resolutions of the House of Commons, was a substitute for the system of the Kildare Place Society, to which the Catholics of Ireland had objected. It was to meet those objections, and in deference to Catholic principles, clearly stated in Mr. Stanley's letter, that the new system was launched—with diffidence, however, and only " *as an experiment*". As no large or general plan of education could be complete which did not make some arrangement for training teachers, the new system, like that of the Kildare Place Society, included a provision for this purpose. The original of Mr. Stanley's letter, which was published in the Dublin *Gazette*, 8th December, 1831, and is preserved in the Irish Office in London, states that the Board " will allow to the individuals or bodies applying for aid, the appointment of their own teacher, subject to (three) regulations", one of which was that " he shall have received previous instruction in a Model School in Dublin, *to be sanctioned by the Board*"; while one of the purposes for which the Commissioners were entrusted with absolute control over the funds annually voted by Parliament was " establishing and maintaining a Model School *in Dublin*, and training teachers for country schools". It appears clearly that the

I. HISTORY.

"Model School" contemplated by the founders of the system was an institution solely for the *training* of teachers; that only *one* such school was intended, that it was to be in Dublin, and that teachers for *country* schools were to be trained in this single Dublin Model School. These provisions were adopted from the Kildare Place Society. At the very first meetings of the Board changes were suggested, some of them of great importance. Mr. Stanley, at the request of the Commissioners, modified his letter, although it had been already published in the *Gazette*, and was in extensive circulation throughout the kingdom. As regards a Model School, the words " to be sanctioned by the Board" were changed into "*to be established in Dublin*". The original letter clearly shows that Mr. Stanley did not in the first instance design that the Commissioners of Education should establish a Model School themselves, but merely extend aid to one which they might sanction; the revised letter, on the other hand, clearly indicates their intention to found and direct the institution themselves—an intention which is further shown by another passage in the letter.

The scheme in its altered form was carried out in 1833 by the establishment of a very modest institution in a lane off Merrion Street, where two primary schools, one for boys and one for girls, were opened; and, in 1834, a few masters from the country were called up for a short course of training of about three months.

In 1838 the present Model Schools in Marlborough Street, were opened for boys, girls, and infants, and the temporary schools near Merrion Street closed; while the number of teachers in training—still consisting of masters only—was increased, and a residence provided for them in Glasnevin. In 1842 a house was erected and opened in Talbot Street for the residence of schoolmistresses. Since that time the whole establishment, consisting of training departments for Masters and for Mistresses, of Model Schools and Residences, has been considerably enlarged and extended.

Although the second report of the Commissioners of National Education, dated June, 1835, contains a project for the gradual establishment of *County Model Schools*, above the grade of ordinary Primary Schools, and designed to afford a preparatory training to candidate teachers previous to their admission to the general training institution in Dublin, no step was taken towards carrying out that enterprise until 1843, when the Board obtained a Charter of Incorporation. This Charter enabled the Commissioners to hold property, and "*erect, maintain, and support in all places . . . . in Ireland, where they shall deem the same most necessary and convenient, such and as many schools as they shall think proper*". The system had then been fourteen years in operation, yet the Commissioners had never established, or felt themselves at liberty to establish, any schools save the Training Department in Dublin, and even this, as above explained, was an innovation on the scheme laid down in Mr. Stanley's original letter, the document accepted by the Catholics of Ireland as the authoritative exposition of the principles of the new system. Any schools founded up to this date with the aid of building grants from the Board were the property of the local patrons and trustees, who had originated and promoted their erection. The Charter now enabled the Board for the first time to erect and support as many schools of their own as they might deem most "convenient and necessary". This enabling clause empowered the Board to establish Model

Schools, or any other schools they thought fit, and for the first time since the fall of the Charter Schools of 1733, revived State Primary Education in Ireland. At the same time the Commissioners, who up to this had given grants towards the erection of schools, the legal property of which was vested in local trustees, now cancelled their rule regulating such grants, and refused any further building aid unless the local patrons, who had to provide a site and one-third of the building and furniture, *vested the premises in the Commissioners in their corporate capacity*. The Board also proposed to accept a transfer of the leases and trust deeds of all the existing school-houses which had been erected in part from local funds. This proposal, if universally acted upon, would have made the Board the legal owners of all the school property connected with them in Ireland. The rule refusing thenceforth building grants towards the erection of schools vested in local trustees, the clause in the Charter enabling the Board to found an indefinite number of its own schools, and the invitation to patrons and trustees of existing vested schools to assign all such schools then in operation to the Commissioners in their corporate capacity, constitute a clear and coherent scheme of direct State Education such as never before had been attempted in this kingdom. The Queen's Colleges' Act received the royal assent on the 31st July, 1845, and within less than a month the Charter of Incorporation of the National Board, dated 26th August, was granted by her Majesty. These two measures must be viewed together as portions of a common scheme of direct State Education --Primary, Intermediate, Collegiate, and University.

Four years afterwards the first District Model Schools and the Queen's Colleges were opened, four of the former in the summer of 1849, and the three latter in the October following. It is only in so far as the National Model Schools are institutions for *Intermediate* education that they fall within our present scope; hence, having sketched their origin, we shall now recapitulate the main facts connected with their extension and operation.

The National Board drew up in 1846 a scheme for the building and management of 32 District Model Schools, in which they estimated that the expense of erecting and furnishing each must not exceed 800*l.*, and that each institution should accommodate 300 scholars; and they laid down that the Model Schools should be "under their sole control in the same manner as the Dublin Model Schools are, without the intervention of local patrons". Another feature in the plan was: "That in each case sufficient space be left for the erection *at a future time of a Middle Class School-house* in connection with the District Model School". The limitations as to expense and the number of scholars, and the separation of the primary from the middle class schools, were soon abandoned. Belfast Model School has accommodation for 1,630 pupils, and its erection cost about 16,000*l.*; Cork, 13,000*l.*; Enniskillen, 11,500*l.*; Newtownards, 10,400*l.*; Sligo, 9,500*l*; Enniscorthy, 9,411*l.*; Athy, 8,224*l.*; Londonderry, 8,895*l.*; and so on. The intermediate character of the Model Schools, both as to the social position of the scholars and the advanced nature of the course of instruction, will be pointed out presently.

According as these institutions spread, and their practical working became known, local opposition to them, on the part of the Catholic bishops and people, soon manifested itself. Although the first District Model Schools were opened only in the summer of

1849, yet, when it was proposed in 1851 to erect a Model School in Drogheda, the Archbishop of Armagh, now Cardinal Cullen, opposed the project, and the corporation of the town cordially sustained him in that opposition, so that the enterprise was abandoned. A similar, but unsuccessful, opposition by the Catholic bishop and several leading citizens, was offered in the same year to the foundation of a model school in Waterford. The opposition, thus commenced, increased from year to year, according as new schools were projected. It extended even to the earlier foundations, some of which had enjoyed toleration, if not favour; so that for many years past nearly all those institutions have been equally shunned by Catholics. The grounds of this opposition to the Model Schools on the part of the Catholic bishops and people are numerous and grave, and will be found stated in the resolutions of the bishops at their general meeting in 1859; in their correspondence with the Rt. Hon. E. Cardwell, when Chief Secretary for Ireland;[*] in their resolutions of 1862, prohibiting the Catholic clergy from sending teachers for training to those schools, or employing any teachers trained there after the date of that prohibition; in their letter, 14th January, 1866, to Sir George Grey, then Secretary of State for the Home Department;[†] in the letters addressed by some of the Bishops to the late Primary Education Commission,[‡] and in the evidence before the same Commission of Cardinal Cullen,[§] Right Rev. Dr. Keane,[||] and Right Rev. Dr. Dorrian,[¶] and in other documents connected with the Education Question.

[*] *Report of Primary Education Commission*, vol. i. pages 160, 170.
[†] *Ibid.*, page 185.   [‡] Vol. viii. pages 15-24.
[§] Vol. iv. pages 1177, et seqq.   [||] Vol. iii. page 670, et seqq.
[¶] *Ibid.*, page 341, et seqq.

In a letter of 10th August, 1860, from nineteen Members of Parliament to Mr. Cardwell, the following passage occurs:—

"How do you propose to realize your engagements? Are we to understand that you will return to the original system?

"There are several other points respecting which we should regard it as a favour if you could supply us with early information. They relate to matters on which you have as yet expressed no definite opinion.

"The system of literary model schools, used also as additional training schools, and educating together, under a common roof, youths removed from all domestic control, and subjected to no adequate collegiate discipline, formed no part of the original scheme of education. In them the State, not content with promoting, directing, and superintending education, assumes the direct function of educator. Is it your intention to maintain or abolish this innovation, which has given rise to grave apprehension, and threatens to spread over the land a net-work of Government education at present scarcely known in any part of the world?"*

Surely this inquiry is still more pressing to-day than it was eleven years ago.

The action of the Bishops having in a great measure paralysed those institutions, and Parliamentary returns moved for by Major O'Reilly and others having shown the extravagant waste of public money, and the general

---

* The following signatures are appended to this letter:—

Castlerosse.
R. More O'Ferrall.
John Francis Maguire.
W. H. F. Cogan.
Laurence Waldron.
John Esmonde.
O'Conor Don.
John Lanigan.
D. O'Connell.
Edward M'Evoy.

O'Donoghoe.
W. Monsell.
G. Gavin.
James M'Cann.
John A. Blake.
GeorgeBowyer.
John Brady
John Dalberg Acton.
J. Pope Hennessy.

failure of the Model Schools, the Government, in 1866, forbade their further extension.

In giving a summary of the cost of erection and of maintenance of the Model Schools, so far only as they are institutions for *Middle Class* and *Intermediate Education*, with which alone we are just now concerned, difficulties present themselves which must be clearly stated.* Every one of those establishments contains school departments for girls and for infants, as well as for boys; and some have in connection with them model farms, where provision is made for agricultural instruction. It is difficult, nay, impossible to discriminate the expenditure in these institutions, so as to separate what is spent upon the literary instruction of the boys only. But as we are here concerned with the education of boys only, we must find out as best we can what is spent upon the boys' departments in Model Schools, in order to compare the amount with the cost of the Grammar Schools and other foundations already noticed.

There are now twenty-nine Model Schools establishments in Ireland, including the Central School. The following table shows the locality, date of opening, cost of erection and repairs, and total cost to the close of 1867 of each Model School, and also the cost for the year 1868:

* The Royal Commissioners on Primary Education complain of the unsatisfactory and contradictory returns of the expenditure on Model Schools made by the National Board. Examples are given (vol. i. part ii. p. 785) in the case of four Model Schools in Ulster, in which the expenditure in the year 1867, as given in the Board's published reports, falls short of that returned to the Royal Commission by the following sums:—Enniskillen, 2,341*l*. 5*s* 5*d*.; Belfast, 432*l*. 12*s*. 8*d*.; Newtownards, 314*l*. 9*s*. 10*d*.; and Bailieborough, 2£9*l*. 19*s*. 3*d*.—making upon one year's expenditure a total inaccuracy amounting to 3,388*l*. 7*s*. 2*d*.

MODEL SCHOOLS.

Name of Town where Model School is situated	Year Opened	Cost of erection and repairs	Total Cost to close of 1867	Cost in the year 1868
Belfast	1857	£15,956	£52,340	£3,147
Ballymena	1849	5,806	17,068	718
Ballymoney	1856	1,879	7,893	593
Carrickfergus	1861	4,495	9,384	735
Lurgan	1863	6,764	12,046	1,012
Newry	1849	6,671	18,342	621
Bailieboro'	1850	5,643	15,797	690
Newtownards	1862	10,395	17,897	1,244
Enniskillen	1867	9,451	10,176	870
Coleraine	1850	6,060	16,493	735
Londonderry	1859	8,896	18,794	1,404
Monaghan	1861	4,415	8,271	549
Newtownstewart	1861	2,039	4,731	435
Omagh	1859	3,622	9,734	778
Total for Ulster	-	96,092	218,966	13,531
Dublin (West Model)	1849	*1,500	*22,500	1,010
Inchicore	1854	2,445	*10,000	490
Athy	1852	8,224	18,370	663
Kilkenny	1854	4,889	15,357	767
Birr or Parsonstown	1860	3,500	6,512	638
Trim	1850	6,830	18,470	705
Enniscorthy	1862	6,636	9,607	472
Total for Leinster	-	34,024	100,816	4,745
Cork	1865	9,842	13,882	1,654
Dunmanway	1849	8,876	20,004	825
Limerick	1855	6,464	20,741	857
Clonmel	1849	7,865	21,084	802
Waterford	1855	7,421	15,925	811
Total for Munster	-	40,468	91,636	4,949
Galway	1852	5,242	18,258	750
Sligo	1863	8,322	12,121	794
Total for Connaught	-	13,564	30,379	1,544
Central Model School, Dublin	1838	*90,000	*150,000	3,772
Total for all Ireland	-	274,148	591,797	28,541

I. HISTORY.

The items in the preceding table are all abstracted from the returns made by the National Board to the Royal Commission on Primary Education, with the exception of a few (marked *), which are estimated.

While the Central Model Schools have been in operation since 1833, the first of the District Model Schools was opened in 1849. Hence it has been necessary, in order to secure a uniform standard of comparison, to restrict the estimate of the total expenses of the former in the second money column to the same period as the return for the latter, dating it no further back than 1849. Our estimate of the expense of the Central Model Schools does not include that of the Training Establishment, although the professors are an important portion of the Model School staff; nor the cost of the Domestic Establishments, in which the students in training reside, although the latter assist in teaching in the schools. The cost of the Training Institution in 1867 amounted to 7,806l.; in this, however, there are not included repairs and many other items which are paid for through the Board of Works. Eight of the twenty-nine institutions—the Central, Athy, Kilkenny, Cork, Dunmanway, Belfast, Ballymoney, and Bailieboro'—have an agricultural department attached, connected with the instruction of the boys or the students in the Model Schools, the expense of which (about 5,000l. a-year) has been excluded from the preceding table. Again, the expenditure by the Board of Works on repairs, furniture, and other matters, and by the National Board on miscellaneous items, which could not well be distributed amongst the several institutions, is not included in the column for 1868. Lastly, the cost of inspection and administration, which is very large, the interest on the immense capital sunk, the deterioration of buildings, and the heavy incumbrance of rent and taxes on sites and land, to which the Commissioners are bound by lease, are all excluded from the Table. We have no intention of investigating the operations of the National Board, except so far as they are concerned with our present purpose, and we may now state in general terms that the erection and repairs of all the buildings connected with the Model Schools, Literary and Agricultural, under the Board's own control, cost at least 400,000*l.*, or much more than twice the sum expended on the erection and repairs of all the ordinary National Schools in the kingdom during nearly forty years.

The total cost of the support of those institutions in 1868 was, as we have already seen, 28,541*l.* If we allow 14,000*l.* (a rather extravagant estimate) for the expenditure on the girls' and infants' schools, we shall have over 14,000*l.* as the expenditure on Boys' Model Schools during the year. These sums do not include any portion of the outlay on the Agricultural Departments connected with the schools, nor on the Central Training Institution. But owing to peculiar circumstances, with which we are not at present concerned, the ranks of the Central Training Establishment have for the last seven or eight years been to a very large extent composed of the pupil-teachers, monitors, and advanced boys from the District Model Schools. There they have a free residence and free education for several months. In this way the Central Training Institution is the complement to the Provincial Model Schools, and they in turn are the feeders which supply it with students; while the inducement of a "*Free Scholarship*" in Dublin must act as a potent stimulant with many youths and draw them to those schools. The Primary Education Commissioners tell us (vol. I., part ii., page 813) that the value of this free scholarship is 28*l*. 10*s*. to each student for each half-yearly session that he remains in residence. Thus the Model Schools and the Central Training Institution occupy towards each other the same relation which binds the Royal and Endowed Schools into one complete educational system with Trinity College

CHAPTER X.

MODEL SCHOOLS.—II. ORGANIZATION.

Date of their Erection. Towns in which Model Schools are situated. One-half of them in Ulster; Model Schools not accepted by Ulster Catholics, who were a majority of the population; only 89 Catholics found present by the Police on 25th June, 1868, in twelve out of the fourteen Model Schools in that province. The Royal Commissioners found only 236 present in the whole fourteen schools. The expenditure of a quarter of a million of the public taxes upon Model Schools in Ulster, less defensible than the expenditure upon previous Protestant educational schemes. The province of Ulster exceptionally treated as regards education—it receives more of the public endowments, while it gives a lower return in the number and proficiency of the scholars, than the other provinces. The localities selected for Model Schools are precisely those already provided with adequate Protestant Institutions. How the Enniskillen Model School was established.

Social position of the Scholars of Model Schools. Occupations of the parents of the children attending Model Schools formerly given in Reports of National Board; not given for some years, attention having been called in Parliament to the superior social position of the scholars. Return obtained by Royal Commissioners of Education; analysis of the Return; children of mill-owners, merchants, magistrates, mayors, deputy-lieutenants, etc., receiving almost gratuitous education under a system originally designed for the poor of Ireland.

Course of instruction. The instruction given in the Model Schools includes all the subjects taught in Intermediate Schools; Return on this subject obtained by Royal Commissioners of Primary Education; analysis of this Return.

School Fees. Rate of payment for children in Model Schools merely nominal; relative proportions of those who pay one penny a week, 2s. 6d., and 5s. a quarter, respectively; surprise of an Inspector of Schools at the respectability of the persons in Belfast who claim exemption even from these nominal fees.

Premiums and Prizes directly or indirectly connected with Model Schools. Literary Results of Model Schools. Staff of teachers excessive in proportion to number of scholars; number of scholars to each teacher in Model Schools. Proportion of space found unoccupied in Provincial Model Schools; cost of accommodation for each child; attendance at some schools when visited by Royal Commissioners; several had an atten-

II. ORGANIZATION.

dance below the average which an ordinary national school should have to entitle it to a grant. Opinion of Royal Commissioners as to literary proficiency of children; they complain of want of discipline and moral training in Model Schools; they notice examples of inaccurate statistics, and mention that there exists an anxiety to manufacture a high average attendance; they condemn the scheme of the State giving a nearly gratuitous education to the children of barristers, mill-owners, etc., which displaces the self-supporting schools they would otherwise have attended; their opinion as to evil effect of the mixture of discordant social grades in a school.

Boarding Institutions connected with Model Schools. Lodging accommodation in excess of wants owing to failure of schools; small proportion of Pupil Teachers who remain in the Board's service. Objection to mixed Boarding Institutions; opinion of Royal Commissioners. Denominational Training Schools recommended by the Royal Commission of 1812; the Model Schools contemplated in the original scheme of National Education of Mr. Stanley were to be *sanctioned*, not founded by the Board. Project of a Denominational Training School in the hands of the State in England abandoned as impracticable; number of Training Colleges in England. Even the Queen's Colleges did not attempt mixed Boarding Houses. Opinions of Royal Commissioners of Primary Education on the difficulties of the mixed Boarding Institutions in connection with the Model Schools, and on the delicate and dangerous position of Inspectors in their relation to Model Schools.

Religious Denominations of the Scholars. Gradual decrease of Catholic children; hardships of Catholics in having to forego educational advantages in order to maintain the principle of religious freedom. Statement of the Royal Commissioners of Primary Education as to attendance of Catholics at Model Schools; their opinion that, after the year 1858, the further extension of Model Schools was wrong. Table showing the ratio of the number of Catholic children attending the Model Schools to the total number of children in them, with the Catholic population in the towns in which they are situated. Analysis of attendance according to religious denomination at Model Schools. The Model Schools a greater failure than the Charter Schools. The Catholics found present not always natives of the place where the Model School is situated.

Conclusion. Model Schools the work of a government department in Dublin; established in open defiance of public opinion of Catholics, and generally at the instance of miserable minorities of Presbyterians and others. Interposition of Government in 1866, forbidding their further extension. Letter of Mr. Fortescue suggesting the appointment of chaplains and creation of vested and non-vested Model Schools; appointment of a Royal Commission to investigate, among other things, the question of the Model Schools; opinion of the Commissioners.

We shall now consider briefly the leading points of interest with regard to the operation of the Model Schools.

DATE OF ERECTION.—The Central Model Schools were founded in 1833, and the other institutions between 1849 and 1867, a period of 18 years. Five of them were opened in 1849, the same year as the Queen's Colleges; three in 1850, two in 1852, two in 1854, two in 1855, one in 1856, one in 1857, two in 1860, three in 1861, three in 1862, two in 1863, one in 1865, and one in 1867. Fourteen, or half of the entire number, were therefore opened within the first six years; the other half during the next twelve years. This slackening of activity on the part of the Board indicates the increasing popular hostility to the working and extension of Model Schools.

LOCALITY OF THE SCHOOLS.—Nothing connected with the Model Schools demands, or will more fully repay consideration, than their local distribution. In dealing with this portion of the question, the Central Establishment must be regarded as wholly exceptional, having been founded so early, and for a legitimate object, namely, the training of teachers. A glance at the table in the preceding chapter will show that fourteen, or one-half of the District Model Schools, are in Ulster; that the erection and repairs of these fourteen schools cost, down to the end of 1867, 96,092*l*.; that their support in 1868 (omitting all charges connected with the agricultural departments) cost 13,531*l*. Thus, although six of those institutions have been opened within the last ten years, the total expenditure on the Model Schools of Ulster, from 1849 to the close of 1868, very nearly reached a quarter of a million sterling; and if the account were carried down to the present time it would be found to have considerably exceeded that sum. Connaught, with its two Model Schools, costing annually one-ninth of the amount spent on those in Ulster, one-eighth of the cost of erection, and less than one-eighth of the total expenditure upon the Ulster Schools, contrasts strangely, if its poverty be considered, with the northern province, which has only double its population, and which is so often held up to the rest of the country as a model specimen of self-reliance. Nor is the contrast much less striking if we compare Ulster with the provinces of Munster and Leinster. It may be urged that, while the Catholic people of these provinces objected to receive Model Schools, the people of Ulster did not. This is an objection which is partially well founded. But it must be remembered that it was a portion only of the population of that province—the Protestant minority—who accepted Model Schools; while, on the other hand, in no part of Ireland has the opposition of the Catholic majority been more uniform, persistent, and eminently successful than in Ulster. In twelve of the fourteen Ulster Model Schools—Londonderry, Coleraine, Omagh, Ballymena, Ballymoney, Carrickfergus, Newtownards, Enniskillen, Newtownstewart, Lurgan, Newry, and Monaghan—the police found present, on the 25th June, 1868, only *eighty-nine Catholic scholars*. The two Royal Commissioners, who subsequently visited these twelve schools in the same year, found in them only *eighty-four* Catholics. Even including Belfast and Bailieborough, the Commissioners found only 236 Catholic children in the fourteen Model Schools of Ulster; the fourteen towns where those schools are placed having had, in 1861, a Catholic population of 79,298, the whole province 966,613 Catholics!

The establishment, at an expenditure of a quarter of a million of the public taxes, of fourteen Model Schools, thus repudiated and shunned by the majority of the population, is, therefore, a creation of foundations which is less defensible—allowance being made for the change of times and of the political treatment of Catholics—than the establishment of the Diocesan Schools of Elizabeth, the Royal Schools of James the First, the Schools of the Irish Society, those of Erasmus Smith, or even the Charter Schools. It is a new and powerful accession to Protestant Intermediate Education, and this, too, in a province abounding with opulent endowments denied to the rest of the kingdom. Ulster has the great Royal Schools of Enniskillen, Armagh, Dungannon, Cavan, and Raphoe, with more than 20,000 acres of land, and an annual net income of 5,000*l*. It has an educational trust fund of over 10,000*l*. a year, for the benefit of a single county, in the hands of the Irish Society, out of which the College in Londonderry and the Grammar School in Coleraine are endowed. It has four of the best of the fifteen Diocesan Schools— Londonderry, Ballymena, Downpatrick, and Monaghan. It has 58 schools on Erasmus Smith's foundation, and some supported by the Incorporated Society. It has many special charities, as the Gwyn Institution, Derry; the Robertson Schools in Donegal; the Tullyvin School, county Cavan; and numerous small foundations. It has a Queen's College endowed with nearly 10,000*l*. a-year, in which there are *only three Catholic Students in the Faculty of Arts.* It

II. ORGANIZATION. 185

receives, through the National Board, a larger share of the grants for Primary Education, while giving a lower return, in the number and proficiency of the scholars, than any of the other provinces. Yet, with this affluence of endowments for 947,571 Protestants, fourteen new institutions have been founded, from which, on conscientious principles, the Catholic majority stands aloof, just as they did from the educational institutions of the penal times, the creations of the sixteenth, seventeenth, and the early part of the eighteenth centuries. Nay, more, as the Primary Education Commission has pointed out, the National Board selected the very localities where those Protestant institutions existed and were most numerous, as the sites for their Model Schools—*e. g.* Enniskillen, Londonderry, Coleraine, Ballymena, Monaghan, and Belfast.

The Enniskillen Model School, founded at the instance of Mr. J. G. Porter, of Belleisle, son of a Protestant clergyman, and of some other Protestants of the neighbourhood, affords an instructive example of the origin of some of those foundations, On receipt of the memorial in 1857, praying for a Model School, the Board referred to their Inspector, Mr. James Brown, a Presbyterian, stationed in the town of Enniskillen, for information as to (1) the number of inhabitants in the town of the different religious denominations; (2) the number of children likely to attend the school; (3) the state of public opinion as to the expediency of establishing the proposed Model School; and (4) the probability of obtaining an eligible site at a moderate rent. The following month the Inspector reported as follows: " According to the Census returns, there were 5,949 inhabitants* in Enniskillen, in the year

* The actual population of Enniskillen in 1851, exclusive of persons in public institutions, was (according to the Census Com-

1851, and the population has been increasing; of the above number about 2,000 are Roman Catholics, the remainder are Protestants—above 1,000 being of the Methodist connexion. Presbyterians are not numerous". Here is an officer who had been resident in Enniskillen for some time, who, in reporting upon the principal points on which the establishment of an important and expensive public institution is made to depend, gives answers which in every material respect are, to say the least, inaccurate. The census of 1861 was taken while the project was under consideration—for the erection of the school was not decided on by the Board till June, 1862, and Mr. Browne was in frequent correspondence with them on the subject. The population of Enniskillen in 1861, instead of having *increased*, is returned as 5,774, being less than in 1851. Of that number 3,235 were Catholics, 2,179 members of the Established Church, 195 Methodists, 610 Presbyterians, and five " others". So that Catholics, who are represented by the Inspector as only 33 per cent., or one-third of the population, form a majority of 56 per cent., while he magnifies the influence of the Methodists more than five-fold—from 195 to "above 1,000". Of course, the Inspector assured the Board that the memorial of 82 persons represented the political and religious sections of the community, and "had much confidence in saying such a school would be very popular and esteemed a great privilege" (*Prim. Ed. Com.*, vol. vii. p. 122). Mr. Brown was of opinion that the attendance at the school might increase until it reached 300 boys, girls, and infants. To provide for these possible 300 scholars the National Board proceeded to erect a splendid building at a cost

missioners of 1861, Part I., vol. III., pp. 212, 214, 223), 5,792 persons.

of 9,471*l*. 9*s*. 3*d*. The rent, so far from being moderate, was at the rate of 10*l*. an acre, or a total of 68*l*. 18*s*. 9*d*. When the Royal Commissioners visited Enniskillen in 1868, they found 188 children present in the three departments of the school, of whom only *six were Catholics!* What a contrast to Mr. Brown's anticipations.

SOCIAL POSITION OF THE SCHOLARS IN THE MODEL SCHOOLS.—Until a few years ago, the reports of the National Board set forth the occupations of the parents of the children attending the Model Schools; but attention having been called in Parliament to the superior social position of the scholars thus indicated, this return has not been published for some years. The Royal Commission on Primary Education obtained, however, from the National Board a classified summary of the occupations of the parents of 9,475 scholars in the Model Schools, exclusive of the central establishment in Dublin.* 9,475 was the *number on the rolls*, and represented an average daily attendance of 6,760 for the last quarter in 1867. Of these 9,475 scholars 100 were the children of clergymen, 23 of barristers and attorneys, 84 of doctors, surgeons, and medical men, 76 of architects and engineers, 77 of captains of ships, 164 of Government *employées*, not clerks, 8 of mill-owners, 527 of merchants and traders, 871 of shopkeepers, 153 of grocers, 51 of hotel-keepers, 294 of agents and managers, 181 of publicans, and 93 of persons of various miscellaneous callings belonging to the middle class, making a total of 2,702 children of parents of whose superior social position there can be little question, and this, exclusive of the children

---

* This return will be found (vol. vii. pp. 94, 95) in the proceedings of the Commission.

of persons living on their private means. What a departure from Mr. Stanley's original scheme of 1831, and even from that for which the Board was chartered in 1845, " to promote the welfare, by providing for the education, of the *POOR* of Ireland!" Under the Privy Council arrangements, in England, no grant is allowed for any pupil whose parents do not get their bread by *manual labour*, even the employment of journeymen, or the farming for profit of the labour of others, being sufficient to exclude from grants. No grant is given, under the department of Science and Art, for any scholar whose parent is assessed for the Income Tax. In the preceding summary we have not included 1,137 children of farmers, 514 children of clerks, 179 children of railway, workhouse, and prison officials, nor 109 children of teachers, being in all 1,977 children. Under the English system these 1,977 children could not be taken into account for the purposes of the state grant. But, in many cases at least, they are the children of parents who, although earning far less than skilled artizans, have a higher social position to maintain out of their smaller incomes, and have, therefore, at least an equal claim to receive from the State that assistance in the matter of education which is granted to artizans. But, it is self-evident that the system of National Education was not intended for the children of mill-owners, merchants, bankers, professional men of every kind, public officers of high rank, mayors and corporators, magistrates, deputy lieutenants, and even members of Parliament, all of whom have had children and near relatives in Model Schools. Cars, carriages, and other fashionable vehicles, are to be found at the schools, and liveried servants escort some of the children, many of whom travel comparatively long distances

—10 to 30 miles daily—by rail, in first or second class carriages, to several of the Model Schools.

COURSE OF INSTRUCTION.—The Model Schools, besides fulfilling the usual functions of primary schools, carry forward the instruction in the subjects usually taught in those schools, to an extent not surpassed by any Intermediate Schools. They include, in their course of studies, pure and mixed mathematics, experimental physics, most of the subjects for which prizes are given by the Science and Art Department, South Kensington, geography, navigation, English language and literature, French, Latin, and Greek, logic and political economy, music, and drawing. Among the subjects, however, one will look in vain for *History;*—even the history of Great Britain is professedly ignored, through the fear of stimulating curiosity on the forbidden subject of Irish history. We do not mean to say that all the subjects enumerated above are taught in every one of the 29 Model Schools, but only that they are taught in those which have pupils who desire such instruction. According to a return which will be found in the proceedings of the Royal Commission on Primary Education (vol. vii. p. 167), vocal music is taught in all, and instrumental in some of the 29 establishments, drawing is taught in 28, arithmetic in all, book-keeping in 27, mensuration in 28, geometry in 27, algebra in 26, trigonometry in 16, navigation in 3, physical and applied science in 26, agriculture in 6, " reasoning" in 11, English and English literature in all; French or other modern languages in 12; and ancient classics in 6 of those institutions. Many scholars and pupil teachers have proceeded directly from these schools to the Queen's Colleges, and some have graduated in Trinity College with marked distinction. The Rev. Dr. Henry, President of the Queen's College, Belfast, and the oldest member of the National Board, in an address which he delivered in December, 1870, on the occasion of the distribution of the premiums in the Belfast Model School, impugned the honesty and fairness of the adverse report of the Royal Commissioners on that institution, citing, in answer, the marked collegiate success of pupils named by him, who had subsequently risen to distinction, if not eminence, in the Queen's Colleges.

SCHOOL FEES.—The rates of payment for this education are merely nominal, 1s. 1d., 2s. 6d., and 5s. per quarter, payable in advance. Of the 9,475 scholars on the rolls, in the return above cited, 3,073, or more than 33 per cent., pay one penny per week; 3,586, or nearly 38 per cent., pay 2s. 6d. per quarter, or little over two pence per week; and 2,816, or less than 30 per cent., pay 5s. per quarter, or below five pence per week, for the superior instruction which those establishments profess to give. Mr. Molloy, the Inspector at Belfast, reports, in 1864, that he was "rather surprised at the number and respectability of the parties who during the year claimed exemption from the higher rates, which are so extremely moderate as compared with the amount and quality of the instruction imparted, and such as can rarely be had, *on any terms*, in non-national schools".

PREMIUMS AND PRIZES.—Examinations are held annually, when money-prizes (from 15*l*. to nearly 100*l*.), parchment certificates, and silver medals, are distributed to the scholars, at public meetings, presided over by persons of local influence, amid all the *eclat* of speeches, music, and an exciting academic display. Nineteen of the twenty-nine institutions

II. ORGANIZATION.

have boarding establishments attached, in which, including the central institution, 108 resident pupil teachers were boarded, lodged, and received small salaries, in 1867, and in which, as well as in the other Model Schools, there were also several hundred paid monitors, all these places being open to the scholars of those institutions. A return supplied to the Royal Commission on Primary Education (vol. vii. p. 95) shows that of 1,268 such resident pupil teachers, who had been boarded, lodged, and supplied with allowance for clothing, for from one to two years, in the Model Schools, only 467, or 36 per cent., were then known to be in the Board's service; while of 1,036 paid monitors, 264, or only 25 per cent., were then employed in National Schools. The free places in the Central Training Establishment, and also those at the Model Farm, Glasnevin, are similarly open to the scholars, monitors, and pupil teachers of the several Model Schools throughout Ireland.

LITERARY RESULTS.—We have seen that the Model Schools are located in collegiate buildings, erected regardless of expense, and furnished with a profusion of apparatus and material aids for instruction superior to any in Ireland of their kind. They are attended by children of the well-to-do classes, as shown above, and have a highly skilled staff, so excessive in proportion to the numbers of scholars, that the instruction may be regarded as detailed and individual as well as *private* tuition. Nevertheless, the Model Schools are a failure. The Royal Commissioners, at their visit to the District Model Schools in 1868, found 6,016 scholars present, taught by a staff of 550 teachers, or, at an average, *one* teacher for every *eleven* children, one-fourth of these being infants. In Coleraine, infants included, they report a teacher for every four and a-half children; in Kilkenny, one for every six; in four others, one teacher for every eight pupils; while eleven schools had a teacher for every nine or ten children. Two of the Royal Commissioners, both Englishmen, her Majesty's Inspectors of Schools— Rev. B. M. Cowie, B.D., Chaplain to the Queen, and S. N. Stokes, Esq.—visited, examined, and reported on all those schools, and also on several of the Primary Schools—National and Denominational—that are in the same towns. Of the 78 departments, boys', girls', and infants', which are contained in the twenty-six Provincial Model Schools, eight have 80 per cent., or more, of their school accommodation unoccupied; while 53 of the 78 have at least 50 per cent., *or more than half their space, vacant.* Allowing ten square feet for each child, instead of six as in the ordinary National Schools, accommodation is provided in the 26 Provincial Model Schools for 12,301 scholars, whereas the Royal Commissioners found present only 5,467, or 45 per cent. of this number, thus furnishing another proof of the inutility of the extravagant outlay spent in their erection. The following items taken from the Report of the Royal Commission, show the extravagant cost of the accommodation per child of those found present:—Coleraine, about 74*l.*; Enniscorthy, 73*l.*; Athy and Clonmel, 60*l.*; Trim, 56*l.*; and Enniskillen, 50*l.* Nine of the departments of these Collegiate Institutions had, at the visit of the Royal Commissioners, the following muster of scholars:—One had 12, one 14, a third 17, a fourth 20, a fifth 21, a sixth, 22, a seventh 23, an eighth 25, and a ninth 29; although, according to the rules of the National Board, aid cannot be given (except in very peculiar circumstances) to an *ordinary National School having a daily average attendance of less than 30 children.*

II. ORGANIZATION.

The two Royal Commissioners charged with the examination of the Model Schools furnish ample details of the proficiency of the pupils in reading, writing, arithmetic, grammar, and geography. Their general estimate of the results is as follows:—

"Our estimate of the literary proficiency of the pupils in Model Schools is not on the whole encouraging. We had hoped that, from the lavish way in which the schools are supplied with every requisite, and the large amount expended by the State on children, most of whom have social advantages far beyond what can fall to the lot of those whom the State intended to assist, we should have found a corresponding benefit. We regret that this just expectation should not have been realised, and that the children exhibit no very great superiority to those who are without these advantages; a great many children get a fair education: but it is only *fair*, not superior"—(*Report*, Vol. I. Part ii. p. 757).

The Commissioners warn their readers against placing reliance on the tabulated particulars of *their own examination*, owing to the want of discipline and moral training in the schools. They say:

"With few exceptions, we were dissatisfied with the class discipline. Some few teachers of superior power of command, managed to keep the children from talking and copying at the examinations; but, *in most cases*, if we had been examining the children *in order to ascertain the amount due by the State for the proficiency of each child, we should have had to dismiss the class, and declare the school unworthy of support.* This is a strong censure, but we are compelled to let it remain as our deliberate conviction. The children never seem to have been examined in a proper manner, and they evidently were surprised at being reproved for consulting over their work. No warnings of the necessity of honesty in examination, or hints as to the discredit which would be brought on the school by disobedience, had any effect.

"The feature of Model Schools, which has already received

frequent notice, viz., the attendance therein of children of the middle class, and professional classes—is probably here to be recalled in explanation. *The children consider themselves much above the teachers, and do not pay attention to them.* They know that there is a great desire to attract them to the schools—and that, consequently, they are the masters of the situation. It is more conspicuous in girls' schools than in boys' schools .. They (the teachers) seemed to be helplessly inefficient in preventing the children from talking, consulting each other, looking over each others' papers, and comparing results of the sums they had worked. So that, though their attainments in elementary subjects are not very creditable, as they stand in our printed tables—we are quite certain that, if we had had time to re-examine, and taken the precautions which would have been necessary to insure accuracy—the percentage of those who passed in arithmetic would have been *much* lower than it is now"—(*Report*, vol. I. part ii. page 749).

We have considered that the most impartial course for us was to give those important extracts from the reports of the two experienced members of the Royal Commission, who are themselves Inspectors of Primary Schools in England, and are charged with the examination of training Colleges in that country, since they afford what, on the face of it, must be recognised as a thoroughly independent and trustworthy account of the working and results of the Model Schools. We have preferred doing this, to quoting evidence or statements of persons, who might be suspected of partiality towards one side or the other. We have been able to touch on a few only of the leading points of the special report of those gentlemen, and are compelled to pass by many others of great interest, referring our readers to the document itself for further information on the subject. They detail (p. 745) several examples of inaccurate statistics, and state "that there is a general anxiety to manufacture a high average attendance by every possible contrivance". They condemn the scheme, which calls on "the State to provide a nearly gratuitous education for children of architects, barristers, clergymen, physicians, mill-owners, etc.", and displaces "the schools to which the children of the higher middle class might have resorted". And they further show that the mixture of discordant social grades is repugnant to all, and injurious to discipline:—

"If children come in private cars to school, or furnished with their season ticket by railway, or are attended by servants in livery (which we have ourselves witnessed*), such children frighten away the poor and bare-footed, who do not like to have their social and fiscal deficiencies made conspicuous by contrast; and in some cases we have actually been requested to recommend that there should be a separation of classes, as the parents of well-dressed children found it offensive to their feelings that they should mix with their inferiors; on both sides the mixture is found unpalatable"—(p. 761 A).

BOARDING INSTITUTIONS.—In nine of the twenty-nine Model Schools, the teaching staff, including the pupil teachers, live in lodgings, an allowance for rent and support being made to them. In the Central Institution, and in the other nineteen Schools, residence is provided for the head master and his assistant, under whom are resident pupil teachers, eight or nine for each of the Provincial Model Schools. Seven of the nineteen boarding establishments are connected with model farms. Owing to the general failure of the Model Schools, the lodging accommodation is almost everywhere in excess, the number of literary pupils in residence having been only 108 in 1867. Ennis-

* " In the Belfast Model School we examined the niece of one of the then Members for the borough".

corthy Model School had no resident pupil teacher, while Athy and Newry had only two each, the large expense on the domestic establishments being in those cases wholly useless. Of 1,268 Pupil Teachers so supported and trained since 1849, only 467, or less than 37 per cent., are still in the Board's service; and unlike the students of the Central Training Department, as their period of training extends from one to two years, the sum thus fruitlessly expended on their education must be enormous. Besides the Pupil Teachers, there is a large staff of non-resident Paid Monitors.

The Catholic Bishops, clergy, and laity, object to Catholic children being taught in *Day* Schools by Protestant Teachers. How much more strongly must they object to Mixed *Boarding* Institutions, under non-Catholic management? After a lengthened and careful examination of the Central Training Institutions, the Royal Commissioners declare :—

" No system, however carefully devised, which ignores the power to be derived, in forming the character, from *unity* of religious conviction, can be effectual.

" In Marlborough Street, at every turn, religious differences are kept before the pupils. It is no happy family which is divided into these sects, continually separating from each other for religious duties, who cannot even say ' *Our Father* ' in common.

" These young people are not any longer children, fresh and light hearted; they have learned to feel already the bitterness and difficulty which religious differences create. Would it not be far better that the training of teachers should be denominational, even if no other part of the system should be altered? This question— so urgently brought before the Commission, and already answered in the affirmative by the Executive Government, in Mr. Chichester Fortescue's letter—has been constantly before us. And we wish to record our decided conviction of the impolicy of the present arrangements, while we are glad to do full justice to the scrupulous

II. ORGANIZATION.

endeavours of those who are entrusted with the administration to make them as effectual as they can, under conditions *essentially wrong in principle*" (*Report*, vol. I. part ii. pp. 813-814).

Nearly 60 years ago, the Royal Commission of 1812, the members of which were all Protestants, recommended *Denominational* Training Schools for Teachers. They said:—

" It fortunately happens that there are in this country existing establishments, as well Roman Catholic as Protestant, which we are persuaded might, with little difficulty, give effectual assistance towards this great national purpose [the training of teachers]. This the Commissioners [of the proposed Board] would find no difficulty in arranging with the Governors of the several institutions. In such arrangements, and indeed in the whole of this part of the scheme, much will, of course, depend upon the discretion of the Commissioners".

This wise recommendation appears to have influenced Mr. Stanley in framing his original scheme in 1831, in which, as already pointed out, he designed that teachers should " have received previous instruction in *a* Model School *to be sanctioned* [not founded or managed] *by the Board*", a recommendation, the setting aside of which has led to bitter contention, and to enormous waste of the public funds, while materially retarding the progress of education in Ireland. The project of a denominational Training College was discussed in England by the Committee of Privy Council, but abandoned as impracticable, as thus reported by the Commission on the State of Popular Education in England.

" The earliest deliberations of the Committee resulted in the adoption of a resolution, that the most efficient means of promoting Popular Education would be, the establishment of a normal school, under the direction of the State, and not placed under the management of a voluntary society; but such difficulty was experienced in providing for the religious instruction of the school, that this design was laid aside, and never resumed" (*Rep.* vol. I. p. 21).

There are in England 39 Training Colleges, all Denominational, having 3,000 students, and enjoying annual State grants of 74,000*l.* towards their support.

Even the Queen's Colleges never attempted a mixture of persons of different religious denominations outside the Lecture Halls, special provision being made in the Act for the establishment of Denominational Boarding Houses for the students, under the moral and religious charge of Deans of Residence, who, it was intended, should be Clergymen of the several religious denominations.

Describing the difficulties of the mixed Boarding Institutions, in connection with the Model Schools, the Royal Commissioners state (vol. I., part ii. pp. 760-61):—

" Brought from distant homes, and so withdrawn from parental and pastoral care, these young men, professing a variety of creeds, pass their days and nights under a schoolmaster who, however skilful as an elementary teacher, has not been selected for ability to mould the character and form the manners of boarders, and who, sincere and well instructed as he may be in his own religion, cannot undertake to enforce the obligations of religions which are not his own. This portion of the Model Schools appears to us to be extremely ill-advised, costly without being effective, and calculated to alienate those most deeply interested in the real welfare of the young men, without securing a sound class of teachers.

" Our disapproval is not based upon the detection of occasional scandals, from which no system can calculate upon being wholly free, but upon general grounds. The responsibility of conducting Boarding-Houses involves a burden which no Government Department should have taken upon itself. Were all the boarders of one creed, the impropriety would be glaring; but not even the Queen's

II. ORGANIZATION. 199

Colleges have attempted Boarding-Houses of *mixed* Religions. Instinctive objections to institutions so novel, so alien to all the customs and traditions of Irishmen, account at once for the unpopularity which has overwhelmed the Commissioners' model schools".

To which may be added their judicious remarks, showing the delicate and dangerous position occupied by the Inspectors in their relation to Model Schools:

"It is obvious that the discharge of the duty of management, exercised possibly by a young unmarried Inspector, over a troop of teachers of both sexes and all ages and creeds, brought from different quarters and working together without perfect subordination among themselves, in schools where boys and girls, often above 13 years of age, occupy adjoining rooms and share a corridor, must be a matter of extreme delicacy. . . .

"In fine, we consider that no Inspector should be placed in a position attended with constant anxiety which must interfere with the regular discharge of his proper functions, and exposed to the risk of mistake, when errors of judgment involve not only his personal character for prudence, but the repute of the Central Government" (*Ibid.*, p. 766).

RELIGIOUS DENOMINATIONS OF THE SCHOLARS.—Since 1858 the number of Catholic children in the Model Schools has become annually less. Each new school brought with it a heavy increase in the expenditure upon this department of the Board's operations, and a relative diminution of the muster roll of the scholars. It has been a repetition of the opposition so successfully waged in 1826, '27, and '28, against the Kildare Place Society. In the later, as in the earlier contest, the victory has remained with the Catholics. But, at what a cost? They have had to hold back their children from schools where the State offered them an education which, in some respects, was not only far beyond what could have been had in their own youth, but far exceeded their utmost desires.

They, the people of the land, had to stand by, and see that education and the advantages which followed in its train, monopolised by an insignificant sect, amounting only to a small fraction of the population of the country. They have maintained the great principle of religious freedom, as their forefathers did in the seventeenth and eighteenth centuries. But they have also had to see their children entering on the race of life at a disadvantage, over-weighted as compared with their Protestant competitors.

Nor was it by educational inferiority alone, that the Catholics of Ireland have had to pay for their loyalty to their faith and country. They have also had to pay for it out of their scanty means. The sheer necessity of holding their own, even in temporal matters, has cast upon them the burden of providing institutions where their sons and daughters can find instruction not inferior to what the State promised to give them in the Model Schools.

At this double price—submitting to the educational injustice of the Government for the sake of religion and country, and spending money lavishly in the establishment of schools for themselves—the Catholics have practically deserted the Model Schools. The Primary Education Commissioners, in their General Report (vol. I. p. 456), state:—" In one or two cases the Roman Catholics virtually have the Model Schools to themselves; from the rest all Roman Catholic pupils have withdrawn, *excepting a few children of the Board's officers, or of mixed marriages*"—marking by their fewness the moral universality of the Catholic protest, and attesting by their own special circumstances the sincerity and honesty of that protest.

The Royal Commissioners, reviewing the history of the Model Schools, point to 1858 as the epoch when all pretext for their establishment ceased, and their further extension became criminal. Adverting to the enlargement of the Central Schools in Marlborough Street, and to the institutions then projected in Londonderry, Enniscorthy, Sligo, Omagh, Carrickfergus, Newtownstewart, and Parsonstown, the Royal Commissioners state :—

" The establishment of these Model Schools, as of others subsequently determined on, received no countenance from Roman Catholics. Of the older Model Schools it is true to say that the ecclesiastical authorities of the Roman Catholic Church regarded them at their first institution with feelings of neutrality, if not of positive favour. Now, however, the experiment involved in the Board's exclusive management of schools was believed to have been worked out, and proved a palpable failure. Henceforward there was no ambiguity, and the Board spent many thousands upon schools at Londonderry, Sligo, Enniscorthy, Omagh, and the rest, without the slightest hope of conducting them as *models of united education*. From this time the Model Schools became for the majority of the people the scene of a contest between the strength of religious principle and the allurements of temporal advantage ; and the Board, appointed ' to superintend a system of education from which should be banished even the suspicion of proselytism', imitated in effect the example of the Charter and Souper schools. The principles of the Roman Catholic Church ' to which in any system intended for general diffusion throughout Ireland, the bulk of the pupils must necessarily belong',* are totally at variance with the principle of exclusive control over schools and boarding houses by the National Board. Previous failures might have taught the Commissioners that 'when this opposition arose, founded on such grounds',† their scheme could not succeed"—(*Rept.*, vol. I. part ii. pp. 739-40).

The following Table‡ indicates, pretty clearly, the extent, position, and relation of the Catholic element in those schools :—

* Lord Stanley's Letter, in *Prim. Educat. Com. Rept.*, Vol. i. page 23.
† *Ibid.*
‡ See *Primary Educat. Com.*, Vol. i., Part ii., page 762, *Table* H.

MODEL SCHOOLS.

MODEL SCHOOL	Catholic Population of Town in 1861	Scholars Found Present		Per Centage of Catholics to	
		Total Number	Catholics	Population of Town	Scholars in School
Bailieboro'	809	178	81	79	46
Ballymena	1,656	176	5	25	3
Ballymoney	795	136	13	31	10
Belfast	41,237	858	71	34	8
Carrickfergus	594	198	7	15	3
Coleraine	1,455	180	26	26	14
Enniskillen	3,235	189	6	56	3
Londonderry	12,036	271	4	58	1
Lurgan	2,752	309	11	36	4
Monaghan	2,667	143	9	70	6
Newry	7,935	138	7	65	5
Newtownards	1,126	311	5	12	1·5
Newtownstewart	604	90	3	49	3
Omagh	2,187	192	4	62	2
Total for Ulster	79,088	3,369	252	38	7·7
Athy	3,688	136	20	90	14
Enniscorthy	4,692	91	5	88	5·5
Kilkenny	12,769	104	19	90	18
Parsonstown	4,234	111	21	78	19
Trim	1,791	123	76	87	62
Total for Leinster	27,174	565	141	87	25
Clonmel	10,209	132	24	88	18
Cork	67,148	445	55	84	12
Dunmanway	1,694	303	284	82	94
Limerick	39,124	278	27	88	10
Waterford	20,429	220	63	88	29
Total for Munster	138,604	1,378	453	86	33
Galway	15,621	147	31	92	21
Sligo	8,313	201	3	79	1
Total for Connaught	23,934	348	34	87	10
Total for Ireland	268,800	5,660	880	63	15

This table shows that these 26 cities and towns, containing a population of 425,632 persons (or about one-twelfth of that of the whole kingdom), of whom 268,800 were Catholics, had 26 Model School Institutions, from which, with a few exceptions, the whole Catholic population stands aloof, although many of those schools have been in operation since 1849.

In the foregoing observations, we have not taken into account the Central, the West Dublin, and the Inchicore Metropolitan establishments, which are peculiarly circumstanced; but, even in these, the decrease in the number of Catholic children, within the last few years, has been considerable. The Model School at Bailieborough, a small town in Cavan, in which there is no other school, and that at Dunmanway, a small town in West Cork, are also peculiarly circumstanced. If these two be excluded, the 880 Catholic children found present in 1868 will be diminished by 365, thus reducing the aggregate muster of Catholics in twenty-four Model Institutions to 524 scholars. In six of the departments no Catholic child was found present; these expensive models of *mixed* education being *unmixed* Protestant schools. Eleven of the departments had a solitary Catholic. Eleven of them had two. Eight others had three each; two had four; six had five; two had six; three had seven; and two had eight Catholic pupils. That is, 51 of the 78 school departments, boys', girls', and infants', in the twenty-six Provincial Model Schools, either had no Catholic pupil present when the Royal Commissioners visited them in 1868, or the number of Catholics found present *was less than nine*. Eleven others had 10, or less than 20 Catholics; seven had 20 to 30; two had 30 to 40; three* had 60 to 100; while only one, the

* One of these is the *boys'* school at Trim—the only *National* School for boys in that place—which had 67 Catholic boys present,

Infants' School at Dunmanway, had 114 Catholics and but 6 Protestants. Indeed Dunmanway can scarcely be regarded as a Model School so far as mixture of religeous denominations is concerned, since there are in the three departments 284 Catholics and only 19 Protestants. Primate Boulter's Charter Schools of 1733 were a triumphant success compared with the Model Schools of 1849, the twin foundation of the Queen's Colleges.

Even the few Catholic children to be found in the Model Schools, are often not natives or regular residents of the localities. Thus, the 12,036 Catholics of the city of Londonderry would feel disgraced, if four of their children should be found in the Model School, just as much as if they were found in the Foyle College, the Magee College, or the Gwyn Institution. The four Catholics who are in the school are strangers, two of them belonging to the family of the Catholic Head Inspector, who come in daily from Donegal, another the child of a railway guard, and the fourth a country child from Culmore. The 8,392 Catholics in the borough of Sligo do not furnish even *one* Catholic pupil, the two returned being the children of the Protestant Inspector, their mother being a Catholic. It is the same story, differing only in degree, in Enniscorthy, Athy, Trim (in part), Kilkenny, Limerick, Cork, Newry, Enniskillen, Omagh, Galway, Clonmel—everywhere.

The importance of these new foundations, to whose history and working we have felt it our duty to devote special attention, consists mainly in their recent origin, expensive character, and total failure. All the previous foundations—Diocesan Schools, Royal Schools,

the Protestants of all denominations being 25. The two others are the boys' and girls' schools at Dunmanway, which we have already observed are peculiarly circumstanced. The attendance in the boys' department at Dunmanway was 79 *Catholics*, and 9 *Protestants* of all denominations; in the girls', 91 *Catholics*, and 4 *Protestants* of all denominations.

Irish Society's Schools, Erasmus Smith's Schools, Charter Schools, and Grammar Schools—were the creation of remote barbarous penal times. The Model Schools were planned and opened twenty years after the passing of the Act of Emancipation, in the face of all the experience of the failure of previous foundations. They were the immediate work of a Government department in Dublin. No previous educational project has been so calamitous. Direct and open defiance was declared against the public opinion of Catholics, and, regardless of expense, these institutions were obtruded into several localities at the instance of miserable minorities of Presbyterians and others. The results of this struggle are now before the world.

At length the Government, in answer to a memorial, dated January, 1866, from the Catholic Bishops, interposed by letter from Mr. Fortescue, Chief Secretary, 19th June, 1866, and objected to any further extension of those institutions, recognising at the same time the fairness and force of the objections made by Catholics to the Boarding Establishments connected with them, and suggesting *Denominational* Training Schools, at least so far as the domestic arrangements for the persons in training. The Board approved the several suggestions of the Government, and proposed the following items in their estimates for the next year (1867-8):

£5,800 capitation allowance to Chaplains of various creeds, to be appointed on the recommendation of the Bishop or other Church authority, and to be placed in charge of religious instruction in the Model Schools.

£5,000 towards the erection of vested Model Schools, under local management.

£6,000 towards the maintenance of non-vested Model Schools under *local* management.

These propositions came, at the close of 1866, under the consideration of Lord Derby's Government, who declined to sanction this partial change without further inquiry. With this view, the late Royal Commission was appointed, and was charged with an examination into all the questions connected with Primary Education, and especially into the Model Schools. We have already referred frequently to their Report for information respecting these institutions. We shall here content ourselves with citing one extract more :

"Many friends of education will lament the opposition shown by the Roman Catholics to the Model Schools, and rest satisfied with the reflection that they were intended for their benefit. This we consider neither wise nor statesmanlike. The ascertained facts are that there was *abundant provision made for the secondary education of Protestants, and that the Model Schools have served practically to increase it*, and have not succeeded in extending the benefits of such superior education to the Roman Catholics"— (*Prim. Ed. Com.*, vol. I. part ii. 772).

British statesmen have annually voted out of the public funds of the empire about 14,000*l*. to maintain in Ireland a net-work of what are practically Intermediate Schools for boys, founded and managed on principles which preclude the Catholic people of the country from availing themselves of the advantages which they offer. Let them, in accomplishing that educational redress which they have been promising us for years, join this sum to the other sums we enumerated in preceding chapters, and reconstruct our Intermediate Education in such a spirit of honesty, that while its blessings shall be open to "all denominations", it shall, at the same time, be "free from all suspicion of proselytism".

CHAPTER XI.

CONSTITUTION OF IRISH EDUCATIONAL BOARDS AND COMMISSIONS.

The public system of Intermediate Education in Ireland being thoroughly Protestant, the authority which controls it would naturally be Protestant; hence discussion on this point would seem to be superfluous. *Legal* equality of Catholics and Protestants, very different from *real* equality. Necessity of noticing the constitution of the bodies which administer the ducational arrangements of the country.

Irish Society, exclusively Protestant, holds in trust for educational purposes property worth £10,000 a year, derived from forfeited estates of Irish Catholics.

Ex officio Governors of Erasmus Smith's schools include, accidentally, three Catholic judges, who may be replaced by three Protestants; but all the elected Governors are Protestants.

Incorporated Society has some Catholic *ex officio* members; but all the Managing Committee are Protestants. No cause of complaint that Protestant institutions should be controlled by Protestants; but that Protestants are provided with schools at the national expense, while Catholics are not so provided. Insult to the Irish people that the Lord Lieutenant is the head of the Incorporated Society; Catholics should be discontinued from being *ex officio* members of it.

The Commissioners of Education have charge of the Royal and other Endowed schools in Ireland. All Protestants, except the Lord Chancellor and Judge Fitzgerald; anomalous position of the latter on such a Board a paradox.

Board of National Education consists of twenty members, all appointed by Government, and removable at pleasure; ten are Catholics; six Protestants; four Presbyterians. *Five* of the Catholics are judges; the other five have occupations which make their regular attendance very difficult. Protestant Commissioners differently circumstanced; they can all attend without much inconvenience. Catholic Commissioners depend for information as to the business of the National Board on Protestant sources. Table showing attendance of each Commissioner at meetings of the Board during seven years. Melancholy record. True nature of complaint in this matter. Government should never have selected persons who could not attend, and, failing a proper attendance, should have required them to resign. Real control of National system in hands of Protestant Resident Commissioner. Secretary's department practically Protestant. Protestant Commissioners representative men. Catholics are not representative men.

Principle on which Irish Commissions are made up by all Governments, whether Whig or Tory. Protestants selected for their fitness for the office; hence Protestant Commissions are effective, e.g. the Church Temporalities Commission. Catholics not so selected for mixed Commissions. Whatever be the business, judges selected, as it were because they have too much to do to attend properly; then barristers; then a few officials or other pliant men. English Judges not appointed to English educational Commissions. The Irish people, if they had a voice in the matter, would not put five judges in charge of education. Irish Catholics appointed on Boards merely to make a show of liberality.

Report for 1870 of "Commissioners of Education". They ask for greater powers of control over the endowed schools, and to reconstitute the system of Intermediate Education. This would be to establish a gigantic scheme of *mixed* education, and to strengthen the Queen's Colleges. Seven signatures to this Report. Judge Fitzgerald appears in the middle of the list, with three Protestants before and three after him. Judge Fitzgerald no representative of Irish Catholic opinion.

In the preceding chapters we have said all that, for our present purpose, we consider sufficient to show the character and the extent of the disability, under which Irish Catholics labour with respect to Intermediate Education; but we have said little, or nothing, about the organization by which the system is administered. As it exists for the benefit of Protestants only, it is obvious that the administration should be in Protestant hands; a Catholic would be as much out of place there as on the "Church Representative Body". Besides, the Boards and Commissions, which manage the educational as well as all other affairs of Ireland, were almost all created at a time when the notion of an Irish Papist holding a post of trust and authority in the government of his own country, would have been a more ridiculous dream than that an Irish exile should be Prime Minister of a great Australian colony. The theory of government has been altered since those arrangements first came into existence. An Irish Catholic is now, except in educational matters, *legally* on a footing of equality with an Irish Protestant. But before this can become a *real* equality, it will be necessary to undo and to reconstruct the whole administrative system of Ireland.

So far, however, as our present object is concerned, we have nothing to say to all this, beyond pointing out, as we hope we have done, how far the public arrangements for giving intermediate education involve injustice to Catholic youth. But parliamentary documents lately published convince us that this matter of the constitution of the bodies by which the educational arrangements of the country are controlled, deserves greater notice and attention than it usually receives. We propose, therefore, to collect together in this chapter a few facts connected with this subject, which, apart from their own importance, have a special significance as illustrating the practical interpretation hitherto given to the theory of religious equality.

" The Irish Society", holding *in trust for the promotion of education* a property of over £10,000 a year, exclusively derived from the confiscated estates of Irish Catholics, is, we need scarcely observe, an exclusively Protestant body. We have seen in our fifth Chapter, that the greater portion of this trust fund is absorbed by the charges of " management and incidental expenses"; and that only about one-fourth is spent on purposes of education, not a penny of which goes to a Catholic school. This, however, is a purely English body, located in London. Its existence is an outrage on the Irish people, just as much as a similar society of Irish Catholics resident in Dublin, dealing with a confiscated Hampshire or Wiltshire, would be an outrage on the English people; and its "disestablishment and disendowment" should be insisted upon, on national and political grounds, quite independently of religious reasons.

The other bodies which control Irish intermediate education, are, the Governors of Erasmus Smith's schools, the Incorporated Society, the Commissioners of Education, and the National Board. All these bodies have certain features in common, while each has some special peculiarity. The constitution of the first two is fixed by Royal Charter, and includes certain *ex-officio* members, the remaining members being chosen as vacancies occur.

The foundation of Erasmus Smith is, as we showed in our sixth Chapter, distinctly intended for Protestant education; the Incorporated Society was instituted expressly for the perversion of the Catholic population of the country. No one could be surprised to find that the "Governors" and the "Society" were exclusively Protestant. The wheel of time has indeed wrought a strange anomaly in the constitution of the *ex-officio* portions of those bodies. Thus, the Lord Chancellor, the Chief Justice of the Common Pleas, and the Chief Baron are *ex officio* governors of Erasmus Smith's Schools; and all three personages happen at this moment to be Catholics. But how vain would be an attempt on their part to interfere with the Protestant character of the foundation, is plain, when we say that the two Protestant Archbishops, the Provost of Trinity College, and Chief Justice Whiteside are joined with them as *ex officio* Governors; while the Protestant Bishops of Killaloe, Meath, and Tuam, the Earls of Erne and Bandon, Rev. Lord O'Neill, Rev. Lord

Plunket, Vice-Chancellor Chatterton, Master Brooke, Dr. Gayer, Mr. A. Lefroy, and Sir Edward Borough, are among the selected Governors.

Similarly, the same three Catholic gentlemen, as well as the Attorney General and the Lord Mayor of Dublin, who are also Catholics, are *ex officio* members of the Incorporated Society. But that in their case it is "*stat nominis umbra*", and no more, is amply guaranteed by the unquestionable Protestantism of the Managing Committee of fifteen

But, as we said above, it is only natural that the control of institutions which exist simply for the education of Protestants, should be in Protestant hands. And, perhaps Protestants may have cause of complaint that the legislative vicissitudes which have placed a few Irish Catholics upon the Bench, should have also included them among the *ex officio* Governors of Protestant institutions. Our objection, as Irish Catholics, is not that the governing bodies of Protestant schools are Protestant, but that while splendid provision is made out of the national property for those Protestant schools, the schools of the Catholic people of the land are destitute of any similar provision.

There is indeed another point connected with the Incorporated Society, to which we will here only allude, having already referred to it in our eighth Chapter, when speaking of that body. It is an insult to the people of Ireland that the Viceroy of the Queen stands first on the list of members of a society founded expressly to pervert poor Irish Catholics. Whatever insolent pretext might have formerly existed for this affront, there is no excuse for the outrage since the disestablishment of the Protestant Church. We will further add, that Lord Chancellor O'Hagan, Chief Justice Monahan, Chief Baron Pigot, and Attorney General

Barry, and the Catholic Lord Mayors of Dublin appear to have very little consideration for what is due to their country, their religion, and their own character, when they take no steps to have their names removed from the register of this infamous society.

The "Commissioners of Education", who are charged with "the regulation" of the Royal and Diocesan Schools and the Endowed Schools of municipal and private foundation, are fifteen in number, of whom eight are *ex officio* under the acts 53 George III, c. 107, and 3 George IV.. c. 79, and seven are appointed by Government. The list of *ex-officio* "Commissioners of Education" is quite sufficient to satisfy any one of the Protestant character of that body. The Lord Chancellor is the only Catholic among them; and the same political vicissitude which places him there to-day might to-morrow substitute a Protestant. The two Protestant Archbishops, the Provost of Trinity College, and the two Members for Trinity College are *ex officio* Commissioners:—thus establishing, according to the mind of the legislature, not only the Protestant character of the schools which they were to "regulate", but also of the Commission itself; and further showing the intimate connection which the Endowed Schools have with Trinity College. A study, however, of the list of the Commissioners appointed by Government on this Board, is eminently suggestive. The seven Commissioners of Education, appointed by Government, are the Protestant Bishops of Meath and Limerick, and the Rev. John Grey Porter; the two Presbyterian ministers, Rev. Lowry E. Berkeley, now Moderator of the General Assembly, and Rev. Dr. Kirkpatrick; Master Brooke; and a solitary Catholic—Mr. Justice Fitzgerald. One is fairly puzzled to imagine how Judge Fitzgerald comes to find himself in such company. His colleagues might certainly be excused were they to ask what business he can have among them. They are all Protestants. The Legislature plainly intended that the schools should be " regulated" for the benefit of Protestants, by a Protestant Commission. It cannot then be for any imaginary advantage to Catholics that he has been placed there. But this only intensifies the paradox, and suggests the question, what brings him there at all?

Now let us turn to the list of " Commissioners of National Education in Ireland", under whose control the Model Schools are placed, and who are incorporated, as their Charter states, for administering the funds for the *Education of the poor in Ireland.* They are twenty in number:—ten Catholics, six Episcopalian Protestants, and four Presbyterians, all appointed directly by Government and removable at pleasure. The Catholics are:—Lord O'Hagan, Chief Justice Monahan, Chief Baron Pigot, Judge Fitzgerald, Judge Morris, Mr. Waldron, Mr. Lentaigne, Inspector General of Prisons, Mr. John O'Hagan, Chairman of Quarter Sessions for Leitrim, and Mr Preston, brother to Lord Gormanstown. There is one vacancy among the Catholic Commissioners, owing to the recent death of the lamented Earl of Dunraven. The Protestants are:— the Marquess of Kildare, Judge Lawson, Judge Longfield, Professor Jellett of Trinity College, and the Right Hon. Alexander Macdonnell, the Resident Commissioner. The vacancy occasioned by the death of Sir Maziere Brady, has not yet been filled up. The Presbyterians are:—Rev. Dr. Henry, President of the Queen's College, Belfast, Rev. Charles Morell, Moderator of the General Assembly at the time of his appointment, Mr. James Gibson, and Mr. James Murland, both barristers, resident in Dublin.*

Of the Catholics, *five* are judges, whose time, it may be fairly presumed, is already fully occupied by

* See note at the end of the chapter.

the business of their courts. Mr. Preston does not reside in Dublin, and his attendance is just what might be expected. Mr. Lentaigne is not only Inspector General of Prisons, but also Inspector of Reformatories, and has the whole charge of bringing into working order the new system of Industrial Schools. Mr. John O'Hagan, besides having his Quarter Sessions to attend to, is in the very front and most active rank of his profession. Mr. Waldron is Chairman of one principal Railway Company, and Director of another, besides being a member of several boards. Surely these three gentlemen might fairly plead the extent and engrossing character of their occupations in explanation of the impossibility of watching all the proceedings of the Education Office and of attending regularly the meetings of the Board. Nevertheless all three, together with Lord O'Hagan, are conspicuous above most of their colleagues for comparative frequency of attendance. Indeed, we believe, of all the unpaid Commissioners, Mr. Lentaigne is oftenest present at the meetings of the National Board.

Now let us look at the Protestant contrasts. Judge Longfield and Professor Jellett have, to say the least, no occupations which ought to prevent their regular attendance. Professor Jellett has the reputation among "outsiders" of being thoroughly acquainted with every thing however trivial that passes through the Education Office. Of Mr. Macdonnell, the Resident Commissioner, we need say nothing. Dr. Henry and Rev. Mr. Morell attend, we believe, to the full satisfaction of their Presbyterian co-religionists; the expenses of their attendance being, we understand, regularly defrayed out of the *Parliamentary vote for National Education.* Mr. Gibson's attendance is second only to that of Mr. Lentaigne. Mr. Murland's is also, we believe, unexceptionable.

Thus, scarcely any of the Catholic Commissioners can attend the meetings of the Board without great inconvenience to themselves or to the public. But the mischief does not stop here. Even when they do attend the meetings, they can exercise no effective or continuous supervision over the course of business, by reason of their necessary dependence for information upon their Protestant colleagues. On the other hand, a majority of the Protestant Commissioners, including *all the Presbyterians*, can attend with regularity.

Those anticipations are fully borne out by the facts. We here subjoin a table showing the total number of meetings of the Board which each Commissioner of National Education attended, during the seven years from 1861 to 1867, and the per-centage which such actual attendance is upon the total number of meetings held. We must premise that Lord Bellew died at the close of 1866, so that he was a member of the Board for only six out of the seven years. Master Murphy resigned in 1863, and Judge Fitzgerald was appointed in succession in 1864; so that together they fill one place of Commissioner; hence their successive attendances are united in the table. Similarly, Dean Meyler died at the beginning of 1864, and was immediately succeeded by Mr Thomas Preston; their successive attendances are consequently united in the table. In the same way, Dr. Andrews was succeeded in 1865 by Mr. Murland, and their attendances are united. The table itself is compiled from a return of the National Board to the Primary Education Commission (vol. vii. p. 7).

We ought perhaps to observe further, that since the date of the return, Mr. Justice Morris has been appointed in succession to Lord Bellew; Professor Jellett, to the Bishop of Derry; and the Rev. Mr. Morell, to the Rev. Mr. Hall, who went to America at the close of 1867.

TABLE

Showing for the Seven Years, from 1861-'67, the total number of meetings of the National Board; the number at which each Commissioner was actually present; and the per-centage which such attendance is of the total number of Meetings held.

Names of the Commissioners of National Education during seven years, from 1861 to 1867.	Religious Denomination of Commissioner.	Ordinary Meetings			Special Meetings.	
		Total Number of Meetings held.	Number actually attended.	Percentage of attendance on total Number of Meetings.	Total Number held.	Number actually attended.
Right Hon. A. Macdonnell	E. C.	289	257	88.9	17	17
Mr. Lentaigne	R. C.	289	198	68.5	17	12
Rev. Dr. Hall	Presb.	289	176	60.9	17	9
Mr. Gibson	Presb.	289	161	55.7	17	11
Mr. John O'Hagan	R. C.	289	146	50.5	17	9
Mr. Waldron	R. C.	289	126	43.6	17	9
Lord O'Hagan	R. C.	289	122	42.2	17	8
Judge Longfield	E. C.	289	110	38	17	10
Mr. Andrews [Four years. Attendance fifty times.] Mr. Murland [Three years. Attendance, fifty-two times.]	Presb.	289	102	35.2	17	8
Right Hon. M. Brady	E. C.	289	99	34.2	17	11
Judge Lawson	E. C.	289	95	32.9	17	6
Marquis of Kildare	E. C.	289	74	25.6	17	5
Rev. Dr. Henry	Presb.	289	73	25.2	17	6
Chief Justice Monahan	R. C.	289	50	17.3	17	5
Master Murphy [Three years. Attendance, seven times.] Judge Fitzgerald [Four years. Attendance, thirty-four times.]	R. C.	289	41	14.2	17	5
Dean Meyler [Three years. Attendance, four times.] Mr. Preston [Four years. Attendance, thirty times.]	R. C.	289	34	11.7	17	2
Earl of Dunraven	R. C.	289	29	10	17	3
Chief Baron Pigot	R C.	289	26	9	17	1
Bishop of Derry (Dr. Higgin)	E. C.	289	25	8.6	17	3
Lord Bellew. [Six years.]	R. C.	250	19	6.5	16	1

We do not think a more melancholy record than this table could be produced. Omitting all reference to the Resident Commissioner, we find that of the nineteen unpaid Commissioners, only *four* have attended half the number of meetings. Of the remaining fifteen, *seven* have attended less than one-fourth. Referring more particularly to the Catholics, *two* only have attended half the number of meetings; while *six* have attended less than one-fourth. Comment would be superfluous upon such figures. At the same time there is a possible misconception, or rather a way of misstating the case, which ought to be guarded against. The Catholics of Ireland have reason for most honest indignation, that out of ten Catholic Commissioners, six have been absent from three-fourths of the meetings of the National Board No one acquainted with those gentlemen, with their characters and their occupations, would think of saying that they have not attended as often as they could, or that they have deliberately absented themselves. The real ground of complaint is, that persons have been selected who could not attend, and that they have been permitted to continue to hold office after the impossibility of their fulfilment of its duties had been demonstrated by experience. Will any one say that a person who can be present at only four meetings of the National Board, out of forty in the year, ought to remain on the list of Commissioners? or that it is not the duty of the Government which nominates the Board, and can remove it at pleasure, to interfere in such cases of conspicuous non-attendance, and find persons better suited to administer the great trust of overseeing the Primary Education of nearly a million of Irish children?

But defective attendance is not the only grave shortcoming of which Catholics have to complain with respect to the organization of the National Board. The whole control of the ordinary administration of the National System is in the hands of the Resident Commissioner, a Protestant; and although he has, deservedly, an unblemished reputation for honourable feeling and high principle, still, as he himself admitted to the Primary Education Commissioners (*Evidence*, 23,970, 23,971), the Catholics of Ireland may justly complain that the control of the funds for the education of over three quarters of a million of Catholic children should be in Protestant hands. We merely note the fact that the Secretary's department is to all purposes exclusively Protestant. There is a nominal Catholic Secretary; but he never attends a meeting of the Board, so that the Commissioners are quite dependent upon the Protestant Secretary, who has also, we believe, the whole charge of the "correspondence" with Managers, etc. We likewise merely note that the chief clerks of the several departments into which the National Education Office is divided, are Protestants. Rumours are rife of Orange and Freemason Lodges finding a congenial home within the precincts, and enjoying all but the highest official countenance, to the great discomfort of those whom conscience keeps without the magic circle of the initiated. These are things, which, of course, no man ventures even to palliate. Yet they have no place in Mr. Gladstone's register of our grievances.

To return to the Commissioners themselves, there is another point which forces itself upon our consideration when we go over the list of the National Board. The Protestants are all truly representative men; they have been by the votes of their co-religionists, or by some equivalent act, placed in a position of a representative character. Can this be said of the Catholic Commissioners? What Catholic Commissioner holds a position in connexion with education equivalent to that of Rev. Dr. Jellett, a Professor and Fellow of Trinity College, and President of the Royal Irish Academy? The total number of the Presbyterian children on the rolls of National Schools in the year 1868, was, according to the report of the National Board for that year, 107.401; while the total of Catholic children was 782,984, or more than seven times the number of Presbyterians. Yet there is not a single Catholic Commissioner who holds, with regard to the body of Irish Catholics, a position in the faintest degree comparable with the representative position of Dr. Henry or Rev. Mr. Morell among Presbyterians; nor with the representative character accorded to Mr. Gibson by the applauding votes of the Presbyterian General Assembly last May. And yet fatal as is this want of truly representative character in the Catholic Commissioners, their poverty of attendance, or the impossibility of their attending properly, is, as we have just seen, even more conspicuous.

The question naturally suggests itself, whence comes this marked difference in the selection of Catholics and Protestants? The Protestants are all, not only eminently representative men, but further they appear to have been selected because they are able to attend to the business entrusted to them. And this at once leads us to the law, or principle, which appears to govern the selection of those Commissioners, and which is faithfully observed by every Government, whether Whig or Tory. When Protestant Commissioners have to be appointed, men are selected who, in general, are qualified for the office, acquainted with the business to be managed, and possessing sufficient leisure to be able to attend to it. Hence a Protestant Commission is always, as a whole, effective and practical:—

witness the Church Temporalities Commission. But when circumstances require the appointment of a mixed Commission, a Mephistophelean ingenuity presides over the choice of Catholics. Whatever be the matter in hand, judges are sure to be selected, and the Chiefs in preference to the others, simply, it would seem, because having most court business, they can have least time to spare for attendance to the duties of the Commission. In this way we find Chief Justice Monahan and Chief Baron Pigot on the Senate of the Queen's University, as well as on the National Board, as if the being a chief judge implied an innate capacity to regulate the whole educational system of the country, from the lowest elementary school to the highest teaching of the University. Next in order of eligibility after judges, come barristers, no matter what may be the subject in hand—from the re-constitution of a Church to the propagation of fishes; from the inspection of the literary condition of schools, to the taking a census of the population—as if the legal profession necessarily implied a profound acquaintance with the *omne scibile*. Next comes a select category of a few high officials who have breathed the Castle air sufficiently long to justify the presumption that they are thoroughly impregnated with its influence, and are imbued with the "*odic*" force which will gently impel and restrain them as may be desirable. And then come such other persons as have already given proof of the requisite pliancy of disposition. A Catholic of original views and independent principles has no chance of selection, even though he were a judge, a barrister, or an official.

If any one questions this description, let him inspect the lists of the several Commissions or Boards upon which Catholics figure along with Protestants. Can it for an instant be pretended that the Catholic members of those bodies have been selected because of their acquaintance with the business, or of their qualifications for managing it properly, and still less for their being representatives of the Catholic body, or of any influential section within it? Is this the way in which the Government in England appoints members of English public boards? Have the English judges charge of the education of their country? Nay, even in Ireland, are Protestant judges selected to fill vacancies on boards?

If the Irish people were polled, will any one say, that five judges would be put in charge of the Primary Education of the nation? There is no use in Irish Catholics disguising to their own souls a truth known to all Europe. The British nation, the British Government, and preëminently the "Great Liberal Party" in England and Scotland, hate our Irish Catholicity. But they like to make a mighty show of liberality in the eyes of Europe, by flaunting the names of a few Irish Catholics as vouchers for it. This costs them nothing; we pay the price.

Do we want any fresh evidence of the evil consequences which flow from the conduct of such Catholics? Let us turn to last year's Report of the Commissioners of Education for the Endowed Schools. In this Report the Commissioners state that in their preceding annual Report they had " brought under the notice of the Government the fact that the powers conferred upon them are very defective"; that they had pressed "certain suggestions, the adoption of which appeared to them to be absolutely necessary". They continue as follows:—

"We then urged the advantage that would arise from conferring upon this Commission much enlarged powers, such as that of appointing, removing, and superannuating the masters and ushers of the different schools and a greater extent of control over the school proceedings, and their arrangements generally. We stated that in our opinion the funds which constitute the respective endowments should be fully confided to this Board, and that the Commissioners should have power to employ them for the benefit of such other schools as they might think judicious, and not to confine them to individual schools, as is now the case; that the Exhibitions and Scholarships conferred by us should not, as is under the present law necessary, be restricted to pupils educated at particular schools, but should, under certain regulations, be thrown open to a general competition amongst youths educated at other schools".

These recommendations, referred to so quietly, and so adroitly, are neither more nor less than a proposal to reconstruct the system of Irish Intermediate Education in the way which was recommended nearly fourteen years ago by *three* out of the *five* Endowed Schools' Commissioners of 1858. This would be the establishment of a great series of Intermediate Schools, all of which should be Seminaries of Mixed Education, all to be feeders of a re-modelled Trinity College and of the Queen's Colleges, all to be constructed on the same principle, and leading to the same object, and all to be administered by "*the Commissioners of Education for Ireland*".

We do not mean to dwell on the cool effrontery of this proposal. We only observe that the report is dated June 1871, and is signed as follows:—

"M. G. Armagh.
James Whiteside, Chief Justice.
H. Lloyd, D.D., Provost T.C.D.
J. D. Fitzgerald.
William Brooke.
Lowry E. Berkeley.
William B. Kirkpatrick, D.D.
  Wm. Cotter Kyle, LL.D. M.R.I.A.,
          Secretary".

It is a symmetrical arrangement; remarkable not merely because the one Catholic of the Commission—Judge Fitzgerald—is preceded and followed by three Protestants, but more so, if possible, on account of the individual names which precede and follow his. The Primate, the Chief Justice, and the Provost are on one side, the two Presbyterians and Master Brooke on the other, and the Catholic judge holding the balance between them!!

That the recommendations of Judge Fitzgerald and his brother " Commissioners of Education" will be adopted is beyond belief. We think we know the temper of our countrymen sufficiently well to feel that the attempt, if made, must fail. But the Government ought to be made to recognize that, when Judge Fitzgerald and other Catholic Commissioners sign similar state-papers, they are not representatives of the Catholic opinion of Ireland.

[While these sheets are passing through the Press, we learn that the vacancies in the National Board have been filled up, and other changes have been made. Mr. Macdonnell, Resident Commissioner since May 1839, has retired. Mr· Keenan, for some years Chief of Inspection, succeeds Lord Dunraven. Lord Monck succeeds Sir M. Brady; and Primate Beresford succeeds Mr. Macdonnell. Mr. Keenan becomes *Resident* in lieu of Mr. Macdonnell. It would be quite foreign to our purpose to comment upon these appointments. We may, however, observe that the appointment of Mr. Keenan cannot alter the facts, to which reference has been made in this chapter.]

CHAPTER XII.

THE EDUCATIONAL PENAL CODE, PAST AND PRESENT.

From the sixteenth century, public instruction exclusively Protestant. Legislation designed to crush all Catholic teaching. Notable declaration of Ulster Catholics in their "Remonstrance" to Charles I., in 1641.

Systematic legislation against Catholic education commenced in 1665. Any Papist teaching subject to imprisoment and fine.

Statute, 7 William III. c. 4, passed in 1695 It deals with two difficulties: prohibits, 1° the sending children of Papists abroad to be educated, under pain of deprivation of all civil rights, the forfeiture of real estates during life, and of "goods and chattels" for ever; 2° Papists to teach either publicly in a school, or in a private family, under penalty of fine and imprisonment. This Act permits *any* justice of the peace to summon any one *suspected* of sending a child abroad, or of remitting money to any foreign place of education, to appear before him, and if he thought the offence probable, to commit him for trial. At the Quarter Sessions *susp cted person required to prove his innocence*; failing to do so, was to be adjudged guilty, and punished accordingly. Similar conviction and penalties to be recorded against the *absent* child.

Act, 2 Anne, c. 6, passed in 1703, prohibits the sending Popish children abroad for any purpose, without license; permits any two justices of the peace to call on any Papist to produce any of his children within two months; failing to do so he was to be adjudged guilty of having sent the child abroad to be educated, with the usual penalties for himself and child. Small chance of justice for an Irish Papist in the half century or more after the Williamite wars.

Act 8th Anne, c. 3, passed in 1709, shews previous legislation to have been ineffective. Even Protestant schoolmasters employed Popish assistants, so that Popery did "continue to grow and was propagated in the realm". Object of this Statute to prohibit any Popish person from teaching publicly or privately, or acting as assistant to a Protestant schoolmaster, under pain of being "taken to be a Popish regular clergyman", and punished accordingly, *i.e.*, by transportation, or a traitor's death; £10 reward for the discovery of a Popish schoolmaster; local magistrates may call on any Papist sixteen years of age to give information.

In 1727, the 1st George II., c. 20, makes "converts" to Protestantism, failing to bring up their children Protestants, sub-

ject to the disabilities of Papists; in 1739, Protestants permitting their children to be educated Papists made subject to all the disabilities imposed upon Papists. In 1745, the 19th George II., c. 7, orders promulgation of Penal Statutes at Assizes and Quarter Sessions.
For thirty-six years no change made in the now completed educational penal code. Penal laws all framed in England, and sent over to Ireland simply to be enacted; Irish Parliament could not alter a word in the bill transmitted from England. Nearly all passed within the half-century following the Revolution of 1688, effected expressly to secure "Civil and Religious Liberty".
First relaxation in 1782. A Papist was permitted to teach, provided he had a license from the Protestant Bishop and did not teach Protestants; but no "Popish university, college, or endowed school" to be allowed "in this realm".
In 1792 Papists admitted to legal profession. Protestants allowed to marry Popish wives and bring up children Papists. Popish schoolmaster dispensed from seeking licence to teach from Protestant Bishops.
In 1793 general removal of disabilities. Power given to establish a second college in the University of Dublin, all offices in which were to be open to Catholics. Catholics admitted to be students in Trinity College, and to take degrees in the University of Dublin, but excluded from the governing body and emoluments of Trinity College. Narrow spirit in which the Act was carried out.
In 1795, Maynooth College established by Act of Parliament; not a complete measure; object of its establishment; only first of a series stopped by the Union. Endowment of cut down to one-half by British Parliament. Act of 1793 never fully carried out. Improvement stopped by Union.
In 1829, Catholic Emancipation Act; only gives power to Catholics to hold *some* of the offices from which they were excluded by the Act of 1793; reënacts several penal disabilities of Catholics; contains a clause disabling Catholics to hold any place in connexion with higher education which they could not have legally held at date of passing of the Act. This disabling clause, still in force, renders a Catholic University, or College for higher education, a violation of the law; Catholics who teach the subjects of higher education still legally liable to the penalties enacted against Popish regulars—*i.e. transportation and death.*
In 1845 Queen's Colleges founded, ostensibly as a boon to Catholics. Principle of every relaxation of the penal code:—Catholics to be educated by Protestants, but not by themselves. With the exception of admission to Trinity College, and the estab-

lishment of Maynooth, Catholic education legally in the same position as eighty years ago. Extract from Report on "the Popery Laws" of Committee of United Irishmen in 1792; applicable to present time.
Protestants have exclusive management of a University and College with an unparalleled endowment. Thirty thousand pounds contributed annually by the State for colleges and university for those who ignore religious teaching. Catholics have no pecuniary help, nor state recognition, and are liable to the severest punishments for teaching their fellow-Catholics.
Acknowledgment by Mr. Gladstone that this is indefensible. Declaration of Mr. Fortescue, that we must have "complete religious equality". This impossible so long as Catholics cannot educate their own youth, and are deprived of the assistance which the State has provided for others.

We have hitherto considered the steps taken by the English Government to pervert the Irish people, by supplying them with a system of education which, had it been received by them, must have brought about a huge national apostasy. We have seen how, steadily and perseveringly, from the sixteenth century, those who ruled Ireland used every effort to render public instruction, from the highest to the lowest branches of it, exclusively Protestant, and to disseminate that instruction over the whole face of the land. For this object statute after statute was passed; public money granted, and private benefactions facilitated and encouraged. Yet, notwithstanding all this, the system failed egregiously, and that for two principal reasons—the wonderful steadfastness of the Irish people in rejecting the gift of the enemy, and the incredible wastefulness and corruption with which the system was administered by those to whom the carrying out of its details was entrusted. We have now to turn our attention to another phase of our subject. Protestant legislation upon this question of Irish education was conceived in no spirit of incompleteness. It was not enough for it to seize upon the public funds, to establish a system, to place a temptation in the way of every Irish Catholic who wished to acquire even the humblest rudiments of learning. All this would have been work but half done. Something more was to be attempted before the plan could be considered complete, and accordingly side by side with the legislation which created or sought to create one system, arose the legislation which had for its aim to crush the other.

We shall have briefly to review this legislation; not for the purpose of recalling the bitter memories of those evil times, but because we cannot complete our sketch of the actual condition of Intermediate Education without considering the obstacles which Catholics have had to overcome in their effort to provide for themselves that education from which the State so persistently excluded them.

For many years after the introduction of Protestantism into Ireland, we do not find in the Irish statute-book any laws directly inflicting penalties upon those who were bold enough to engage in the business of Catholic education. Considering, however, the height the royal perogative had attained during the reigns of Elizabeth, James I., and Charles I., the spirit which animated as well those sovereigns as their representatives in this country, and the stringent nature of Queen Elizabeth's Act of Uniformity, we can have no doubt that when it suited the purposes of our governors, they had means enough always at hand to close any Catholic school, at all events in the cities where their authority was best settled. In fact we find the northern Catholics in 1641, in their "humble remonstrance" to the King, stating as one of the grievances which had driven them to take up arms, that the "youth of this kingdom, especially of us Catholics, is debarred from education and learning, in that no schoolmaster of our religion is admitted to be bred beyond the seas, and the one only university of Ireland doth exclude all Catholics, thereby to make us utterly ignorant of literature and civil breeding, which always followeth learning and arts, insomuch that we boldly affirm we are the most miserable and most unhappy nation of the Christian world".

It is needless, of course, to say that during the melancholy years which elapsed from the downfall of the Kilkenny Confederation to the Restoration, the whole policy of the law was the sternest repression of everything which savoured of Catholicism. But the regular systematic legislation against any education, save that which was protected by the government itself, commenced in the reign of Charles II., and continued down to that of the second George. During this period we find a chain of acts of Parliament, the provisions of which can only be designated as ferocious, levelled, directly or indirectly, against Catholic Education. The first of them is the 17 and 18 Car. II., c. 6 (A.D. 1665) intituled, "An act for the Uniformity of Public Prayers and Administration of the Sacraments, etc." By the 5th section of this statute "Every public Professor and Reader in any Universities, Colledge, or Colledges, which are, or shall be within this realm . . . and every Schoolmaster keeping any publique or private school, and every person instructing, or teaching any youth in any house or private family as a tutor or schoolmaster", is required to subscribe a declaration or acknowledgment, declaring, among other matters, that he will "conform to the liturgie of the Church of Ireland, as it is now by law established". The 6th section enacts "that every schoolmaster or other person instructing or teaching youth in any private house or familie as a tutor, or schoolmaster, be required to take the oath of allegiance and supremacie, which oath is to be administered by the ordinarie". And

"If any person shall instruct or teach any youth as a tutor or schoolmaster before licence obtained from his respective ordinarie of the diocess . . . and before such subscription . . . as aforesaid, and before such taking of the oaths of allegiance and supremacie . . . he shall for the first offence suffer three months' imprisonment without bail or mainprize, and for every second and other such offence shall suffer three months' imprisonment without bail or mainprize, and also forfeit to his Majesty the sum of five pounds".

It may, perhaps, be said that this statute was directed rather against the Presbyterians and other Protestant Dissenters than against the Catholics, but its terms were wide enough to embrace all, and the 6th Geo. I., c 5, relieved Dissenters (excepting Unitarians) from the penalties inflicted by it, expressly leaving "Papists" subject to those penalties (sect. 13.)

The Act of Charles II., to which we have just referred, was passed in 1665. Just thirty years later, in 1695, was passed the statute 7 Wm. III., c. 4, intituled "An Act to Restrain Foreign Education". This enactment grapples with two mischiefs. Some of the unhappy Irish had got accustomed to send their children to foreign schools; others, it would seem, found means, in spite of the Act of Uniformity, to have them educated at home. Both were crimes intolerable in a land which had just been delivered by the ever blessed William from the thraldom of Popery, brass money, and wooden shoes. Accordingly, the first section of the act deals with the question of "foreign education", which it was desirable to restrain. It recites that—

"Many of the subjects of this kingdom have accustomed themselves to send their children and other persons under their care into France, Spain, and other foreign parts not under his Majesty's obedience, to be educated, instructed, and brought up; by means and occasion whereof the said children and other persons have, in process of time, engaged themselves in foreign interests, and been prevailed upon to forget the natural duty and allegiance due from them to the Kings and Queens of this realm, and the affection which they owe to the established religion and laws of this their native country, and returning so evilly disposed into this kingdom, have been in all times past the movers and promoters of many dangerous seditions, and oftentimes of open rebellion".

It then enumerates various classes of persons who are the objects of the enactment. One consists of his Majesty's subjects who shall go, or shall convey or send any child or other person, into any foreign country, "to the intent and purpose to enter into or be resident or trained up in any priory, abbey, nunnery, Popish university, college, or school, or house of Jesuits or Priests". Another consists of those subjects who shall go or be conveyed

"into any parts beyond the seas out of the King's obedience, to the intent and purpose, to be resident or trained up in any Popish family, and shall be, in such parts beyond the seas, by any jesuite, seminary priest, fryar, monk, or other Popish person, instructed, persuaded, or strengthened in the Popish religion, in any sort to profess the same".

And finally we have the offenders who shall presume to " convey or send or cause to be conveyed or sent . . . any sum or sums of money or other thing", for the maintenance of any child or other person who is being educated abroad. All these persons are subjected to the following penalties:

"They shall be for ever disabled to sue, bring, or prosecute any action, bill, plaint, or information in course of law, or to prosecute any suit in any court of equity, or to be guardian or executor, or administrator to any person, or capable of any legacy or deed of gift, or to bear any office within the realm".

In a word they are to be deprived of every civil right. Even the right to existence is reduced as far as possible to a shadow; for the offender is not only made incapable of receiving property, or of defending it if it is attacked, he is further to lose "all his goods and chattels which he has, or which any person has in trust for him", and is to forfeit all his real estate during his life. This certainly was a formidable body of penalties to risk for the sake of education. At the same time, we can imagine that if the unfortunate Irish Papist had been allowed to find instruction for his children in schools or colleges at home, he might have taken heart, and, regretfully though it might be, have renounced the advantages to be derived from the lectures of renowned continental professors. But it was resolved, in the words of the old northern Catholics, "to make them utterly ignorant of literature and civil breeding". The Catholic was no more to be educated at home than abroad, unless he chose to barter his faith for the learning of the stranger, *et propter vitam vivendi perdere causas;* and the question of home education comes to be dealt with, in its turn, in the ninth section of the same statute. This section recites that—

"It is found by experience that tolerating and conniving at Papists keeping schools or instructing youth in literature, is one great reason of many of the natives of this kingdom continuing ignorant of the principles of true religion, and strangers to the Scriptures, and of their neglecting to conform themselves to the laws and statutes of this realm, and of their not using the English habit and language, to the great prejudice of the public weal thereof".

Having thus stated the mischief to be remedied, it enacts:

" that no person whatsoever of the Popish religion shall publicly teach school, or instruct youth in learning, or in private houses teach or instruct youth in learning within this realm from henceforth, except only the children or others under the guardianship of the master or mistress of such private house or family, upon pain of £20, and also being committed to prison without bail or mainprize for the space of three months for every such offence".

So determined was the legislature to cut off every chance of receiving a Catholic education, that *any justice* of the peace was empowered, by this same Act, 7th Wm. III., ch. 4, sec. 2, to summon before him any one *suspected* of having sent a child to be educated abroad, or money to defray the expenses of such education, or to help in any way to support a foreign place of education, and to examine him concerning the grounds of such suspicion. If the justice considered it probable that the suspected person had committed any of those heinous deeds, he was to bind him over in sufficient sureties to appear before the next quarter sessions. If it should appear *probable* that the sending of either child or money was for the purposes of Catholic education, then the suspected person was called upon to show where the child was, and to clear up the purpose for which the money was sent. Failing to do so, a conviction was to be recorded against him, and he became liable to all the penalties of the act, including the forfeiture of all goods and chattels *for ever*, and lands for life. Further, a similar conviction, with the same penalties, was to be recorded against the *child sent*, although necessarily absent.

But in spite of this Act, the Popish schoolmaster appears to have been as irrepressible as the Popish priest. Popish parents, too, *would* run the risk of loss of property and civil rights, and send their children to seek instruction abroad. The Protestant citizen also either was not so cruel as the Protestant ruler, or else found that it was for his interest not to enforce these cruel laws too severely. The complaint of connivance at Popish teaching is common in the penal statutes, and is often put forward as the motive for passing them The result was that in 1703, an Act was passed, 2nd of Anne, c. 6, " to prevent the further growth of Popery", the first section of which provides that any Popish person sending his child abroad, without special license of the Lord Lieutenant *and four Privy Councillors*, was to be deemed guilty of sending him to receive a Popish education, and to incur all the penalties of the 7th William III., section 4. And by the second section of this Act of Anne, it was provided that any of the judges of the courts of law, or any two justices of the peace, may call before them the parent or guardian of any child *suspected* to have been so sent abroad without license, and require that the child be produced within two months. If the child be not so produced, and *proof be not given* that the child is in England, Scotland, or Ireland, *and not abroad*, then " *such child* shall be deemed to be then educated in foreign parts, contrary to the aforesaid act, and shall incur all the penalties and disabilities in said acts mentioned".

What damning evidence of the ruthlessness of penal legislation is borne by those two acts, the 7th William III., c. 4, and the 2nd Anne, c. 6! The ascendant faction which then governed this country were so bent on rooting out the religion of the people, that they scrupled not to employ any means, however at variance with their own principles, which could help them to their end. One of the great principles of British law is, that every man is assumed to be innocent until proved to be guilty. But where Papists were concerned this was to be read backwards. The suspicion of their having transgressed the law was *prima facie* sufficient to uphold their guilt in a court of justice. They were assumed to be guilty, unless they could prove to the satisfaction of their tyrants the legal innocence of their acts. They were further called upon to give evidence against themselves, and to disprove suspicions. Nay, more, the *absent child*, who would not in any rational system of jurisprudence be held responsible for acts which he could not control, was *convicted*, and penalties decreed against him which amounted to a wiping out of his civil existence. It requires no great acquaintance with Irish affairs, nor great force of imagination, to understand whether "suspicions" could be lightly raised against Papists in the half-century succeeding the Williamite wars, and whether once raised they could be easily dispelled. We need not go far for an impartial witness. The Cornwallis correspondence gives terrible evidence of the poor chance an Irish Papist had, even a hundred and ten years after the battle of the Boyne, of justifying himself in the eyes of the "loyal" Protestants of the time.

In 1709 we find a statute which bears witness at once to the comparative impotence of the efforts theretofore made against Catholic education, and to the determination of the government to suppress it at any cost to humanity and national feeling. This statute, the 8th Anne, c. 3, is of curious interest, were it only for the picture which it gives of the means adopted to evade the previous laws. From its recitals it appears that the ninth section of the act (7th William III., c. 4), "to restrain foreign education", had proved utterly ineffectual; that in spite of the penalties imposed by it, many of the Popish religion did continue to keep public schools for the instruction of youth; and that when prosecuted for the offence in one county, they betook themselves to another and kept school there. Further, it would seem that not merely did Popish schools, properly so called, continue to exist, but that many Protestant schools were running great danger of losing their Protestant character and drifting into downright Popery. It complains in the sixteenth section that—

"Several Protestant schoolmasters, to increase the numbers of their scholars, do chuse to combine with such Papists rather than prosecute such Popish schoolmasters, and, to elude the said act, do entertain such persons professing the Popish religion to be ushers, under-masters, or assistants, to teach and instruct youth in learning under such *Protestant schoolmasters, who frequently thereby become negligeut of their said schools, and leave the instruction of the youth, as well the Protestant as Popish scholars, to the care and instruction of such Popish under-schoolmaster, usher, or assistant, so by them entertained and allowed, whereby Popery doth continue to grow and is propagated in this kingdom*".

Of course such an evil as this required a strong remedy, and it was unhesitatingly applied; for the section enacts that—

"Whatsoever person of the Popish religion shall publicly teach school, or shall instruct youth in learning in any private house within this realm, or shall be entertained to instruct youth in learning as usher, under-master, or assistant, by any Protestant schoolmaster, he shall be esteemed and taken to be a Popish regular clergyman, and be prosecuted as such, and incur such pains, penalties and forfeitures as any Popish regular convict is liable to by the laws and statutes of this realm".

And by the 9th Wm. III., c. 1, those penalties were *transportation*, and in case of return to the country, *death*, with drawing and quartering, as for the crime of high treason. The Act (8th Anne, c. 3) contains provisions for compelling schoolmasters to take the oaths of allegiance and abjuration, under a penalty of 10*l.*, recoverable at the suit of a common informer, and also gives minute directions for carrying out the penalty of transportation against " Popish schoolmasters", with which, after the point at which we have arrived, it is scarcely necessary to trouble our readers.

By the twenty-first section of this same Act, it was also provided that every person "making discovery" of a Popish schoolmaster, shall receive a reward of 10*l.*, to be " levied from the Popish inhabitants of the county where the schoolmaster taught" or resided. Further, any two justices of the peace were authorised to summon before them any " Popish person of the age of sixteen years and upwards", and examine such person "touching the being, residence, and abode of any Popish schoolmaster, tutor, usher, under-master, or assistant to any Protestant schoolmaster, who may be disguised, concealed. or itinerant in the country", and if such person refuse to appear, or to be examined as aforesaid, *such person shall be imprisoned for one year*, unless such person *pays a sum* not above 20*l.* to the poor of the parish. By the twelfth section of this act, all converts to Protestantism who held office under the Crown, or were Members of Parliament, or barristers, attorneys, etc., were required to bring up their children Protestants, under penalty of forfeiture of office, or being incapable to sit in Parliament, or to practise their professions or other avocations.

By the 1st Geo. II., ch. 20, passed in 1727, " converts" not bringing up their children Protestants, were made subject to all the penalties imposed upon Papists; and by the 13th Geo. II., c. 6, section 16, passed in 1739—the same year in which the Charter School system was brought into full operation, by giving it aid from the public funds—it was provided that all Protestants whatsoever, "educating or willingly or knowingly permitting their children to be educated Papists, shall be subject to such disabilities as Papists are". We have already seen that these "disabilities" amounted to a wiping out of civil existence, and a reduction to absolute beggary.

The last act to which we will refer is 19th Geo. II. c. 7, passed in 1745. It recites, sec. 6, that the Act Wm. III. "to restrain foreign education" had not been duly executed, and "to the end that by the strict observance of the said act, and of this present act, the peace of the kingdom may be preserved", it enacts that both acts shall at the assizes for the several counties in Ireland, and at the Dublin quarter sessions, be publicly read in open court by the Clerks of the Crown and Peace respectively, after the grand jury is empanelled and before the charge is given.

The educational penal code was now complete. So far as the law was concerned, in the year 1745, and for thirty-six years afterwards, no person could give his child a Catholic education either at home or abroad. We have designedly confined ourselves to the statutes which had the extirpation of such Catholic education for their avowed object. But, of course, each and every one of the penal laws—especially those which were directed against the Catholic clergy—had indirectly the same end. Where the statute law was animated by this atrocious spirit, it is needless to say that bequests and donations for purposes of Catholic education were against the policy of the law, and were therefore unlawful, and whenever made, the courts of equity discountenanced them by every means in their power. Surely the Catholic who lived when the 8th of Anne, c. 3, was passed, might well repeat the remonstrance of his ancestors, and say, " We may boldly affirm that we are the most miserable and most unhappy nation of the Christian world".

Nearly all those laws, it must not be forgotten, were passed within the half-century after the revolution of 1688, which had been expressly effected in order to secure complete " Civil and Religious Liberty". They were passed during a period of, so far as Ireland was concerned, perfect political calm, without the slightest excuse being afforded by the hapless people, whom the defeat of 1691 had given over to the will of their tyrants. But we ought also, in fairness, to remember that those laws were all planned and every detail of their provisions settled in England, and were only sent over here to be registered as statutes by the Irish Parliament, which had no power to make the slightest alteration in their provisions. Ninety years have not yet passed away since that code was in full vigour. Much of it still remains behind, a legacy of hatred bequeathed by the evil spirit of those bad times to vex posterity. And men exist, and are in high places too, who marvel that its memory rankles still, and that the people of this country have not quite forgotten the terrible legislation, by which it was sought to rob them of their faith and their nationality.

We need not trace in detail the subsequent legislation. The influence of civilization and the force of political circumstance made some relaxation of the penal code inevitable. But how grudgingly and sparingly was it effected! There was no generous measure of enfranchisement, conceived in the spirit of large-hearted statesmanship. Shreds and patches of freedom were all that the intolerance of the age could be induced to concede. And even in granting those mendicant pittances, the traditional thread of the ascendency policy was carefully kept in hand, as the clue that was to guide through the untrodden paths of a halting liberality.

The first relaxation came in 1782, when the efforts of the revolted American colonies had been crowned with success, and the Irish Volunteers had secured the legislative independence of their country. The 21st and 22nd George III., c. 62, after admitting that the laws " relative to the education of Papists . . are considered as too severe", permits Catholics to teach a school. But this pedagogical manumission was subject to two conditions. In the first place, before he could teach, the intending schoolmaster should secure a license from the Protestant bishop of the diocese. In the next place he was prohibited, under all the severe old penalties, to teach a Protestant. Moreover, it was provided that this relaxation was not to " be construed to allow the erection or endowment of any Popish university, college, or endowed school, in this realm".

Ten years passed by without any change, so feeble was Catholic influence, so inveterate was the strength of penal ascendency. In 1792 the first remission of penal legislation worth speaking of took place. By the 32nd of Geo. III. c. xxi., intituled an " Act to remove certain restraints and disabilities, etc.", Papists were permitted to become barristers, attorneys, notaries, and attorneys' clerks. The great condescension was shewn of allowing *Protestant barristers to marry Catholic wives*, and bring up their children Papists, without being debarred from practising their profession:—provided, however, the marriage ceremony was performed by a clergyman of the Established Church. Further, Popish schoolmasters were relieved of the obligation of obtaining a licence to teach from the Protestant bishop, provided the other conditions required by the Act of 1782 were complied with. And, greatest gain of all—the terrible statute, 7 Wm. III., c. 3, was wholly repealed. But it was carefully stipulated that no one should take any benefit under this act, unless he had taken the elaborate oaths of allegiance and abjuration formulated for the special use of Papists in 1773; and Catholics still continued to be forbidden to teach Protestants.

In order to estimate the motives and character of these relaxations, and of others to which we shall presently refer, we must not forget that the French revolution was in course of transaction in 1792; that the Austrians and Prussians were obliged to fall back before the revolutionary armies; and that before the year 1793 was three months old, England was already engaged in a gigantic struggle which strained all her energies and abilities to the utmost.

This year, 1793, was marked by the largest measure of social and political emancipation, which has ever, at one time, been accorded to Catholics in these kingdoms. The Act 33rd Geo., III., c. xxi., accomplishing this result, is intituled, emphatically, "An Act for the *Relief* of his Majesty's Popish or Roman Catholic subjects". The first section enacts that

"His Majesty's subjects being Papists......shall not be subject to any penalties, forfeitures, disabilities, or incapacities......save such as His Majesty's subjects being of the Protestant religion are liable to".

The seventh section enables Roman Catholics

"to hold or take degrees, or any professorship in, or be masters or fellows of any college *to be hereafter founded* in this kingdom, provided that such college shall be a member of the University of

Dublin, [and shall not be founded exclusively for the education of Papists or persons professing the Popish or Roman Catholic religion, nor consist exclusively of masters, fellows, or other persons to be named or elected on the foundation of such college, being persons professing the Popish or Roman Catholic religion,]* or to hold any office or place of trust in, and to be a member of any lay-body corporate, except the college of the holy and undivided Trinity, of Queen Elizabeth, near Dublin",

provided they shall have taken and subscribed the oaths of allegiance and abjuration of 1773, and a further oath and declaration,† specially framed for the occasion, and enacted by this new statute. The words which we have given in italics, excluded Catholics from the governing body and the real honours of Trinity College, even without the special enactment to that effect at the close of the section.

* It is surely noteworthy at the present crisis that the University question, so far as Catholics are concerned, would receive a complete and satisfactory *legal* settlement by the simple repeal of the words which are above included within brackets. In the resolutions, adopted last October by the Irish Catholic Bishops, the same solution was pointed out—perhaps, without advertence to the fact that an Act, passed by the Irish Parliament seventy-nine years ago, made the task an easy one.

† The Declaration contained in this Act, 33 Geo. III. c. xxi., is of singular interest, for the minuteness of its doctrinal engagements, as well as for other reasons. The subscribers to it declare that "it is not an article of the Catholick faith, neither am I thereby required to believe or profess that the Pope is infallible". They also state that "a sincere sorrow for past sins, a firm and sincere resolution to avoid future guilt and to atone to God, are previous and indispensable requisites to establish a well founded expectation of forgiveness; and that any person who receives absolution without these previous requisites, so far from obtaining thereby any remission of his sins, incurs the additional guilt of violating a sacrament". It is rather startling to find a Protestant Parliament imposing a declaration of belief in the efficacy and conditions of the sacrament of penance. Probably there was, at bottom, a more genuine spirit of fair-dealing towards their Catholic fellow-subjects in the Irish Parliament of 1793, than in the Imperial Parliament of 1871.

The eighth section declares Catholics capable of holding any of the professorships of Sir Patrick Dun's hospital, " any law or statute to the contrary notwithstanding". One will naturally ask:—how many Catholics have held those professorships, during the seventy-eight years that have passed by since 1793? The "relief" remained a dead letter; the spirit of exclusion has been as potent and active, as when the statute-book clothed it with legality.

The ninth section enumerates all the positions from which Catholics are to continue to be excluded. They include both Houses of Parliament, every office of trust, emolument, or honour, connected with the government of the country,* and the legal profession, and specifically that of " Provost or fellow of the College of the holy and undivided Trinity of Queen Elizabeth, near Dublin". This last was an excessive precaution, inasmuch as Catholics had been already excluded—both explicitly and by implication—from all offices in Trinity College.

The thirteenth section was, for a long time, looked upon as a sort of Magna Charta by the Catholic middle and professional classes: nay, it still continues to be so regarded by some, who have not been able to rid themselves of the feeling of subserviency, which was the natural inheritance of the penal days. It is as follows:—

"Whereas it may be expedient, in case His Majesty, his heirs and successors, shall be pleased so to alter the statutes of the College of the holy and undivided Trinity, near Dublin, and of the University of Dublin, as to enable persons professing the Roman Catholic religion to enter into or to take degrees in the said University, to remove any obstacle which now exists by statute law; be it

* The measure of 1829 was really only a partial repeal of this ninth section of the act of 1793.

enacted, That from and after the 1st day of June, 1793, it shall not be necessary for any person, upon taking any of the degrees usually conferred by the said University, to make or subscribe any declaration, or to take any oath, save the oaths of allegiance and abjuration ".

The necessary changes in the statutes of Trinity College were immediately made by the royal authority, and Catholics were admitted to study and to take degrees in the University of Dublin; but, as we have just seen, they were specifically excluded from all share in its government and emoluments.

The fourteenth section enacts, that no persons shall take any benefit under the Act, unless they shall have first taken and subscribed the oaths of allegiance and abjuration, enacted in 1773, and also the new declaration first imposed by this present act of 1793. Moreover, the two highly penal acts, 2nd Anne, c. 6, and 8th Anne, c. 3, were only partially repealed, some of their most stringent clauses being left in full force.

It is, really, not possible to exaggerate the boon this imperfect measure of relief must have been felt to be by the Irish Catholics of 1793. Its benefits would indeed have been much greater, than they were actually proved to be in results, had it been interpreted in the large-heartedness which inspired the sweeping reform of the first section. But the cramped and narrow bigotry, which had kept the people of the land in the condition of Helots for 235 years—since the accession of Elizabeth—restricted, as much as possible, the meaning and force of the enabling clauses of the act, and read them side by side with the letter and spirit of the penal laws still unrepealed. The relief granted by the first section would, so far as the natural sense of the words reaches, seem wide enough to include the religious orders, Catholic education in its widest sense, and every Catholic charity and purpose. But the courts of law held, and still hold, otherwise. And—worst of all—this restricted interpretation of what reads like a complete measure of emancipation, bore most pernicious fruit in the imperfect knowledge, the mean ideas, and narrow views of the statesmen of 1800-1829, and in the grudging and paltry concession of 1829.

"In the year 1795, at the opening of the Session of Parliament in Ireland, Lord Fitzwilliam, in his Speech from the Throne, recommended to both Houses to take into serious consideration the imperfect system of education in Ireland, more particularly with respect to persons of the Roman Catholic religion. And Dr. Hussey very soon after came into this country, under the patronage of the Irish Government, to be put at the head of a college, to be founded exclusively for the education of persons of that persuasion of all descriptions. Nothing further passed during Lord Fitzwilliam's stay in Ireland, but soon after Lord Camden's arrival, an Act was passed, appointing Trustees to found a college in Ireland for the education indiscriminately of persons of the Popish religion. An immediate grant was made by Parliament of £8,000 to the trustees, to enable them to purchase a house and other necessary buildings for the accommodation of students....In the Session of 1796 a further grant of £7,000 was made by Parliament to the trustees to enable them to enlarge the accommodations for students, and in the Sessions of 1797 and 1798 two further grants of £10,000 each, were made for the same purpose".*

This Act of 1795, 35 Geo. III., c. xxi., establishing

* Official Memorandum by Lord Clare, then Lord Chancellor of Ireland, dated 28th Dec., 1801, in the *Cornwallis Correspondence*, vol. iii. page 371.

a college for the exclusive education of Catholics, would have been a great step in advance, had it been a complete measure. It was, however, only the first link of what might have become a great educational chain. There is no doubt that it was intended as a sort of fulfilment of the promise of relief, in the matter of higher education, which had been held out to Catholics by the seventh section of the Act of 1793, just referred to. It "was clearly and distinctly understood, as the Act of 1795 imports, to be the foundation of a college for the education of persons of the Popish religion, indiscriminately".* The first section recites:—

"Whereas, by the laws now in force in this Kingdom, it is not lawful to endow any College or Seminary for the education exclusively of persons professing the Roman Catholic religion, and it is now become expedient that a Seminary should be established for that purpose".

It then enacts that certain public personages who were Protestants, six Catholic laymen, ten Catholic bishops, all named, and Dr. Hussey shall be trustees

"for the purpose of establishing, endowing, and maintaining one Academy for the education only of persons professing the Roman Catholic religion;...and to erect and maintain all such buildings as may be necessary for the lodging and accommodation of the president, masters, professors, fellows and students who shall from time to time be admitted into or reside in such academy".

The second section empowers the trustees, or any seven of them, to "appoint one president, and so many masters, *fellows*, professors, and *scholars on the foundation*", as they may consider advisable, and to make such regulations for the filling up of vacancies in those positions, as they may deem proper. The gene-

* *Cornwallis Correspondence*, vol. iii., page 372.

ral purport of the language throughout the whole enactment; the precise enumeration of *masters, fellows,* and *scholars on the foundation,* as distinct from professors and students; the provision as to filling up vacancies;—all suggest, as Lord Clare seems to imply, that the institution was intended to be a college of university studies, and not exclusively for professional training for the priesthood. It was to be allowed to grow, and develope in time, into an institution for Catholics, analogous to what Trinity College was for Protestants, and would thus have been a great improvement on the second *mixed* college contemplated by the seventh section of the Act of 1793. The only restriction imposed was set out in the ninth section, which prohibits "to receive into, or educate, or instruct in the said academy, any person professing the Protestant religion, or whose father professed the Protestant religion", under the usual penalties. But this prohibition is not surprising with respect to an institution founded at that time "for the education exclusively of persons professing the Roman Catholic religion".

On 16th April, 1799, a debate took place in the Irish House of Lords on the proposal of a grant "of 8,000l. to complete the establishment of the Roman Catholic College at Maynooth, for one year, ended on the 25th March, 1800".[*] Objection was taken that hitherto it was a place of purely clerical education, contrary to the intentions of the Legislature when passing the Act of 1795. In this debate, the Chancellor, Lord Clare, admitted that it was understood, "on the original foundation of the College at Maynooth, that it was to be made a seminary for educating the Catholic gentry as well as priests". And in a letter to the Lord-Lieutenant,

* *Cornwallis Correspondence*, vol. iii., page 872.

dated April 18, 1799, he " considered it essential to the public security that there should be a well regulated academy in Ireland for the education of the Roman Catholics".* In the course of the year, an understanding was arrived at, between the Government and the Catholic Bishops, that Maynooth was to be henceforward an institution for lay as well as clerical education; and money was granted by the Irish Parliament to carry out the arrangement. But the Union effectually interfered to prevent the completion of a scheme, which promised fair to secure, in time, a thorough system of higher Catholic education for Irish Catholics. The unreasoning terror of Popery, and the rancorous opposition to what were known as " the Catholic claims", that were so conspicuous in the British Parliament, rekindled the bigotry of the Protestant party in Ireland, which had been fast dying out towards the end of the eighteenth century; so that the men, who had helped to pass the relief acts of 1793 and 1795, resumed a hostility to Catholic interests which they seemed to have abandoned. We have a sad proof of this most melancholy effect of the Union in the solemn and deliberate expression of opinion, addressed on 25th December, 1801, to the then Chief Secretary, Mr. Abbott, by Lord Kilwarden—a man whom tradition has surrounded with a halo of amiability and tender-heartedness

"Lord K [ilwarden] would advise the Crown and Parliament, with a view only to the present race, to govern by a strong military force, and keep down the Catholics by the bayonet; but with a view to posterity, he should wish to educate the Protestants and Catholics together: and such was the object of opening Trinity College to the Catholics".†

* *Cornwallis Correspondence*, vol. iii., pages 91, 92.
† *Ibid.*, vol. iii. page 371.

Thus we find that, seventy years ago, Protestant intolerance was as averse to the education of Catholics by Catholics, as Presbyterian fanaticism is at the present hour. Just as, in the time of James I., men trusted to the Royal Schools for gaining over Catholic youth to Protestantism, while indoctrinating them in the "English habite and order", so, in 1801, they trusted to the influence of Trinity College, and since, and now, to the influence of the Queen's Colleges and the Mixed Model Schools.

It is scarcely necessary to add, that the lay department at Maynooth existed for a very few years only. One of the early legislative effects of the Union was the cutting down the Maynooth endowment by one-half. Thenceforward, for nearly forty years the college had to struggle for existence; so that the ideas which suggested to the Irish Parliament the Maynooth Act of 1795 produced no fruit.

Nor can it be necessary to remind our readers that, beyond the incomplete and abortive attempt of the Act of 1795, the other "college to be hereafter founded", of which, by the seventh section of the Act of 1793, Catholics were permitted to be fellows, etc., has never had more than the ideal existence given to it by that Act.* And thus the measure of educational enfranchisement vouchsafed to Catholics, became really confined to the power to teach a school and to take degrees in the University of Dublin; and it remained so limited down to 1829, nay, even to our own day! With respect to educational liberty, as in political matters, the Union proved an impenetrable barrier to all progress.

* It remains to be seen whether the Government will avail of the easy method of solving the difficulty of Irish University Education, which has been left ready to their hand by the Irish Act of 1793.

The next political relaxation was the great measure of "Catholic Emancipation" in 1829, which was really believed at the time by most persons, and is still regarded by many, as a sort of universal legal rehabilitation of Catholics; whereas, its only relieving effect was to permit Catholics to occupy *some* of the positions and offices from which they had remained excluded under the ninth section of the Relief Act of 1793, while by re-enacting sundry pieces of penal legislation, especially with regard to the regular clergy, it was a reversal of the spirit and the letter of the legislation of 1793. The Emancipation Act contains a clause expressly declaring that Catholics shall not be enabled

"otherwise than they are now by law enabled, to hold, enjoy, or exercise, any office or place whatever, of, in, or belonging to any of the universities of this realm; or any office or place whatever, and by whatever name the same may be called, of, in, or belonging to any of the colleges or halls of the said universities'—10 George IV., cap. vii., sec. 16.

To appreciate exactly the educational position of Catholics, as it has been fixed by this clause—for it is still unaltered, after nearly forty-three years—we must recall how far, in 1829, Catholics were "by law enabled to hold, enjoy, or exercise any office or place" connected with superior education. By the charter granted by Elizabeth to Trinity College, Dublin, it is expressly provided "especially that no other person (but the Provost and Fellows) should teach or profess the liberal arts in Ireland without special license" from the Crown. The Act of 1782 distinctly provided, that the educational relaxations therein granted were not to "be construed to allow the erection or endowment of *any Popish university, college, or endowed school in this realm*". The powers granted by the Maynooth Acts of 1795 and 1800, were expressly limited to the one College. Thus, in 1829, no Catholic could teach the subjects of higher education anywhere outside Maynooth. The operation of the Emancipation Act has been to rivet this educational disfranchisement. Nay, more, since the Act of 1782 repealed the savage penalties of the 8th Anne, c. 3, only in the case of those Catholic teachers who should comply with its provisions,* it follows that any Catholic engaged in superior teaching outside the walls of Maynooth IS TO THIS DAY LIABLE TO THE PENALTIES decreed by the Act of Anne:—

"*Whatsoever person of the Popish religion shall publicly teach school, or shall instruct youth in learning in any private house within this realm,...he shall be esteemed and taken to be a Popish regular clergyman, and to be prosecuted as such, and incur such penalties as any Popish regular convict is liable unto by the laws of this realm*".

This is one of many still existing Catholic disabilities "not generally known". Catholic barristers may climb to the highest legal position in the land; they may fill the bench and hold the great seal. Catholic civilians may hold great offices of trust and influence in the public administration. But a Catholic Professor of the liberal arts—of Greek, of Political Economy, of Mathematics, of Natural Philosophy—is liable, at the whim of any one who may be able to set the law in motion, to severe punishment—even to the

* The Act of 1792 affords no further relief, except the dispensation from procuring a licence to teach from the Protestant Bishop. Neither it, nor the "Relief Act" of 1793, has abrogated the enactment of 1782, which expressly forbids "the erection of any Popish university college or endowed school in this realm"; or the other clauses which continue the prohibition that Papists should teach Protestants.

length of *transportation* and *death*—for his presumption in communicating to his fellow-Catholics the literary information or scientific knowledge which he may have acquired.

The last measure of educational freedom, we are usually told, was the establishment of the Queen's Colleges, where Catholics are offered the benefits of a higher education, subject to the very trifling condition that they shall lay aside all reference to their religion while following their studies; although the Protestant youth, who frequent the halls of Trinity College, have academical opportunities of pursuing their religious and secular studies side by side.

Throughout all these successive relaxations of the old educational penal code we find one idea consistently adhered to. Catholics were never to be allowed to instruct themselves—at least in the subjects of higher education. They might be admitted to receive intellectual alms in the halls belonging as of right to their favoured Protestant fellow-countrymen. But not only were they, and *are they*, forbidden to set up an establishment of their own for higher education, but they are not permitted to pick up the crumbs of emolument, place, and preferment, which fall from the Protestant rich man's table.

It is not with any mischievous desire to rake up evil memories, that we have cast our nets into the bitter waters of the past, and brought those statutes under public notice. But no review of the education question could be complete, without showing over what the Irish people have triumphed, or without calling attention to the heavy educational disabilities which, at the present hour, press upon Catholics. With the exception of admission to Trinity

College, and the establishment of the College of Maynooth—concessions, the value of which we have seen above—the legal position of Catholic education is, at this hour, exactly the same as it was in 1792, or *almost eighty years ago*. In that year the Society of United Irishmen appointed a committee "to inquire and report the Popery laws enacted in this realm", and on the 21st January, the Hon. Simon Butler in the chair, the report of this committee was read and adopted. We quote its concluding paragraphs:—

" Your Committee submit to you this view of the Catholic Penal Statutes, under the galling yoke of which your country has so long, and so patiently languished; statutes unexampled for their inhumanity, their unwarrantableness, and their impolicy. The legislature, which is instituted to protect and cherish the people, has here overspread the land with laws, as with so many traps, to ensnare the subject in the performance of the necessary duties of life. We recognize a free state in the right, exercised by its inhabitants, of framing laws for the security of their liberty and property against all invasion; but with us the order of civil association is reversed, and the law becomes the foe, the ruffian, that violates the rights, and destroys the harmony of society. That this infamous system of political torture, was not warranted by any alleged delinquency on the part of our Catholic brethren, is notorious; for it was devised in times of profound tranquillity. We cannot, then, refrain from acknowledging with sympathy that signal forbearance in our oppressed countrymen, which, joined with a laudable sense of shame in the persons insidiously authorised to give efficacy to these acts, has preserved our country from the calamitous consequences of such flagitious misgovernment.

" As for the *favoured* part of the community, your Committee considering that this code, in its expanded operations over this realm, is utterly subversive of the fundamental principles of the constitution, feel it their duty seriously to inculcate this truth, that our liberties must ever rest on the most precarious foundation, while seven-eighths of our fellow-citizens remain palsied in the exercise of those rights, which were our common inheritance.

"A divided people, governed by foreign influence and domestic corruption, . . . we submit to laws enacted, not only without our consent, but against our declared sense".

This state of things still, in great part, remains. Protestants have a network of institutions for Intermediate Education spread over the land of which they have practically exclusive possession, and absolutely exclusive management. They have the exclusive government of a great university and college, and the exclusive enjoyment of an unparalleled endowment. The State has provided for those who ignore all religious influences in education, three colleges and a university, at an expense of £30,000 a year out of the public taxes, besides Model Schools as seminaries for intermediate instruction, at a further expense, for this purpose alone, to the country of £10,000 a year. But Catholics not only have no pecuniary assistance from the State, to provide them with higher education; they not only have no State recognition of the courses of study and lectures of the University, which at such a heavy cost they have set up and continue to maintain; but they have been driven to do this in spite of the law. It is probable that many, if not all, the Catholic colleges come within the prohibition of the Act of 1782, which forbids any " Popish college, or endowed school"; while the colleges conducted by religious communities are under the further ban of those penal clauses of the Emancipation Act, which proscribe all the regular clergy. At all events, the Professors of the Catholic University deliver their lectures, in defiance of an express clause in that Catholic Relief Act which has made it possible to have Catholic judges. At any moment Dr. Woodlock and his professors may be brought into the Queen's Bench, for daring to teach the Liberal Arts to young Catholics, without having previously secured the legal licence to do so from the Crown. Here is a "sentimental grievance", with a vengeance, which does not seem to have hitherto caught the attention of Mr. Gladstone; and yet this is not the worst feature of the case.

On the 20th June, 1865, in their place in the House of Commons, Mr. Gladstone and Sir George Grey, then Ministers of the Crown, announced that the Government had arrived at the conclusion that Catholics did labour under educational disabilities which ought to be removed. Mr. Gladstone, when out of office, in July, 1866, and again in 1867, repeated the same conclusion as his personal conviction. Again, on the 1st April, 1870, in his place in the House, as Prime Minister, he declared that the government had "taken office for a variety of purposes; . . . but the *first and greatest* of these purposes was to find a solution for the Irish Church, the Irish Land, and the Irish Education questions, *the latter including especially the subject of higher education in that country*".

More than six years have passed since June, 1865; but the disabilities, which were then declared to be unjust, exist still in full vigour. Can we conceive a more cruel wrong to the Catholic youth, and therefore to the best interests of the country? What is this, but indirectly to perpetuate the worst features of the penal code? We are pretty sure that a Catholic professor of mathematics will not be transported or hanged, as the barbarous law would authorise. But Catholic higher education—a "Popish university, college, or endowed school"—is as much a subject of legal ostracism in 1871, as it was in 1782. Ought any thinking man to be surprised, if the people of Ireland look upon the bungling educational experiments of the last twenty-five years as illusory, even for the very reason that they have been abortive, and seem not to have been intended to succeed? How many generations of youths, who might have received a higher education, have passed away, waiting for the everlastingly deferred removal of their disabilities, while those experiments were running their course to their foreknown failure? How many students have seen their reasonable hopes disappointed, since, in June, 1865, Mr. Gladstone promised that those disabilities should be removed? And all this time, Protestants, by having preserved to them their monopoly of great educational advantages, have had practically secured to them the further monopoly of middle-class employment.

We have been told by no less an authority than Mr. Fortescue, the late Chief Secretary for Ireland, that "the Irish Church Act has restored the people of this country to a true state of political equality". Surely when Mr Fortescue, on the 6th January 1871, addressed those words to the electors of Louth, he cannot have been acquainted with the facts, which it has been our painful duty to place before the public in this and the foregoing chapters He could not have reflected on the string of disadvantages and disabilities, which alternately worry and sting, dishearten and exasperate, the Catholic youth of this country, and place them under most unfair conditions in their competition with their Protestant fellows. Equality—" a true state of equality"—is what Catholics ask, in education as in all else besides. In Intermediate Education, in the Public Schools, in the Colleges, in the Universities, they expect to be put upon a footing of equality with Protestants. So much they insist upon as their right. More they do not ask, but with less they will never be content.

CHAPTER XIII.

CATHOLIC INTERMEDIATE SCHOOLS.

Deplorable condition of Irish Catholics in 1793. Public education wholly Protestant. In spite of penal legislation, Irish Catholics strove to secure some kind of education. Suppression of Irish Educational establishments on the Continent, gave an impetus to Catholic Intermediate Education in Ireland. Foundation of Carlow College in 1793; of Maynooth by Government in 1795.

Queries addressed to heads of existing Catholic colleges and schools in Ireland. Returns received afford a sketch of the condition of those establishments, the first of its kind. Forty-seven colleges and schools belonging to dioceses or to religious communities. Their geographical distribution.

Periods within which those schools were founded. Cost for purchases, buildings, etc.

Extent of accommodation. Number of professors and permanent teachers. All presided over by priests. Hostility of enemies of Catholic education has concentrated the management of Catholic education in the hands of the clergy. Distribution of schools by provinces.

Number of scholars in 1870, in the forty-seven schools:—boarders and day-boys. Total number of boys in exclusively Irish Catholic Intermediate Schools. Number of Irish boys in English and foreign Catholic schools and colleges. Number of Catholic boys in Protestant endowed schools. Not easy to determine how many Catholic boys are receiving an intermediate education in Model Schools. This number estimated from Returns to Primary Education Commission. Total number of Catholic boys receiving intermediate education in Protestant, public or private schools and in Model Schools. Probable number of Irish Catholic boys receiving Intermediate Education.

Return of age of scholars in Irish Catholic schools; proportion over sixteen. Total number of Irish Catholic boys, of sixteen and upwards, receiving an Intermediate Education in Irish, English, and Foreign Catholic schools. Per-centage of all the boys in Irish Catholic Intermediate Schools learning classics.

Amount paid for rent and taxes of schools; annual repairs. Annual receipts from boarders' pensions and day-boys' fees. Amount paid by Irish Catholics for Intermediate Education in exclusively Catholic schools, exclusive of travelling charges,

cost of books, etc. Amount paid for Catholics in Protestant and Model Schools.
Irish Catholics have reason to feel proud of their exertions; their system of Intermediate Schools far surpassing those created by the Government. A University the natural complement of a system of Intermediate Schools. Without such a head, school-system a headless trunk. Irish Catholics suffer from the want of this educational head every way. The University Question concerns all classes of Irishmen alike.

It is scarcely necessary to remind our readers, that the condition of Irish Catholics in 1793 was deplorable. Almost the whole of the landed property of the kingdom had, long since, passed into the hands of Protestants, most of whom were of English birth or of recent English extraction. The ecclesiastical and educational endowments, intended for the benefit of the whole nation, had been transferred to a hostile minority. The people themselves were shut out from all public employment, the learned professions, and skilled trades, and almost from their own corporate towns. As regards education, outside the Protestant institutions, there were no schools in the country, save the few private classical schools which had crept into existence since 1782. The sons of the few Catholic nobility and gentry, who had survived the wholesale confiscations, and the clerical students, obtained education in various colleges abroad. Some, who could not afford the expense of sending their children to the Continent, sent them to private Protestant schools, or to some of the endowed schools; while numbers of the poorer Catholics were obliged to risk the faith of their children at the less obnoxious of the Protestant parish and other endowed primary schools. Where such schools did not exist, and even alongside them, the so-called "hedge schools", grew up, providing elementary education for the farmers' children, and even for those of many of the country gentlemen. The houses of the farmers were always open to the "poor scholars", or poor youths, who, attracted by the reputation in classics or mathematics of some schoolmaster who kept a school in spite of the law, flocked thither, as in the olden time students gathered round some distinguished teacher and founded a school—the true *Mater Universitatis*. Counties often contended for the possession of such a teacher, or, failing to obtain permanent possession of the treasure, borrowed him for a time.

No sooner, however, was even the restricted liberty of teaching granted in 1782, as we explained in the preceding chapter, than the Catholics began to make provision for intermediate education. The suppression of the Irish colleges in France and the Low Countries, and the unsettled state of affairs on the Continent, by depriving the clergy and gentry of the only means of obtaining superior or intermediate education, gave an additional impulse to the educational movement, which was further fostered and helped by the larger measures of relief of 1792 and 1793. The College of Saint Patrick, at Carlow, led the van among the more important establishments, being founded in 1793; and the Government was induced, in 1795, to found and endow the College of Maynooth "for the education exclusively of persons professing the Roman Catholic religion", and with the views which we explained at length in the preceding chapter. Since then, the establishment of Diocesan and other Intermediate schools has kept pace with the growing wealth and enlightenment of the people.

With the view of showing what the faith and self-reliance of the Catholic people of Ireland have effected for Intermediate Education, in the face of dangers and under difficulties, before which almost any other people would have sunk into nearly hopeless barbarism, the heads of the principal Catholic schools were requested, by a friend of our Committee to supply certain statistical information regarding their several institutions. This information was furnished with a readiness which deserves our thanks. The answers to our queries enable us to present, for the first time, a reliable and satisfactory account of the *unendowed* public institutions for Intermediate Education which Irish Catholics have provided for themselves not only without the aid, but in spite of the action of the State.

Besides the regular Diocesan schools, which are the property of the dioceses, and the schools and colleges established by Religious communities, which may be considered, in a certain sense, public schools, there are a few schools which, although conducted by private persons, possess a certain semi-public character, due either to their being more or less connected with public institutions, or to their masters receiving aid from the Bishop of the Diocese or from the Parish Priest. Among the former, may be cited the Rathmines Catholic School of Mr. R. Campbell, M.A., while several classical schools in various parts of the country belong to the latter category. We thought it right to send queries to the teachers of these schools, and to include the scholars that attend them in the general total.

The following table is a list of the Diocesan schools and schools of Religious Orders, arranged according to provinces and counties, with the dates of their foundation.

CATHOLIC INTERMEDIATE SCHOOLS.

Locality of School.	Name of School or College.	Character of the Management	Date of Establishment.
ULSTER.			
Armagh	St. Patrick's	Diocesan, but conducted by Vincentian Fathers	1838
Belfast	St. Malachy's	Diocesan	1833
Cavan	St. Augustine's	Do.	1839
Letterkenny	Seminary	Do.	1860
Monaghan	St. M'Cartan's	Do.	1848
Newry	St. Colman's	Do.	1851
MUNSTER.			
Cahir	Our Lady's of Rockwell	Fathers of the Holy Ghost	1864
Cappoquin	Mount Melleray	Cistercians	1844
Cork	St. Vincent's	Vincentian Fathers	1845
Ennis	Seminary	Diocesan	1866
Fermoy	St. Colman's	Diocesan	1858
Killarney	St. Brendan's	Do.	1860
Limerick	St. Munchin's	Jesuit Fathers	1859
Do	Diocesan School	Diocesan	1869
Thurles	St. Patrick's	Diocesan	1820
Tralee	Holycross	Dominican Fathers	1862
Waterford	St. John's	Diocesan	1807
LEINSTER.*			
Blackrock	Immaculate Conception	Fathers of the Holy Ghost	1860
Carlow	St. Patrick's College	Diocesan	1793
Castleknock	St. Vincent's	Vincentian Fathers	1835
Clane	Clongowes College	Jesuit Fathers	1814
Clondalkin	St. Joseph's	Carmelite Brothers	1830
Clonliffe	Holycross	Diocesan	1859
Dublin, City	St. Francis Xavier	Jesuit Fathers	1839
Do	St. Lawrence O'Toole	Augustinian Fathers	1852
Do	Our Lady of Mt. Carmel	Carmelite Fathers	1853
Do	Catholic Univ. School	Marist Fathers	1867
Dundalk	St. Mary's	Marist Fathers	1861
Kildare	Mount Carmel	Carmelite Fathers	1864
Kilkenny	St. Kyran's	Diocesan	1836
Knoctopher	Mount Carmel	Carmelite Fathers	1852
Longford	St. Mel's	Diocesan	1865
Mountrath]	St. Patrick's	Brothers of St. Patrick	1810
Mullingar	St. Mary's	Diocesan	1856
Navan	St. Finian's	Do.	1802
Newbridge	St. Thomas's	Dominican Fathers	1852
Rahan	Tullabeg	Jesuit Fathers	1818
Terenure	Immaculate Conception	Carmelite Fathers	1860
Tullow	St. Patrick's	Brothers of St. Patrick	1808
Wexford	St. Peter's	Diocesan	1819
CONNAUGHT.			
Athlone	Summer Hill College	Diocesan	1857
Ballaghaderreen	Diocesan School	Do	1810
Ballina	St. Muredach's	Do	1851
Galway	St. Joseph's	Patrician Brothers	1862
Do	St. Ignatius'	Jesuit Fathers	1863
Sligo	St. John's	Marist Brothers	1857
Tuam	St. Jarlath's	Diocesan	1818

* A new school was opened at the beginning of October in Athlone, by the Franciscan Fathers.

LOCAL DISTRIBUTION.

Of these forty-seven Catholic Intermediate Schools and Colleges, which may be considered in a certain sense as public foundations, six are in Ulster, eleven in Munster, twenty-three in Leinster, and seven in Connaught.

Of the Ulster schools there is one in each of the following counties:—Antrim, Armagh, Cavan, Donegal, Down, and Monaghan. Three Ulster counties have no Intermediate Catholic school or Diocesan seminary —namely, Derry, Fermanagh, and Tyrone.

Of the six Munster counties five have two schools each, and one, Clare, has one.

Of the twelve Leinster counties, seven have one school each—namely, King's, Longford, Louth, Meath, Queen's, Westmeath, and Wexford; two, Carlow and Kilkenny, have two each; one, Kildare, has three; the city and county of Dublin have nine. The only Leinster county without a Diocesan or Intermediate school is Wicklow; but, as the Archbishop of Dublin is also Bishop of Glendalough, Clonliffe seminary is intended to be the Diocesan school for the clerical students of the united dioceses, while the proximity to Dublin and its neighbourhood affords the lay youth adequate educational facilities.

Of the Connaught counties, Galway has three schools, Mayo two, Roscommon and Sligo have each one. The only county without a school is the poor and mountainous one of Leitrim; this county, however, forms part of the diocese of Ardagh, which has a Diocesan school at Longford.

Of the thirty-two counties, therefore, twenty-seven have Diocesan or other Intermediate schools; and five only are as yet unprovided with them.

DATE OF ESTABLISHMENT.

Two important events divide into three periods, the seventy-nine years which have elapsed since Catholics were first allowed to teach—Catholic Emancipation, and the Famine. The first period, from 1792 to 1829, embraced thirty-seven years; the second, from 1829 to 1850, twenty-one years; and the third, from 1850 to the present time, also twenty-one years. During the first period, ten schools and colleges were established. In the second period, ten schools were also established; and in the third, twenty-seven. Thus, within the last twenty-one years, a greater number of schools have been established than in the preceding fifty-seven. During the first period, the country was only awaking from its enforced intellectual sleep, and working out its further emancipation. During the second period, all the energies of Catholics were absorbed in political struggles which have been chiefly beneficial to the Irish Presbyterians and English Dissenters. After the passing of the Emancipation Act, Irish Catholics naturally expected that the whole education of the country would be re-organized, so as to put them on a footing of equality with their Protestant fellow-countrymen. This, as well as the political agitation for legislative independence, no doubt retarded the growth of Catholic intermediate schools. The establishment of the Queen's Colleges, and the spirit in which they were being worked by the Government, opened the eyes of the country, and stimulated the Bishops and clergy to fresh exertions in providing Catholic Intermediate Schools. They thus forestalled the efforts of the friends of mixed education, who were silently organizing, under the name of Model Schools, a complete net-work of Intermediate Schools, which it was hoped would, in time, completely supersede the Catholic

Middle Schools, and would not only take the control of the education of Irish Catholic youth out of the hands of the clergy, but even, in the end, wholly withdraw it from their influence.

PURCHASE OF SITES, COST OF BUILDING, ETC.

Many of the sites of the schools are held in fee; others are held on long leases, and a few only are held in premises rented for the purpose. The total cost of sites, buildings, etc., up to the present time, amounts, so far as the returns furnished to us supply data, to 362,750*l*.

CHARACTER OF THE BUILDINGS.

The nineteen schools of Clonliffe, Kilkenny, Carlow, Waterford, Wexford, Fermoy, Thurles, Summerhill, Longford, Monaghan, Tuam, Belfast, Castleknock, Clongowes, Tullabeg, Terenure, Blackrock, Navan, and Armagh, may be favourably compared with any buildings for similar objects in these countries. The sites are, in most cases, good, the grounds generally extensive and often well planted, and the architecture of those which have been recently built tasteful. Of the forty-seven colleges and schools in our list, the cost for site, buildings, etc., of thirteen, has been from 1,000*l*. to 5,000*l*, each; of nine, from 5,000*l*. to 10,000*l*., each; of eleven, from 10,000*l*. to 20,000*l*., each; and of five, upwards of 20,000*l*., each. The remaining nine include those which originally cost for building, etc., under 1,000*l*., or which occupy premises for which an annual rent is paid. The Cavan School, though a good building, erected in 1839, at an expense of several thousand pounds, is about to be superseded by a fine building, the site and grounds for which have cost 14,000*l*., while the estimate for the building itself is placed at 12,000*l*. In Waterford a new Diocesan College has also just been built, at a cost of several thousand pounds, on a fine site purchased for the purpose. The furniture, fittings, apparatus, and material aids for instruction are, in most of the schools, ample, and in some of them quite up to the present requirements of teaching. Several have fair libraries. The domestic arrangements for boarders are, in general, superior to those in the majority of the Endowed schools in this country.

EXTENT OF ACCOMMODATION.

Of those forty-seven public schools, eight are for boarders only, twenty-four receive boarders and day scholars, and fifteen day scholars only; so that thirty-two may be described as boarding schools, and fifteen as day schools. The following table shows the distribution of these schools according to provinces:

Province.	No. of Colleges and Schools for			Total.
	Boarders only.	Boarders and Day-Scholars.	Day Scholars only.	
Ulster	1	5	0	6
Munster	0	8	3	11
Leinster	6	10	7	23
Connaught	1	1	5	7
Total	8	24	15	47

The six Ulster schools have accommodation for 360 boarders and 320 day-boys; the eleven Munster schools for 628 boarders and 995 day-boys; the twenty-three Leinster schools for 1,467 boarders and 1,297 day-boys; and the seven Connaught schools for 230 boarders and 504 day-boys. So that the existing Catholic public Intermediate Colleges and Schools afford accommodation for 2,685 boarders and 3,116 day-boys, or together 5,801 boys. In the forty-seven schools there are 247 lecture and class-rooms, or an average of one lecture or class-room for every 23·5 scholars.

TEACHING STAFF.

In the forty-seven schools included in our list, there are three hundred and eight professors and permanent teachers, exclusive of visiting or occasional teachers. If we add the teachers in the seven or eight private schools to which we have already referred, as possessing a semi-public character, the total number of professors and teachers engaged in Intermediate Education in strictly Catholic schools amounts to three hundred and twenty. The whole of the forty-seven schools are presided over by priests or members of religious communities and they also form the chief portion of the staff, although in a large number laymen are employed as masters. In the absence of endowments, and of opportunities of Catholic higher education for laymen, it would have been impossible to create a system of Catholic schools conducted by laymen. Thus the enemies of Catholicity have, by their opposition to the rights of Catholics in matters of education, unconsciously contributed in a large degree to exclude lay Catholics from the office of teachers in Intermediate schools, and given clergymen and religious communities a virtual monopoly of Catholic education.

Twenty-two of the forty-seven schools are "diocesan", and are, therefore, under the immediate direction of the Bishop of the diocese in which they are situated; the remaining twenty-five have been established by religious communities. The following table shows the number of schools belonging to each religious community, and their distribution, as well as that of the diocesan schools, according to provinces:—

No.	Governing Body.	Number of Schools in				Total
		Ulster.	Munster.	Leinster.	Connaught.	
1	Diocesan	5	6	7	4	22
2	Jesuit Fathers	0	1	3	1	5
3	Carmelite Fathers	0	0	5	0	5
4	Vincentian Fathers	1*	1	1	0	3
5	Marist Fathers	0	0	2	0	2
6	Fathers of the Holy Ghost	0	1	1	0	2
7	Dominican Fathers	0	1	0	0	1
8	Augustinian Fathers	0	0	1	0	1
9	Cistercians	0	1	0	0	1
10	Marist Brothers	0	0	0	1	1
11	Patrician Brothers	0	0	2	1	3
12	Carmelite Brothers	0	0	1	0	1
	Total	6	11	23	7	47

NUMBER OF STUDENTS.

During the year 1870, the number of scholars who attended those forty-seven Catholic colleges and schools was 4,950, of whom 2,484 were boarders, and 2,466 were day-boys. As in many of the returns sent to us the numbers given were those of the boys actually in the institution at the time, the real number of boys at school, during the year, will have been somewhat higher. If we add the number of boys attending the Catholic semi-public schools from which we received returns, and which either enjoy aid from bishops or priests, or are more or less connected with Catholic public institutions, the total number of boys in exclusively Catholic schools was 5,178, of whom 2,485 were

* This (Armagh) is really a Diocesan School, though conducted by the Vincentian Fathers. Strictly speaking, there are 23 Diocesan Schools, and 24 schools established by Religious Communities.

boarders, there being only one boarder in the private schools

In order to make our account of Catholic Intermediate Education as complete as possible, we applied to the heads of English Catholic schools and colleges for a return of the number of boys from Ireland in their schools. We thank those gentlemen for the readiness with which they complied with our request, and for the trouble they took in supplying the information. According to those returns the number of boys from Ireland at the colleges and schools of Oscott, Stoneyhurst, Ushaw, Ratcliffe, Downside, Sedgley Park, Edgbaston, Beaumont Lodge, Ampleforth, St. Augustine's (Ramsgate), etc., may be set down at about 250. If to these we add the boys sent to Catholic schools in France, Belgium, Switzerland, and Germany, who on an average do not exceed about 50, the total number of Irish boys in exclusively Catholic Intermediate schools at the date of our returns was 5,478, or in round numbers 5,500.

In the foregoing chapters we have given the number of Catholics attending the Protestant schools of public foundation in the year 1857. Assuming that the same number still attend them, which is doubtful, the number to be found in each class of schools would stand thus :—

In Diocesan Schools	38
„ Royal Schools	3
„ Erasmus Smith's Schools	23
„ all other Endowed Schools	27
Total	91

It is not easy to determine the number of Catholics who may be set down as attending Mixed Intermediate Schools, since the only schools of public foundation of this class are the Model Schools, which also fulfil the functions of Primary schools. Indeed some of them can scarcely be said to be more than efficient primary schools. The total number of Catholic scholars found, by the Royal Commissioners,* present in the boys' departments of *all* the Model Schools, exclusive of the Central Institution in Marlborough Street, was 503, of whom not more than 144 can be assigned to the category of youths who ought to be found in Intermediate Schools. If to these we add the 44 Catholics at the Glasnevin institution, we have 188, as the number of such youths found by the Royal Commissioners in the Model Schools and Agricultural establishments of the Board, exclusive of the Institution in Marlborough Street.

Let us now refer to another source of information— viz., the educational Census taken by the Constabulary and Police on the 25th June, 1868. On that day the Police found present† in all the Model Schools, including the Central Schools in Marlborough Street, 7,751 children, of whom 3,279 were boys, while 2,807 of the entire number, or 36·2 per cent., were Catholics. If we assume that the proportion of these 7,751 children, who were of a superior social position, was the same as among the 9,475 children on the rolls of all the Model Schools (exclusive of the Central), in 1867, namely, 28·5 per cent.,— then we may estimate 338 to be the number of Catholic boys of superior social position, who may be considered to have been receiving intermediate instruction on the 25th June, 1868, in all the Model Schools, exclu-

---

* *Primary Education Commission*, vol. I., part ii., page 762.
† *Ibid.*, vol. vi., page li.

sive of the Model Farm at Glasnevin, but inclusive of the Central Model Schools. If to this we add the 44 Catholic youths at the Model Farm at Glasnevin, we have 382 as the total number of boys who may be considered to have been in any sense receiving secondary instruction, at that date, in *all* the Model Schools and Agricultural establishments of the National Board. Any one at all acquainted with the Model Schools will at once admit, that the proportion of Catholics, who use them as Intermediate Schools, is relatively much smaller than that of the other religious bodies, and much less than the total proportion of Catholics on the rolls, and consequently, that the calculated number of Catholic boys just given, as receiving Intermediate instruction, is too high. We may, then, safely say, that the proportion of Catholic boys on the rolls of all the Model Schools, who are receiving Intermediate instruction in those establishments, does not exceed—probably does not even amount to—400.

If we allow that 50 Catholic boys attend Protestant private intermediate schools, and add the 300 Irish Catholic boys, whom we have ascertained to be at English and Foreign Catholic schools and colleges, the numbers will stand thus:

In Catholic Schools,	... ...	5,478
In Protestant Schools, {Endowed, 91 / Private, 50} 141	}	... 541
In Mixed Schools (Model Schools), 400		
	Total,	6,019

That is to say:—of Irish Catholic boys receiving Intermediate Education, 91·01 per cent. do so in exclusively Catholic Schools; 1·51 per cent. in Protestant Endowed Schools; 0·83 per cent. in private Protestant Schools; and 6·65 per cent. in Model Schools.

Although, when estimating the total number of Catholic boys who are receiving an intermediate education, it is right to take into account the number of boys who receive this kind of instruction in Model Schools, yet the parents of those boys are not to be taken as preferring Mixed Schools to Catholic ones. In most cases they have no option; there may be no good Catholic schools in the neighbourhood, and most of them are not able to afford to pay for their sons as boarders at the large Catholic schools.

Allowing for boys at home at the date of our returns, and for those studying with tutors, etc., the total number of Irish Catholic boys receiving what may be strictly described as Intermediate instruction, exceeds, therefore, 6,000.

AGES AND COURSE OF STUDY.

As regards the ages of the Scholars, the returns were complete for only forty-one out of the forty-seven schools. As these schools, however, included 4,195 out of 4,950 scholars, the returns for them afford us the means of arriving at a sufficiently close approximation to the ages of all the boys in the Catholic Intermediate Schools of Ireland. Of those 4,195 students, 396, or 9·43 per cent., were under ten years of age; 1,593, or 38 per cent., were between the ages of ten and fifteen years; 793, or nearly 19 per cent., were between the ages of fifteen and sixteen years; 727, or 17·3 per cent., between the ages of sixteen and eighteen years; and 686, or 16·3 per cent., were eighteen years of age and upwards. We may, therefore, conclude, that about 10 per cent. of the boys in Catholic Intermediate Schools are under ten years old; 57 per cent., or more than half, between the ages of ten and sixteen years; and 33 per cent., or about one-third, of sixteen years or upwards.

From the foregoing figures it is evident, that boys are not generally sent to the higher schools, until after the age of ten years; that the school period, or time spent at those schools, for a large number of boys, is eight years; and, lastly, that a considerable number remain at school beyond the age of sixteen and even of eighteen years. These last represent the boys who, in Germany and other continental countries, would be at universities, or polytechnic, agricultural, veterinary, and forestry schools of university rank. Assuming, therefore, that one-third of the students in all Catholic Intermediate Schools are sixteen years of age and upwards, the 5,178 who were present in them at the date of the returns, would give 1,726 students of University age. To this we must add one-third of the boys at English and foreign schools—say 100. There were, thus, in 1870, in Catholic Intermediate Schools and Colleges, at least 1,800 Irish Catholic boys, who, in other countries, would be either attending universities or technical academies of equivalent rank, or preparing to enter them immediately.

Of the 5,178 boys in the Irish Catholic Intermediate Schools, 3,188, or 61·5 per cent., were stated to be learning classics; in this number are not, however, included some of the more advanced students, in what is called the Philosophy Class, who, though continuing their classical studies, are not usually included among the Grammar Classes. We may, therefore, fairly assume that in our Irish Catholic Intermediate schools fully 70 per cent. study Greek and Latin.

COST OF ANNUAL SUPPORT.

The sites of many of the forty-seven public schools, as has been above stated, have been purchased in fee, and the rent of others fined down; nevertheless, the annual amount paid in rent according to our returns is 1,694*l.* As a few of the schools made no return on the subject, we may put the annual rent and taxes at about 2,500*l.*, to which must be added the interest on 362,750*l.*, sunk in purchase of sites and in buildings. The annual repairs cost at least 1,500*l.*

To meet this annual charge of 4,000*l.* for rent, taxes, and repairs, as well as the payments to teachers and the support of the institutions generally, there is, first, the annual income from boarders' pensions and day-boys' school fees. If we estimate the boarders' pensions at an average of 30*l.* each, and the school fees at the moderate estimate of 5*l.*, the annual income of the forty-seven public schools from these two sources would be 86,850*l.* If we estimate the cost of each boarder in the English and Foreign schools at 40*l.* a-year, and add the exclusively Catholic private schools, we find that Irish Catholics pay for the education of their children in middle-class Catholic schools a sum of at least 100,000*l.* per annum, exclusive of travelling expenses, cost of books, etc., and of some moderate endowments. If we add this to the interest of the sum sunk in buildings and in sites, the annual expenditure of Irish Catholics for Catholic Intermediate Education amounts to more than 120,000*l.* per annum. As all, or certainly nearly all, the Catholics who attend Protestant Endowed Schools are day-scholars, the school fees of the 91 Catholic scholars in those endowed schools, and of the Catholic boys who attend the Model Schools for the purposes of intermediate education, do not amount to more than 500*l.* to 600*l.* a-year, if even they reach that sum.

Irish Catholics have reason to feel proud of their independence and self-reliance. Plundered of their lands by successive confiscations; excluded from civil rights and the practice of skilled trades, until the traditions of technical skill were nearly forgotten; forbidden, under severe penalties, to teach school or to acquire the merest rudiments of learning, except at the sacrifice of religion and personal honour—this people, thus made one of the poorest in the world, and all but barbarised in craft of hand and work of brain, has, within the eighty years which have elapsed since the brutalizing influence of English law and Government was first relaxed, created for itself an organisation of Intermediate Education better and more complete, than all the power, wealth, and cunning of the English Protestant Government have been able to effect in more than 300 years.

Intermediate Schools naturally culminate in a University, which acts as the educational brain, and centre of the intellectual force of the country, whence the educational energy which vivifies the schools, diffuses itself over the land. Without a kindred University, our Catholic Intermediate system, complete as it otherwise is, would be a mere headless trunk. The students would have no higher intellectual goal than the mechanical learning or teaching of the merest rudiments of knowledge. No stimulating influence from above would set them in motion. It is true that scientific discoveries are often the work of men who have never been at a university. Art-creators—poets, painters, sculptors and musicians—are generally strangers to university halls; and not a few great orators and statesmen have arisen, whose education was begun and completed at a parish school. Nevertheless, we affirm that even those exoteric results are the indirect products of universities; for science, art, and statesmanship are inseparable from the higher culture which the action of universities alone produces. The influence, for instance, of the Universities of Oxford and Cambridge, on the social, political, intellectual, and religious life of England has been incalculable. On the other hand, the loss to Irish Catholics, or rather to all Irishmen, from the absence of an educational head for Catholic education, is equally incalculable. We suffer from this want, physically as well as intellectually, but, perhaps, politically more than in any other way. The university question thus concerns every one, rich and poor, in the country; indeed, none have a more direct interest in the existence of flourishing universities than the civic and middle classes.

Having now described the various classes of intermediate schools in Ireland, it only remains to briefly review the principal results of our inquiry in order to complete the first part of our task—namely, the history and present state of the Institutions for Intermediate Education in Ireland. This we propose to do in our next Chapter.

CHAPTER XIV.

SUMMARY.

Existing Intermediate Schools of two classes; endowed and unendowed. Former of two kinds.

Protestant Endowed Schools.

DIOCESAN SCHOOLS. Support of a school a charge imposed on bishop and clergy of every diocese by Act of Parliament still in force. Number of Diocesan Schools in existence. Amount actually contributed to them. Neglect. Arrears owing on account of those schools, and recoverable from living persons or from Church Temporalities Commission. Amount which Protestant Clergy could fairly be called upon to contribute. Those schools quite Protestant, contrary to intention of foundation. Endowments applicable to new arrangement of Intermediate Education.

ROYAL SCHOOLS. Endowed magnificently out of confiscated estates of Irish Catholics. Acreage; annual value; school premises, value of, accommodation. Number of scholars—*only three Catholics.*

IRISH SOCIETY. Endowed out of confiscated towns and lands, etc., in Derry. Amount of annual income. Extravagant management. *Not a penny contributed to a Catholic school.* This fund ought to be applied to a new system of intermediate education.

ERASMUS SMITH'S SCHOOLS. Title to the property. Situation of property, of schools. Departure from original purposes. Scandalous and unjust nature of this departure. Future destination of this fund.

OTHER ENDOWED SCHOOLS. Number of; nature of foundation; value of premises; annual income; character of schools; number of scholars; number of Catholic boys.

INCORPORATED SOCIETY. Founded for education of poor Catholics, now educates well-to-do Protestants. Parliament should apply the funds to Intermediate Education.

Mixed State Schools.

Object of Protestant Endowed Schools; of Mixed Schools of the State. Strange law of locality with respect to Irish educational endowments. Cost of Model Schools. Annual cost for salaries, etc. Number of boys in Model Schools. Number of such boys receiving an intermediate education. Amount spent by National Board on intermediate education. Very small proportion of Catholic children in Model Schools.

Catholic Intermediate Schools.

Catholics shut out from all public educational endowments, had to found intermediate schools. Particulars connected with those schools. Number of their scholars. Number of Catholic boys who are being educated in Catholic intermediate schools. Cost of their education. Contrasted with number of Catholic boys in public endowed or mixed schools.

Laws regarding Catholic education in same condition as left by Irish Parliament eighty-six years ago. Imperial Parliament has only riveted the educational disabilities of Catholics. Penalties against Catholic teachers.

The first part of our task being now ended, we propose to sum up the chief results of our inquiry into the existing institutions for Intermediate Education in Ireland. In making this summary, we shall endeavour to keep in view the practical object of our whole inquiry, and confine ourselves as far as possible to such matters as bear directly on the present state of the schools, and on the future organization of a system of Intermediate Education.

The existing Intermediate Schools may be divided into two classes:

1. Endowed Schools of public foundation, and State Schools; *i.e.* those which are maintained out of funds granted by the Crown or by Parliament.
2. Unendowed Schools.

The former may be again subdivided into:—

A. Protestant Endowed Schools, which have a permanent endowment.
B. "United", or Mixed, State Schools, which have been established, and are controlled and supported directly by the State.

By "Unendowed Schools" we mean all schools which receive no assistance from public funds under the direct or indirect control of Parliament, whether they possess private endowments or not. We shall take each group of schools in the order in which we have described them in the foregoing chapters.

ENDOWED AND STATE SCHOOLS OF PUBLIC FOUNDATION.

A. Endowed Schools.

The Protestant Endowed Schools are maintained by permanent endowments granted by the Crown or by Parliament out of the national property, or what was treated at least as the national property. Five classes of them may be distinguished.

DIOCESAN SCHOOLS. The Endowed Schools Commissioners in 1858 give the number of such schools said to be in existence as sixteen, or rather fifteen, as two of them had been united. The masterships of two were temporarily vacant; another had been closed for several years; so that only twelve were in actual operation. The tax on the incomes of the bishops and clergy of twenty dioceses for the support of these twelve schools amounted to 1,179l, 12s. 11d. The total number of boys on the rolls was 304; the average daily attendance 240, or only 20 per school. Five had no Catholic boy on the rolls, one had three, one five, and another six; while the schools of Rosscarbery and Elphin, situated in localities almost entirely Catholic, had nine and thirteen Catholics respectively. The total number of Catholics in the twelve schools was thirty-eight, or 12·5 per cent. of the whole number of boys on the rolls. If the Act 12 Eliz., c. 1, had been carried out, there would have been thirty-four such schools. Up to the present, however, the Lord-Lieutenant's warrants have given a legal existence to only nineteen, towards the support of which the diocesan contributions were fixed at 1,670*l.* 15*s.* 3*d.*; and even of these nineteen schools, only sixteen have ever had a real existence, towards the support of which the diocesan tax was fixed at 1,384*l.* 12*s.* 3*d.*

The payment of salaries for the masters of those schools is a charge, imposed upon the Bishops and Clergy of the Irish Episcopal Protestant Church by an Act of Parliament still in full legal force. We have shown in our third chapter, that, for forty-seven years, since 1824, the arrears of this tax, legally due from the bishops and clergy of those dioceses whose contributions had been fixed by warrant of the Lord Lieutenant, amount to 20,720*l.*, part of which is recoverable from the present occupants of several sees, or the representatives of former bishops. We have further shown that the arrears for the period previous to 1824, might be estimated at 188,450*l.*, making, together with the previous sum, 209,170*l.* —part of which, as just stated, is recoverable from living persons, namely, the Archbishop of Dublin, and the Bishops of Cashel and Limerick; and the remainder ought to be considered as an equitable charge on the church property now vested in the Commissioners of Irish Church Temporalities. We have also pointed out that, instead of the 1,670*l.* 15*s.* 3*d.* now annually leviable on the bishops and clergy, the tax may be increased to at least 5,000*l.* a-year at the discretion of the Lord-Lieutenant.

Finally, we have shown that it has been declared several times by Royal Commissions and Parliamentary Committees, that boys of all religious denominations are entitled to admission to those schools; that the master has no right to give religious instruction to children not of his own religion; and that the master may be of any religious denomination. The endowments, dormant as well as active, of this class of schools belong, therefore, to the nation at large, and may be applied by Parliament for the purposes of an equitable scheme of Intermediate Education.

ROYAL SCHOOLS.—These schools have been endowed by the Crown out of confiscated estates of Irish Catholics, situated chiefly in the Province of Ulster. Omitting all reference to Carysfort, which is a Primary school, the endowments of the other six Royal Schools comprise 21,334*a*. 3*r*. 3*p*., exclusive of 100 acres given to Clogher and 300 to Londonderry which have been diverted from their original purposes, but which may possibly be still made available. The net annual income from land amounted in 1857 to 5,747*l*. 0*s*. 9*d*.—a sum which could be easily augmented. The school premises are valued at 1,083*l*. 1*s*. 8*d*. per annum, and afford accommodation for 651 boys, the actual number on the roll in 1857 being, however, only 311, of whom *three only were Catholics.*

It is unnecessary to repeat here that all these funds, etc., amounting at present to nearly 7,000*l*. a-year, are available towards the establishment of a system of Intermediate Education on a basis of honest equality for all classes of Irishmen.

THE IRISH SOCIETY.—The anomalous institution known as " The Society of the Governors and Assistants in London, of the New Plantation in Ulster within the Realm of Ireland", representing the common interests of the London Guilds, was endowed by James I., with the city of Derry, the town of Coleraine, 7,000 plantation acres of land adjacent to these towns, besides bog and mountain, the fisheries and the slob lands of the Foyle and Bann, the advowsons of several church livings, and other properties, in trust, " to provide for the Protestant religion, the Protestant Establishment of the district, and the education of the inhabitants of the district". The income of the Society was stated in evidence, in 1868, to be about 14,000$l.$ a-year, of which about one-half appears to be spent in the cost of management and incidental expenses. The Society give aid to about 100 primary schools and benevolent institutions. They contribute largely to the maintenance of the Diocesan School known as Foyle College, upon the building of which they expended 13,000$l.$ They expended recently 5,000$l.$ upon the Coleraine Academical Institution, and contribute annually to its support. They also contributed 1,000$l.$ to the building of Magee College, and pay 500$l.$ annually towards its support. It seems almost unnecessary to add, that the Irish Society, while contributing to the schools of Protestants of all denominations, *have never given a single shilling to a Catholic* school, or Catholic institution of any kind. Since the Protestant religion has ceased to be the established religion of the country, it is clear that one branch of the Society's trusts has terminated, so that its revenues ought henceforward to be devoted solely to the purposes of education. And since Primary Education is already amply provided for, in the neighbourhood of Derry and Coleraine, Intermediate Education ought to have the benefit of this fund. We have shown that a sum of at least 10,000$l.$ a year might, by good management, be made available for the purpose.

ERASMUS SMITH'S SCHOOLS.—A certain Erasmus

Smith, who became an alderman of London, obtained under the Cromwellian government a grant of some of the forfeited lands. This grant not having been perfected before the Restoration of Charles II., Smith's title was impeached. A compromise was, however, permitted by the Crown, under which the estates were assigned to trustees for the foundation and endowment of Grammar Schools. Various Acts of Parliament, both Irish and Imperial, have dealt with those estates and their trustees. The estates comprise over 11,000 acres of land, situated in the counties of Limerick, Tipperary, Westmeath and Sligo, the town and liberties of Galway, besides a large tract of mountain and two rent charges. In 1854 the revenues from these estates amounted to a little over 9,400*l*. There are five Grammar Schools on Erasmus Smith's foundation—Drogheda, Ennis, Tipperary, Galway, and the new one in Dublin. Exclusive of the last, which is of very recent foundation, the total number of scholars in these Grammar Schools in 1858 was 160, of whom only 23 were Catholics, and of these 12 were in the single school of Tipperary, which is placed in an eminently Catholic district. Only 30 of the 160 scholars were free. The annual value of the school premises of those four Grammar Schools was, in 1868, 706*l*. 16*s*. 1*d*.

The Governors of Erasmus Smith's Schools have deliberately departed from the intentions of the original foundation. In connection with their Grammar Schools, they maintain several paltry, and some good exhibitions in Trinity College. This is a legitimate application of the funds, as a university is the natural goal of a successful school career. But they have also established several University professorships, spent 10,000*l*. in the purchase of a library for the same College, and have built the present Examination Hall.

But the greatest departure from the original trust is the expenditure of 4,500*l.* a-year, nearly one-half their revenue, in the maintenance of about 107 Primary Schools. The following table* shows the distribution of these schools according to provinces; the number of scholars in them, distinguished according to religious denominations; and the income derived by the Governors from estates in each province:—

Province.	Annual income from Estates in Province.	Number of Primary Schools maintained in Province.	Number of Scholars on the Rolls in such Primary Schools half-year ended 30th November, 1868.	
			Protestants.	Catholics.
Munster ...	£5,712	9	600	5
Connaught	2,976	6	164	7
Leinster ...	535	34	1423	30
Ulster ...	*Nil.*	58	4190	295

It thus appears that while the Catholic tenant-farmers of Munster pay almost 6,000*l.* a-year to this educational corporation, the "self-reliant" Protestants of Ulster, *who contribute nothing*, are nevertheless provided by the Governors with more than six times as many schools!

It would be superfluous to shew that Parliament may again resume its control over confiscated estates originally destined to promote Intermediate Education, and may remodel the distribution of the income to as to bring home its benefits to the descendants of the original owners of the property.

* *Primary Education Commission,* vol. viii., page 100. Returns from Governors of Erasmus Smith's Schools.

VARIOUS OTHER ENDOWED SCHOOLS.—This group of schools comprised sixteen schools, some founded by political personages as part of the state policy of the day; some founded or in part endowed by municipalities; and some by private persons. The land belonging to these schools is over 4,000 acres; the annual value of the school premises exceeds 550*l.*; and the annual income from the land or other endowments exceeds 1,700*l.* Some of these schools were expressly founded for the benefit of the people of a certain locality; and as regards almost all of them, there are special circumstances which take them out of the category of private schools, as we fully explained in our seventh chapter. In 1857 three of the schools were not in operation; in ten of the schools there was not a single Catholic; and out of a total of 298 boys attending the schools in operation, only 27 were Catholics.

THE INCORPORATED SOCIETY.—This body has an income of about 8000*l.* a-year, originally intended for the education of poor Catholic children, but now, as we believe, illegally diverted to the education of the children of well-to-do Protestants. In our eighth chapter above we showed that one of the original objects of this Corporation could not be carried out, and that Parliament should now deal with the funds; and we suggested that they might be applied to the purposes of Intermediate Education, without losing sight of another object for which they were intended— viz., the education of the poor.

B. *Mixed or United State Schools.*

The several groups of Endowed Schools which we have noticed above, were intended in the first place to denationalize Catholic youth, and if possible to Protestantize them. The system by which it was sought to effect this double object having failed, a new and more insidious one was next tried. Instead of the offensive plan of direct bribery and intimidation, Catholics were invited to throw aside their legitimate distrust of British statesmen, and partake of the benefits of an education which, under the assumption of social liberality, ignored the religion, the traditions, and the history of Ireland. This new system was intended to be more complete than the preceding one—it was to embrace all degrees from the Primary School to the University. The National Schools, which, it was hoped, would all gradually pass into the hands of the Government, were to form a great system of State Primary Schools, in which the Irish working classes were in time to be purged of all dross of Catholicism and Irishism. The Model Schools and the Queen's Colleges were to perform the same offices for those requiring Intermediate and University Education. As we were concerned, in this first part of our task, only with the Intermediate Schools, we discussed in the ninth and tenth chapters above, the Model Schools of the National Board in their aspect as Intermediate Schools, and we shall here briefly recapitulate what we said there at some length.

MODEL SCHOOLS OF THE NATIONAL BOARD.—Following the mysterious law which seems to have persistently governed the geographical distribution of all Irish Educational foundations, half of the twenty-eight Model Schools have been established in Ulster. The total cost of the erection and repairs of all the Model Schools up to the close of 1867 was over 270,000*l*. Their total cost to the end of 1867 is estimated at little short of 600,000*l*. The cost for salaries,

SUMMARY. 285

etc. in the year 1868 exceeded 28,000*l*. We explained in our ninth chapter that the expenditure on the boys' Model Schools must be set down at the half of this sum at least, or over 14,000*l*. For reasons given at length in their proper place, above, we will exclude from consideration the Central Model School establishments in Marlborough Street, and confine what we have to say to the other twenty-eight Model Schools. They cost, for erection and repairs, down to the close of 1867, over 180,000*l*.; their total cost to same date being about 440,000*l*. The salaries and maintenance of these twenty-eight establishments, in 1868, amounted to nearly 25,000*l*. Allowing only the half of this for the expenses of the boys' departments, we find that the boys' Model Schools (always excluding Marlborough Street) cost in 1868 almost 12,500*l*.

The total number of boys on the rolls of the twenty-six provincial Model Schools on the 31st December, 1867, was, according to the Board's Return to the Primary Schools Commission,* 3,240. The corresponding numbers for the Inchicore and West Dublin establishments are not anywhere given, but may be estimated, from the Board's Report for 1867,† at 79 and 276 respectively. This will give the total number of boys on the rolls of the twenty-eight Model Schools, on the 31st December, at 3,595, the total number of scholars in the boys', girls', and infants' departments of those schools being, at the same date, 9,475. Of this total number, as we shall presently see, 2,702 were children of superior social position, whose proper place is in Intermediate Schools. If we assume that the proportion of boys, girls, and infants

---

* *Primary Education Commission*, vol. vii., pages 74–89. Returns of National Board. Section iv. Part 2.

† *Report for* 1867, page 25.

during the last quarter of 1867 was the same throughout all the classes, it would appear that of these 2,702 children of superior social position, 1,025 were boys. Thus we find that in the boys' departments of the twenty-eight Model Schools, which in 1867 cost almost 12,500*l.*, there were not more than 2,570 scholars who can be fairly said to use them as Primary Schools. It is surely no exaggeration to say that the annual cost of good ordinary National Schools for 2,570 scholars "*on the Rolls*" ought not to exceed 2,500*l.* It thus appears that, in 1867, at least 10,000*l.* were spent by the National Board, on boys alone, for the purposes of Intermediate Education.

The course of instruction in the Model Schools is not surpassed in extent by any Intermediate Schools. It includes Greek, Latin, French, "Reasoning", Political Economy, Pure and Mixed Mathematics, Experimental Physics, Music, etc.

Accommodation for 12,301 scholars is provided, on a most liberal scale, in the twenty-six provincial Model Schools. The Royal Commissioners found only 5,660 children present. Out of the 78 departments (boys', girls', and infants') in those provincial Model Schools, 53 *have more than half their space vacant.*

In *nine* out of the 78 departments of the Provincial Schools, the attendance was *less than* 30. That is to say, over one-ninth of those institutions, if treated as ordinary National Schools, would be struck off the roll for insufficient attendance.

The circumstances of the Model Schools at Dunmanway, Bailieborough, and Trim are so special—these schools being practically Catholic Schools—that we may leave them out of consideration in discussing the religion of the scholars. In the remaining

23 Provincial Model Schools, the Royal Commissioners found present 4,956 children, of whom *only* 439, *or less than nine per cent., were Catholics.* Taking the circumstances of the present time into account, this is as emphatic a repudiation of the Model Schools by Catholics as took place in the case of the Charter Schools.

Exclusive of the Central Establishment in Dublin, there were 9,475 scholars on the rolls of those institutions,* of whom only 2,583, or 27·3 per cent., are Catholics. Of those 9,475 scholars, 2,702, or 28·5 per cent.,

* As an instance of the difficulty of arriving at any reliable conclusions respecting the Model Schools even from official returns, we will just cite a specimen.

In the *Returns* furnished by the National Board to the Royal Commission on Primary Education, we find, that the total "number of Pupils on the Roll for the *last quarter*, 1867", in all the Model Schools, excluding Marlborough Street alone, was 9,475 (Vol. vii. page 95).

In the *Report* for 1867 of the Commissioners of National Education, laid before Parliament, we are told (page 25) that "the total number of pupils on the rolls of these [Model] Schools for the *year* ended 31st December, 1867, was (excluding Marlborough Street) 13,854.

A similar contrast of figures is furnished to us in another matter.

In their Report for 1868, laid before Parliament, the Commissioners of National Education tell the public (page 22) that "the total number of pupils on the rolls of these [Model] Schools for the year ended 31st December, 1868, was (excluding the Agricultural Institution at Glasnevin only) 17,619.

But the Constabulary and Police found *present* on the 25th June, 1868, in all the Model Schools and Agricultural Institutions of the Board (excepting only Glasnevin) 7,751.

Persons familiar with the language and statistical methods of the National Board understand what is implied, by the difference between the two sets of figures. But, for purposes of comparison, this necessity of referring different sets of facts to two different and heterogeneous standards of comparison is always perplexing and troublesome, and must always prevent anything like a complete grasp of the complicated considerations connected with the Model Schools. Perhaps this result is not unintentional. For any one not acquainted with the Board's statistical methods, it is hopeless to attempt to trace an intelligible path through the figures.

were children of superior social position—their parents or near relations, including mill-owners, merchants, bankers, professional men, magistrates, deputy-lieutenants, and even members of parliament—whom no one could expect to find in National Primary Schools maintained and managed by the State.

Any one who has the slightest acquaintance with the feelings and habits of Irish Catholics of the well-to-do classes, will at once recognize that the proportion of Catholics to be found among these 2,702 children of superior social position must be very small. It will be considerably less than the proportion upon the total number of scholars on the rolls. Nevertheless, even were we to assume that the same relative proportion of numbers exists throughout all the classes of the Model Schools, so that the proportion of Catholic children of well-to-do parents was as large as that of the poorer classes—which we know is not a fact—we find that in all the Model Schools and Agricultural establishments of every kind, excepting the Central Institutions, there could not have been at the close of 1867, more than 738 Catholic children, who ought to be in Intermediate Schools, and of these, at the utmost, 279 were boys.

Further, we have explained fully above (page 269) the grounds which justify us in assuming, that the total number of Catholic boys who are receiving an Intermediate Education in all the Model Schools (including the Central Institution and Glasnevin) does not exceed—probably does not even amount to—400.

CATHOLIC PUBLIC INTERMEDIATE SCHOOLS.

Catholics, shut out alike from the old and the new public educational endowments—although the former consist of parts of the confiscated estates of their ancestors, and the latter come out of he public taxes which they pay like other citizens of the State—have been obliged to provide Intermediate schools for themselves. In our thirteenth chapter we explained very summarily what they have done in this way. We showed that, in the purchase of sites, and in the building of schools, etc., they have expended 362,750*l.*; that there is accommodation in those schools for 5,801 boys (day-scholars and boarders); that the number in attendance during 1870 was 4,950, more than the half of whom were boarders; that the annual cost of maintaining those 47 establishments is about 86,850*l.*; that about 300 boys are being educated in schools and colleges in England and on the Continent; and about 250 in semi-public Catholic Intermediate schools in Ireland. If we add the annual cost of the education of those 550 boys to the sum set down for maintaining the quasi-public Catholic Schools and Colleges, we find that at least 120,000*l.* a-year are annually spent by Irish Catholics on the education of about 5,500 boys in Catholic Intermediate Schools and Colleges; and lastly, that the number of Catholic boys who are being educated in Protestant or Mixed Public Intermediate Schools cannot exceed 541 !!!

We have no means of determining the number of Private Intermediate schools in Ireland, nor of ascertaining the number of Catholic boys in them. We are not, however, concerned here with this class of schools, especially as there are not many Catholic boys in them.

EXISTING EDUCATIONAL DISABILITIES.

In order to put in a clear light the state of the Catholic people, when they began the work of reconstructing their educational institutions, and the difficulties they had to contend with, we sketched in our twelfth Chapter the penal legislation against Catholic education, and we showed that no real advance in this matter has been made since the relaxations of 1782 and 1793. It is an almost incredible fact—but none the less a fact for being almost incredible—that the laws regarding Catholic education are in precisely the condition in which they were left by the Irish Parliament seventy-six years ago. The only step taken on the subject by the Imperial Legislature was, to rivet the educational fetters, then left remaining, while "emancipating" what are commonly called the professional classes from their legal disabilities. At this moment, every Catholic engaged in teaching or professing the liberal arts in Ireland, without the special license of the crown, is liable to all the penalties enacted against " Popish regular convicts":—*i.e. transportation* and *death*.

The following Tables put the position of the Catholics of Ireland, as regards public educational endowments for Intermediate Education, in a striking light. We commend them to the attention of our fellow countrymen.

(A) CATHOLIC UNENDOWED PUBLIC SCHOOLS IN IRELAND.

Classes of Schools	Total Annual Value of Public Endowments	Total No. of Scholars	No. of Catholics
	£ s. d.		
Diocesan Schools	Nil.		
Schools of Religious Orders	Nil.	5,178*	5,178
Semi-Public Schools	Nil.		
Total	Nil.	5,178	5,178

* Exclusive of Irish boys in similar schools in England, etc.

SUMMARY.

(B) PROTESTANT AND MIXED ENDOWED PUBLIC SCHOOLS IN IRELAND.

Protestant Endowed Schools — Classes of Schools	Total Annual Value of Endowments	Total No. of Scholars	No. of Catholics
	£ s. d.		
Diocesan Schools	1,670 15 3	304	38
Royal Schools	6,830 2 5	311	3
Irish Society	10,000 0 0	—*	—
Grammar Schools of Erasmus Smith	10,114 8 6	160	23
Various other Endowed Schools	2,390 19 11	313	27
The Incorporated Society	10,934 1 4	541	—
	£41,940 7 5	1,629†	91
State Endowed Mixed Schools			
Model Schools	10,000 0 0‡	1,228	400¶
Total	£51,940 7 . 5	2,857	491

* Only two Grammar Schools are aided or maintained by this Society: the Foyle College, which is included among the Diocesan Schools, and the new Academical Institution, Coleraine, which was only recently opened.

† Exclusive of Coleraine Academical Institution.

‡ This sum, £10,000, is the proportion of the entire sum annually spent on Model Schools (£28,000) which we have shown to be their cost as institutions for the *Intermediate education of boys*. Hence, this sum of £10,000 is the annual expenditure on Boys' Model Schools, considered as *Intermediate Schools only*, independently of their further cost as Primary Schools, and the cost of the Model Schools for girls and infants. We have also not taken into account a proportionate share of the large outlay for buildings and sites, the interest upon which, at 4 per cent. per annum, would alone amount to £7,200.

¶ This is the estimated highest possible number of Catholic boys who can be said to be receiving an Intermediate education in *all* the Model Schools and Agricultural Establishments of the National Board. It should be remembered, however, that they are, in great part, the children of parents who could not afford to send their sons away to Boarding Schools.

www.ingramcontent.com/pod-product-compliance
Lightning Source LLC
Chambersburg PA
CBHW032046230426

43672CB00009B/1490